INSTITUTIONAL INVESTORS AND CORPORATE GOVERNANCE

Best Practices for Increasing Corporate Value

CAROLYN KAY BRANCATO

IRWIN
Professional Publishing®
Chicago · London · Singapore

This publication is designed to provide accurate and
authoritative information in regard to the subject matter
covered. It is sold with the understanding that neither the
author nor the publisher is engaged in rendering legal, accounting,
or other professional service. If legal advice or other expert
assistance is required, the services of a competent professional
person should be sought.

*From a Declaration of Principles jointly adopted by a Committee of the
American Bar Association and a Committee of Publishers.*

Library of Congress Cataloging-in-Publication Data

Brancato, Carolyn Kay.
   Institutional investors and corporate governance : best
practices for increasing corporate value / Carolyn Kay Brancato.
     p.   cm.
   Includes index.
   ISBN 0-7863-0558-4
   1. Insitutional investors.   2. Stockbrokers.   3. Corporate
governance.   I. Title.
HG4521.B6458   1997
332.6 ' 725—dc20   96–32589

Printed in the United States of America

2 3 4 5 6 7 8 9 0 DOC 3 2 1 0 9 8 7 6

For Howard

CONTENTS

Part II

Best Practices in Corporate Governance

Chapter 3

Institutional Investors Become Activists   81

PREFACE

Research for this book began during the 1980s takeover period while I was head of the Industry Analysis and Finance Section of The Congressional Research Service in the Library of Congress, Washington D.C. In that capacity, I met key players in the 1980s takeover wars and wrote numerous Congressional Committee Prints for the House of Representatives and the Senate on mergers and acquisitions, leveraged buyouts, and junk bonds. My research continued from 1988 through 1992 at the Columbia Institutional Investor Project (chaired by Ira M. Millstein), where I had an invaluable opportunity to see leaders of major public pension funds interact with key corporate executives. I discovered the role Ira Millstein played as diplomat, urging each side to air its problems and searching for common ground, and I decided that it was essential to continue this work in some manner. One of the founders of the Columbia Institutional Investor Project, then New York State Comptroller Edward V. Regan, asked me to become the Staff Director for the Subcouncil on Corporate Governance and Financial Markets of the federally legislated Competitiveness Policy Council, where we continued this round table approach, gathering together the best minds from the corporate and institutional investor arenas and producing a report in December 1992. Shortly thereafter, the late Preston Townley invited me to join The Conference Board (a global business and research organization) where, as Research Director for Corporate Governance and Strategy, I was fortunate to have been able to conduct a major international study entitled *New Corporate Performance Measures*. At this writing, I am in the process of directing another international Conference Board study entitled *Communicating Corporate Performance: Closing the Loop Between Shareholders, Managements and Boards of Directors*. Both Conference Board efforts involve the round table participation of key corporate and institutional investor representatives.

The corporate governance world is rather small, and a number of key individuals have clearly shaped my thinking on these issues: Ira Millstein from Weil, Gotshal & Manges; Elmer Johnson, formerly with General Motors; Jonathan Charkham, formerly from The Bank of England; Ned Regan, formerly with The State of New York; Joseph Spadaford of First Chicago Trust of New York; John Wilcox from Georgeson & Company,

Inc.; Richard Koppes and William Crist from the California Public Employees' Retirement System; Nell Minow and Robert Monks from LENS; Martin Coyle from TRW; Howard Sherman from ISS; and Cathy Dixon from the SEC. The author is grateful to Kevin Crum for continued and excellent research assistance, to Irwin editor Ralph Rieves for his faith, and to Howard Greenhalgh for sailing into my life.

Carolyn Kay Brancato

INTRODUCTION

Since the early 1980s, mutual mistrust has developed between corporate executives and their major shareholders. Moreover, as shareholder activism has spread from the United States to Europe, then to farther reaches of the globe, the circle of mistrust is alarmingly widening. The classic Berle and Means corporate model (with separation of ownership and control, where management runs the corporation with little input from a passive shareholder base) has become outmoded. A new model of the corporation has evolved, which reflects a shift in balance of power within the corporation derived from the substantial increase in the economic and political power now wielded by institutional investors. In this new model, institutional investors view executives and boards of directors with various degrees of mistrust—views which are swiftly returned by corporate executives and boards. Much of this mistrust is based on escalating corporate governance demands by institutional investors. Corporate executives have been used to receiving implicit votes of confidence accompanied by passive and tacit approval (which if not forthcoming prompted the institution to observe the "Wall Street Walk" and sell shares in the company). Now, companies must contend with *investors* who consider themselves *owners.*

Notwithstanding this climate of mistrust, both sides have, to their credit, worked over the past decade to accept and institute a wide variety of changes in corporate governance processes and, on that score, both companies and institutions seem to be coming to a better understanding. Now, however, the major gulf between the companies and those who own their stock is centered on concepts surrounding the creation of shareholder value. Executives continue to express enormous frustration that the markets are so volatile and that their attempts to create value for the long term are not fully appreciated by a roller-coaster stock market, which temperamentally and sometimes perversely reacts to general economic and company-specific financial news. Executives at major corporations complain that, while they have struggled so long to finally attain some degree of confidence that the corporate governance ground rules will be known to both sides, the whole subject of creating shareholder value for institutional investors is still maddeningly elusive.

This book is intended to explore shareholder and firm value from the perspective of what institutional investors want from corporations and what corporations can be expected to give back. It is based on a new model of the corporation, which not only adjusts for a shift in the balance of corporate power towards institutional investors but also makes critical distinctions among portions of the shareholder base. This new model is based on the recognition that there are a series of very different types of shareholders, ranging from *investors* to *traders*. Understanding the behavioral distinctions between institutional investors versus institutional traders is key to minimizing the current tensions between corporations and institutions. Moreover, this knowledge can provide corporations with an unprecedented opportunity to engender confidence and attract the new breed of institutional investor (rather than traders). Furthermore, if investors themselves are forced to make the distinctions described in this book, it will help them to clarify their own objectives and take responsibility for actions consistent with improving the corporation's intrinsic growth and its potential to provide them with sustained returns. Investors who are truly interested in the sustained viability of the corporation have, given sufficient confidence in management, rejected the promise of higher immediate returns to take sides against traders who fashion short-term payout strategies to harm the viability of the company. In these cases, the new breed of institutional investor may be the corporation's best chance to realize its goals of creating sustained investor value—to the mutual benefit of both corporation and investor.

Creating shareholder and firm value, however, depends more than ever on the company's ability to weather the vicissitudes of a volatile financial marketplace. This, in turn, depends on its ability to enhance performance and achieve success through expansion, especially in areas where investments must be made to position the company for future sustained growth—such as investments in intellectual capital, workplace practices, research and development, quality processes, and environmental compliance. The new institutional investors also present the company with the potential for providing a stable capital base, reducing the company's stock price volatility and lowering its cost of capital. In order for corporations and institutional investors to achieve mutual growth and success, however, both will have to develop methods for aligning their financial interests and for communicating their expectations for creating investor value.

With over $10 trillion in assets, U.S. institutional investors are clearly vital to the capital formation needs of corporations throughout the world.

Similarly, the ability of corporations to achieve success and generate shareholder value is vital to the capability of these institutional investors to provide returns to their beneficiaries. Instead of synergy, however, acrimony frequently surrounds the relationships between corporations and their institutional investors. This threatens both sides by impairing important decisions corporations must make in order to generate value and reducing critical communication between institutional investors, managements, and boards of directors.

Corporations sometimes perceive that institutional investors make unreasonable demands and may therefore adopt a variety of counterproductive tactics to alienate the very shareholders they need to assure their own viability. And some of these shareholders, in their quest for a say in corporate affairs, risk making demands that can actually reduce the corporation's ability to achieve success. This book will help both corporations and institutional investors clarify their objectives and take action to meet their *mutual* needs to achieve success and generate investor value.

Companies should:

- Understand that the institutional investor community is comprised of investors with a wide range of investment objectives and corporate governance goals and strategies.
- Organize their corporate governance structures to enhance corporate value.
- Organize their strategic corporate planning processes to measure and enhance future corporate value.
- Appropriately align the interests of their managers and boards of directors with those investors who are most important to the company.
- Target specific shareholders they would like to hold their stock based on common investment and corporate governance perspectives.
- Communicate in a constructive manner with institutional investors to achieve their mutual goals.

Institutional investors should:

- Clarify their investment objectives with respect to the corporations in their portfolios.
- Take responsibility for investment and proxy voting decisions if they wish to have a say in corporate affairs.

- Press managements and boards of directors for corporate governance structures and processes that will generate value and not be distracted by other types of initiatives.
- Communicate in a constructive manner with managements and boards of directors to achieve their mutual goals.

VALUE FOR WHICH SHAREHOLDERS?

The first step in generating shareholder value requires corporations to fully understand the complex nature of the institutional shareholder community. Some corporations tend to generalize by saying that institutional investors sell them out in the short term, act like commodity traders rather than owners, grandstand for the media, or interject themselves in the running of companies without having the requisite managerial skills. The institutional investor universe is, however, comprised of a "marble cake" of types of institutions with varied investment objectives and strategies. Corporate pension funds and public pension funds control about half of the total $10 trillion in institutional investor assets. Pension fund investment strategies and payout requirements vary considerably from those of money managers, venture capitalists, and arbitrageurs (who, for example, in a takeover situation might buy the target company's stock hoping that the takeover will be completed at the full premium).

It is crucial to remember that creating shareholder value means different things to different shareholders. As Figure 1 shows, shareholders navigate quite different routes through the stock market. Much like sailing from the United States across the Altantic Ocean, there is a choice whether to take a northern route to the United Kingdom and Europe or a southern route by way of the Azores. The northern route to Ireland follows the Gulf Stream northward to Nova Scotia and Newfoundland, where the sailor will encounter fog and must keep watch for icebergs even during the summer months. An analogy might be the "northern" route taken by investors who pay close attention to corporate governance, the elements of corporate performance which generate intrinsic value, and the capability of generating a future stream of profits. A less daunting, southerly route proceeds along an arc to Bermuda and then to the Azores, where fewer obstacles are likely to be encountered. By comparison, traders will follow this "southern" route as they look for trends in net profits without necessarily engaging in corporate governance or fundamental, performance-oriented research. They may, therefore, have an immediate and quite different time horizon

FIGURE 1

Investors and Traders Sail Different Courses Through the Stock Market

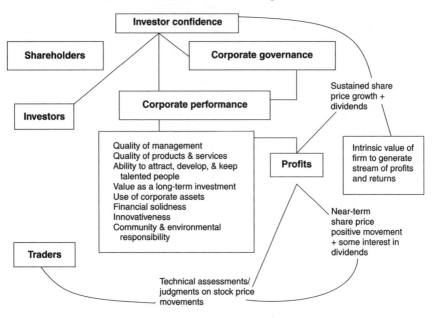

over which to measure returns than a future-oriented pension fund investor who measures success in terms of the corporation's ability to generate a consistent stream of payout benefits.

The all-purpose term *shareholder value,* meaning price appreciation plus reinvested dividend return, therefore no longer accurately reflects the varied expectations and demands of different segments of the investment community. It is time to recognize this milestone in the evolution of financial markets and split shareholders into groups which reflect a more precise understanding of their varied investment objectives and strategies.

Thus, the concept of shareholder value should now be defined along a spectrum with *trading value* at one end and *investor value* at the other. Trading value should be defined to focus on immediate return on investment, while investor value should be focused on a corporation's ability to generate a stream of profits from which investors will reap sustained returns. Corporations interested in creating sustained investor value (from among the types of possible shareholder values) could then concentrate on what it takes to satisfy these investors; they would not focus on the investment horizons required to appeal to the traders. Making a practical distinction between the objectives of traders and those of investors should assist both corporations and certain types of investors to clarify their mutual demands and expectations and achieve successful results over their various investment horizons.

SHORT-TERMISM CHALLENGED

This book also challenges two myths of *short termism.* The first myth is that shareholders are in the markets only for the short term. Careful analysis of the portfolios of institutional investors indicates that some institutions may hold stock for very long periods, while others trade much more rapidly. Moreover, even within one portfolio of a single institutional investor, several different investment strategies may be pursued, each accompanied by varying turnover periods.

The second myth dispelled in this book is that corporations are not making long-term investments because of shareholder pressures to obtain short-term profits. In fact, there is strong evidence that a growing number of major global corporations are putting less and less emphasis on bolstering short-term financial returns and are specifically looking to enhance long-term success and firm value. They are putting aside an obsession with quarterly financial returns and gearing their businesses to the investors, not the traders, in the market. They are factoring in not only strategic plans for future financial growth, but also new concepts of measuring corporate performance which embody investments in intellectual capital, research and development, customer satisfaction, environmental compliance, and other intangibles necessary for future sustained corporate growth—precisely the kind of growth that appeals to future oriented investors.

Finally, it is time to recognize that an important debate has, for many years, been unproductively sidetracked by focusing on the concept of *time of investment commitment,* such as short versus long term. Corporations are now recognizing that it is not the length of time for investment commitment that is critical—the concept of time is meaningless, as illustrated by the fact that a short-term time horizon for a utility would be a long-term horizon for a toy company. The real issue is that, regardless of how long an investment is made, it should be made considering the *depth of investment commitment* as measured by the *credibility* that the investment will yield returns over the time period expected. An in-depth commitment by an investor for a toy company will be anticipated for a much shorter time horizon than an in-depth investment in a utility, yet both are made by investors interested in the future success of each corporation within its own time frame. Proponents of the theory of short-termism do not recognize this important distinction. They miss the fundamental premise that investors hold their positions in accordance with their investment objectives only so long as confidence is maintained, and not according to some arbitrary short- or long-term unit of time.

INSTITUTIONAL INVESTOR ACTIVISM: FROM STRUCTURE TO PERFORMANCE

The major activist public pension funds have led the institutional investor movement to challenge corporate managements and boards of directors on a number of grounds. During the last decade, institutions on the forefront of the movement have shifted their focus first from antitakeover issues such as the payment of *greenmail* (e.g., payments made to one "raider" who would threaten a takeover unless bought out at a premium), then to procedural proxy voting issues, and finally to issues that are now related to the fundamental performance of the corporation. This activism further reinforces the need to split the concept of shareholder value along a spectrum with investors at one end and traders at the other. Some of these institutions have more clearly become investors rather than traders as they argue for performance-related changes in corporations which will ensure sustained corporate viability and, in turn, a sustained stream of investment return.

Moreover, there is evidence that certain, future-oriented institutional investors can act to counterbalance the traders in the market to provide a solid corporate ownership base. These investors have been known to rally to the aid of corporate managements against hostile raiders, if managements have demonstrated and communicated viable and credible strategies for future growth. One example is Time Warner which, in 1993, sought approval for a *poison pill* (rights given to current shareholders to receive additional shares of stock if a company is taken over, thus forcing a raider to swallow a bitter pill in the form of unacceptable dilution of company shares). Time Warner's management sought shareholder approval to institute the poison pill, which was necessary to thwart a hostile takeover by Seagram. In this case, a large group of institutional investors had confidence in existing management and voted with management in favor of the pill, resisting short-term trading pressures for an immediate and higher takeover premium. All segments of the shareholder community, therefore, do not behave in the same manner; some investors can become valuable allies to the corporation against traders who are less concerned with the sustained viability of the corporation.

CORPORATE GOVERNANCE STRUCTURES AND PROCESSES

If both corporations and institutions are to achieve sustained growth, effort is required on both their parts, not only with regard to investing but also with regard to corporate structure and decision-making processes, e.g., *corporate governance.* Some corporations have become frustrated by groups of demanding shareholders who press for a variety of changes, including altering the structure and election practices of company boards of directors, increasing current dividend payout, getting out of certain businesses (such as tobacco), and altering executives' and directors' compensation packages. Will these demands, if met, enhance or detract from management's future growth plans? What are the motives of various groups of shareholders, and which ones should managements and boards listen to in shaping their strategic investment plans? Will changing corporate governance structures and processes increase the value of the firm?

In answering these questions, it is critical to remember that future sustained growth and success require the efforts of both the corporations and the institutional investor. If institutional investors accept responsibility as investors they will have more credibility to make demands for a say in the strategic future of the enterprise. They may come to be regarded as allies of management if they have confidence and can support certain plans by management to, for example, reinvest excess cash in the company for training, research and development, and so on, rather than use excess cash to provide more immediate returns from repurchasing stock or issuing higher dividends.

Institutional investors interested in corporate governance are, generally speaking, those most likely to be willing to expend the energy to monitor their investment for future growth. They are also the ones who tend to operate under the assumption that attracting management's attention and making sure there are "lights on in the boardroom" will lead to both measured and unmeasured benefits. Traders will never stay around long enough to perform this monitoring function, nor can corporations hope to establish a viable dialogue with them over their strategic investments and future prospects.

In the realm of corporate governance, institutional investors must also focus on their role in ensuring the success of the corporation. They must take responsibility for participating as owners and not traders, and for monitoring their investments and proxy voting processes to ensure that their strategic goals are met and not ignored, or worse, inadvertently subverted by fiduciaries to whom they have delegated their stock who may have a different corporate governance focus. Pension funds should ensure that a delegated money manager acting on their behalf to generate investor value does so. Furthermore, pension funds should rate their money managers' performance accordingly and not hold them to performance standards more appropriate to traders interested in more immediate results. While pension funds and other future-oriented segments of the institutional investor market do not control the entire market (money managers invest vast sums on behalf of individual investors, and individuals are entering markets directly via on-line personal computers in unprecedented numbers), they hold approximately 50 percent of all institutional assets. Moreover, pension funds control far in excess of their share of assets in exercised voting power (money managers and individuals tend not to vote their stock, making the vote by the pension fund that much more influential).

The role of the institutional investor in the affairs of the corporation now transcends conventional legal wisdom. The legal system assures individual shareholders limited liability and immunity from being sued for wrongdoings of the corporation; shareholders put only their money at risk. In this system, individual shareholders who did not control enough stock to be owners had little direct leverage over the company's strategic plans. Their only recourse was to observe the classic "Wall Street Walk" and sell their shares. The current economic and political power now wielded by institutional investors has made this legal model obsolete. Indeed, some institutions have political power well beyond their economic power, as measured by the number of shares in a company they control.

As with investment practices, best practices in corporate governance should be designed to improve corporate performance for a select group of investors—in this case, for those investors who are *economically and politically targeted* investors as opposed to the more general universe of shareholders. Critical to this governance process is structuring a method of positive communication between investors and corporations to focus both sides on the benefits of these in-depth investments and the corresponding generation of a stream of investor returns.

INVESTOR TARGETING: MAKING MARKETS MORE EFFICIENT

Once the corporation and the investor have clarified that they share the mutual goals of achieving sustained corporate growth, corporations can successfully target and attract the investors who best match their strategic profile. The key is to understand that, while markets may be efficient in the aggregate, they may not necessarily be efficient in a particular instance. In order to assure efficiency individually, corporations must analyze which shareholder segments they want to have as their primary shareholder base, such as, for example, investors interested in future sustained growth. They can then cater their strategies to appeal to them and not necessarily to the remaining, trading-oriented shareholders.

Trading shareholders provide needed liquidity in the markets. Thus, making distinctions among shareholders does not imply that traders have no place in the markets. Furthermore, corporations that pursue sustained corporate growth objectives may appeal to traders for periods of time. But the managers and boards of directors of the corporations interested in achieving future growth should be clear and focused on their goals to achieve value for the shareholder base they deem most essential to achieve that future success.

Investor targeting challenges the conventional wisdom that markets are efficient and that managements should just tell their story and let market forces operate. Rather, it forces companies to clarify their strategies and enables them to communicate their goals to those investors who share their objectives. Companies that successfully employ investor targeting enjoy less stock price volatility and a lower cost of capital, enabling them to make the *in-depth* investments necessary to achieve sustained growth.

ALIGNING THE INTERESTS OF INVESTORS AND CORPORATIONS

Finally, in order to engender the confidence of their investors, corporations will need to find ways to link the success of the corporation to that of these targeted investors. Corporations should examine their executives' and directors' compensation practices in this light. A full alignment of the interests of managements, boards, and investors is the key to improving *sustained corporate performance* for the enduring benefit of corporations and their investors alike.

In challenging key elements of economic and legal conventional wisdom, this book argues in favor of six major propositions:

1. Corporations cannot create *shareholder value* through one all-purpose strategy. They must define which shareholders they intend to create value for and design strategies accordingly.

2. Markets are not short-term oriented; they are made up of complex groups of shareholders with different investment objectives and trading patterns. Corporations must analyze the investment community and target those subsegments they believe share their goals for sustained success. They must construct their strategic plans accordingly.

3. Companies do not necessarily neglect needed long-term investments to please short-term investors. Many reject the obsession with quarterly earnings. They increasingly undertake future oriented investments in areas formerly thought to be "intangible" (such as improving intellectual capital and increasing customer satisfaction) which enhances their potential to achieve future success.

4. Stock markets are not necessarily efficient when it comes to matching the needs of the individual corporation with the investing public. Targeting the shareholders a corporation wants as its shareholder base, however, can improve this efficiency and reduce a corporation's stock price volatility and cost of capital.

5. Investors may have political clout far beyond what their economic concentration of holdings would suggest. In order to have a meaningful say in corporate affairs, however, these institutions should ask that corporations fashion their growth and corporate governance strategies to generate sustained value and resist being distracted by other political issues.

6. The corporation should ensure that its major drivers of success and compensation schemes are inextricably linked to measures that also satisfy its investors.

This book provides a road map for corporations and institutions alike to achieve their mutual goals of sustainable success. Part I, *Creating Firm Value,* describes how corporations can create not just shareholder value but true investor value which, in turn, enables them to enhance their strategic success. As companies measure and communicate this success in both financial and nonfinancial ways, there will be a self-reinforcing cycle of positive investments made in areas and over investment horizons, which will stimulate still more rounds of future success and growth. Part II, *Best Corporate Governance Practices for Investors and Companies,* traces the rise of institutional investor activism and how economically powerful these institutional investors have become. It also describes how the institutional investor activism movement has evolved from a focus on procedural to performance issues and how this concentration of institutional investor power can be turned from a negative feature to provide companies with a supportive capital base. Part III, *How Companies Can Attract the Investors They Want,* describes how companies can target the investors they want in their capital base. Successful investor targeting can provide the corporation with a more stable environment for expansion by lowering its stock price volatility and its cost of capital. Finally, this book discusses corporate governance processes and compensation procedures that further align the mutual interests of institutional investors and corporations and strengthen investor confidence that the destinies of the companies and their investors are inextricably linked.

I

CREATING FIRM VALUE

CHAPTER

1

SHAREHOLDER VALUE: FOR INVESTORS OR TRADERS?

At the turn of the 20th century, large shareholder/owners such as the Rockefellers and the DuPonts dominated the U.S. corporate landscape. Thirty years later, Columbia Professors Adolph A. Berle and Gardiner C. Means recognized that a separation of ownership and control had developed in the large, modern corporation. Shareholders had become largely dispersed and passive, while companies were being run by professional managers with comparatively small financial stakes in these corporations. This separation of the functions of owners and managers was reinforced by explicit provisions of corporate law:

> The shareholder has the exclusive control of the stock itself. But as a condition of the shareholder's limited liability, the shareholder gives up the right to control use of the corporation's property by others. That right is delegated to the management of the corporation. Indeed, it is one of the benefits of the corporate organization to the investor; he can entrust his money to people who have expertise and time that he does not. . . .
>
> The rights of a shareholder are classically defined as (1) the right to sell the stock, (2) the right to vote the proxy, (3) the right to bring suit for damages if the corporation's directors or managers fail to meet their obligations, (4) the right to certain information from the company, and (5) certain residual

3

rights following the company's liquidation (or its filing for reorganization under bankruptcy laws), once creditors and other claimants are paid off.[1]

Although this strictly legal definition implies that all shareholders possess exactly the same rights, financial markets have developed into a complex web of relationships between corporations and varying types of institutional investors. A new, 21st century model of the corporation (see Figure 1–1) is, therefore, shaped by the economic and political power exerted by certain individual institutions who sometimes act in concert, thereby magnifying their economic clout.

Moreover, it can no longer be assumed that all shareholders are the same. Shareholders should now be classified according to their investment objectives and corporate governance behavior along a spectrum, with investors at one end and traders at the other. Investors are those whose interests are more fully aligned with the success of the corporation, and traders are those whose interests are more narrowly focused on achieving rates of return over a more limited duration, regardless of the ultimate effect on the corporation. The development of two groups (and the innumerable gradations in between) challenges the Berle and Means model of a passive, widely diffuse shareholder base. If corporations cling to this outmoded corporate model and its strict legal framework, they will operate as if shareholders were a single dimension, dispersed and largely unimportant. This will have serious negative consequences for the corporation's ability to raise capital in the markets of the 21st century. Moreover, a stable and knowledgeable institutional shareholder base can be management's best ally against the 1990s style of takeovers. In commenting on the Chrysler/Kerkorian battle for control, John Wilcox, Chairman of Georgeson & Company, Inc.—a major proxy solicitation company which counts major corporations among its clients—noted:

> . . . this is a good example of a power struggle in which institutional investors demonstrated that a great deal has changed since the 1980s when takeover bids virtually always succeeded. In this case the market agreed with Chrysler management, taking a long-term approach to value, rather than granting a major investor's request for immediate return.[2]

The 1995–1996 attempted raid on Chrysler started out like a typical 1980s-style takeover, but ended up establishing a new 1990s model for corporate interaction, with institutional investor owners rather than traders. The elements were all there—the large "beachhead position" taken by a well-known raider, a cash rich company selling at a low ratio of stock price

FIGURE 1–1

Models of the Corporation

Turn of the 20th century model

Berle and Means model—1930s

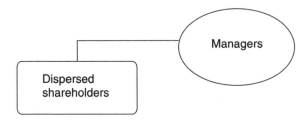

The 21st century model

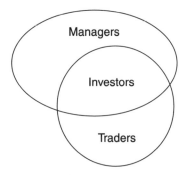

to earnings, a company whose second largest holding of company stock was in the hands of a large manager of mutual funds, and a promised premium over the current stock market price. In the 1980s, the deal would have been inevitable. Once the company was put into play, the funds and institutional investors holding the stock would have sold to arbitrageurs, who would have given them a small premium which reflected the probability of the deal concluding at the announced premium. The "arbs" would then have completed the cycle, tendering the shares.

The Chrysler deal is perhaps the first to defy the model of the 1980s, primarily because the company managed to convince its institutional investors to back current management. The Council of Institutional Investors, representing nearly 100 public and private corporate pension funds, wrote to Chrysler that it did not support actions to increase current returns at the expense of ongoing returns or long-term viability. Even FMC, a major shareholder which runs several Fidelity mutual funds and is not an "activist" player on governance issues, sent signals that it was inclined to back Chrysler on financial grounds. Just as important was the role of the investment banks. Following the collapse of the junk bond market in the late 1980s, lining up financing for hostile deals was no longer a foregone conclusion. The fact that major investors initially hesitated to embrace the raider's terms clearly contributed to the collapse of the raider's financing prospects, which were slim even going into the deal—perhaps because the raider was still playing by the 1980s rules, which generally dictated that once a company had gone into play, financing was obtainable, even if it involved "bridge loans" from the investment banks themselves. Perhaps the most important element in the transaction was Chrysler's communication process—both management's and the board's—with major long-term oriented institutional investors and its ability to convince them that current management had a much better chance of generating value for them than the immediate returns promised by the raider. Box 1–1 contains a brief chronology of the deal. There were certain major differences between the 1980s style leveraged buyouts and the 1995–6 Chrysler bid.

1. Most 1980s leveraged buyouts (LBOs) were for "cash cow" companies which were not in cyclical businesses and could be expected to generate a steady stream of cash with which to pay down debt incurred in the leveraged buyout transaction. Chrysler was in a cyclical industry with peaks and troughs depending on the economy, although it had adopted a strategy to accumulate $7.5 billion in reserves, which would be used to weather the next recession while maintaining new product growth and paying dividends.

2. During the mid-1980s, with junk bond financing available, investment bankers had little trouble amassing the funds

BOX 1-1

Chrysler: Institutional Investors Side With Management

January 3, 1995	Kirk Kerkorian, through the Tracinda Corporation, increases his stake in Chrysler from 9.2 percent to 10.16 percent. Throughout the fall of 1994, Kerkorian pressured Chrysler to raise the value of its stock price by increasing dividends and repurchasing shares with excess cash.
	The company announced on December 1, 1994 that it intended to increase its dividend by 60 percent and to initiate a $1 billion stock buyback program to begin during the first quarter. Chrysler also initiated plans to increase the trigger level for its "poison pill" from 10 to 15 percent. This is a defense intended to make an acquisition prohibitively expensive for an unwanted suitor. (Chrysler believed that most of its institutional investors would not oppose raising the trigger point for the pill, in the face of Tracinda's announced intention to exceed the 10 percent threshold—Chrysler was right.)
April 12, 1995	Kirk Kerkorian, through Tracinda and backed by former Chrysler CEO Lee A. Iaocca, offers $22.8 billion or $55 per share for a leveraged buyout of Chrysler. The stock price is approximately $50 per share, having traded since April 1994 in the range of $45 to $50 per share. The bidder contemplates borrowing $10 billion, then using the company's own cash reserves and possible sale of assets to complete the deal. The bare outlines of the transaction are very much in the style of the 1980s leveraged buyouts.
April 20, 1995	Bear, Stearns & Company, which had been widely expected to represent Tracinda, announces that it has decided not to represent him, or any other bidder, in the hostile takeover bid. This causes the financing part of the bid to collapse.
April 28, 1995	With the financing for the leveraged buyout in trouble, Tracinda hires proxy solicitation firm D.F. King &

(continued)

Chrysler—Continued

	Company, setting the stage for a proxy fight for control of the company through the election of a board of directors.
May 31, 1995	Tracinda announces that it has dropped its buyout bid and that it has hired the merger specialist investment banking firm Wasserstein & Perella to develop a new strategy.
June 26, 1995	Perhaps testing the waters prior to mounting another full-fledged attack, Tracinda announces its intention to spend $700 million to purchase, via an open market tender offer, another 4 percent of Chrysler.
September 5, 1995	To bolster its forthcoming proxy battle, Tracinda hires Jerome B. York, Chief Financial Officer of IBM, and the former Chrysler CFO. This lends credibility to Tracinda's proxy battle intentions, since most observers believe that York would not have joined Tracinda had he not had his sights on becoming the CEO of Chrysler.
October 3, 1995	Chrysler Chairman Robert Eaton delivers a presentation to the Council of Institutional Investors which is well received; influential fund managers begin to vocally support Chrysler's management.
November 2, 1995	Chrysler discloses a strategy of having a "90-day consultation period" during which it will review the company's "corporate governance procedures and board membership."
November 20, 1995	Tracinda asks that former Kmart Chairman and CEO Joseph E. Antonini be removed from the Chrysler

(continued)

necessary to complete even the largest transactions—especially since many of those transactions relied on utilizing the company's cash and sale of assets to pay down the debt. Tracinda had not, apparently, firmed up its financing for Chrysler, although it announced that Bear, Stearns & Company

Chrysler—Concluded

	board. Subsequently Antonini resigns, and Tracinda announces it intends to pursue a proxy solicitation for two seats on the board, including one for former Chrysler CFO Jerome York. Chrysler's board accepts Antonini's resignation.
February 7, 1996	Chrysler's nominating committee endorses John B. Neff as a new member of the board. Neff is the recently retired manager of the Wellington Management Company's Windsor Fund.
February 8, 1996	The battle ends as Chrysler enters into a five-year standstill agreement with Kerkorian and Tracinda Corporation under which they agree: (1) not to increase their beneficial ownership of beneficial securities beyond 13.75 percent; (2) not to solicit proxies or enter into any activity aimed at a change of control of the corporation or its board; (3) that during the term of the agreement, as long as Tracinda or Mr. Kerkorian beneficially own more than 5 percent of the outstanding voting securities of Chrysler, the corporation's board of directors will nominate Mr. James D. Aljian (or a successor) for election at each meeting of stockholders at which directors are to be elected; (4) to terminate within 30 days of the agreement all arrangements with its financial, corporate governance, and proxy solicitation advisors. Chrysler announces the results of its 90-day corporate governance consultation, which include governance improvments, as well as its intention to repurchase an additional $2.0 billion of common stock in 1996 and $1.0 billion in 1997.

would advise it to solicit $3 billion in equity and more than $10 billion in credit. When a major institutional investor (John Neff from Wellington-Windsor Funds) expressed reservations about the transaction, the financing did not merely "fall in place" as it would have during the 1980s.

3. It hardly mattered that a company was in sound shape in the 1980s—indeed it appeared that the better off the company was, the more likely a target it would be, especially if it had substantial cash reserves. Fundamentals, however, appeared to have more bearing in the Chrysler case. Chrysler had already experienced a major turnaround and, despite some declines in earnings primarily associated with new minivan product introductions, it appeared to be in sound shape. The cash reserve of $7.5 billion which the company had accumulated was to be used to weather a possible recession in the highly cyclical automobile industry, without affecting a stream of new products and quality improvement efforts. At the time of the LBO bid, Chrysler was selling for an extremely low earnings multiple. Such a prominent investor as John Neff, then-manager of Vanguard Windsor, was reported by the *New York Times* on April 13, 1995 (p. D-7) to have been a "vocal supporter of the notion that Chrysler shares are undervalued." Moreover, the bid appeared too low, and, coupled with the lack of firm financing, this prompted speculation on Wall Street that Kerkorian was not serious and merely meant to attract another bidder or to get the company to buy him out at a premium (e.g., pay "greenmail").

4. During the 1980s, once the company went into play, the change of control was inevitable as blocks of stock rapidly moved into traders' hands. In Chrysler's situation, there was a fortunate lack of immediate volatility when the bid was announced, primarily because large blocks of momentum traders had already fled the company's cyclical stock in favor of the "hot technology" stocks.

Stability of ownership was also evidenced by major institutions including FMC, the parent for a series of Fidelity funds, which held the second largest position in Chrysler after Tracinda. Behind the scenes discussions were also later reported to have occurred between the company and the College Retirement Equity Fund (CREF), as the company's board appealed to this major institution by agreeing to adopt a policy to restrict the company's ability to issue "blank-check" preferred stock, which can weaken the voting power of common shareholders.

The critical factor in the Chrysler-Tracinda battle, however, appears to have been communications between the company and its investors. Discussions between Chrysler's Chairman and CEO Robert J. Eaton were held with major institutional investors, as well as with outside board members. Eaton, in a speech before the Economic Club of Detroit on March 18, 1996 said of these communications:

> On a number of occasions, I would leave and let the board member and the fund manager talk one on one. We had a simple story that combined solid performance over the past few years with a compelling strategy for the future. None of our institutional owners asked us to change direction. Not one of them told us to compromise the future for the sake of today.[3]

VARIATIONS AMONG SHAREHOLDERS

If corporate executives fail to understand the complex variety of shareholders' investment behavior in securities markets, they can unnecessarily antagonize their institutional investors. For example, some CEOs claim that institutional investors, such as public pension funds, are "only in the market for short-term gain." But the large public employee pension fund, with a portfolio which is largely indexed (i.e., it contains a wide range of stocks generally replicating the Standard and Poor's 500 stocks or some other even larger "basket of stocks"), will generally invest on behalf of long-term beneficiaries. This type of fund may rarely if ever sell stock and is understandably annoyed at the charge that it is a "short-term trader"—a charge which clearly implies the fund has no standing to be concerned about the governance of the corporation. Although the corporation thinks of the fund as a trader, its investment behavior actually puts it closer to the investor end of the shareholder spectrum. It is critical for both corporations and institutions to correctly distinguish the investment characteristics and behavior patterns of the various shareholders along a spectrum consisting of investors at one end and traders at the other; this is the only way for these corporations and institutional investors to build a mutually acceptable and understood frame of reference regarding investment strategy and corporate governance. Only then will corporations be able to deal with their shareholder constituencies not as monolithic, passive shareholders, but with regard to the highly individualized blocks of economic and political power they exert in the market.

The distinctions between investors and traders made in this book are not intended to cast dispersion on any one group of shareholders. Traders as well as investors occupy a critical place in an efficient securities market, since some mix of both is necessary to ensure the combined efficiencies of immediate liquidity and sustained investment. Some have advocated imposing a transactions tax on each trade of stock in order to dampen perceived trading excesses. This approach ignores that traders are vital to the markets and should not (and cannot) be eliminated. It is more important, therefore, for corporate managers to accept that traders exist and, within the new 21st century model of the corporation, differentiate between types of shareholders—investors or traders—in order to formulate strategic plans to build shareholder value that will appeal to the right kind of shareholder base.

Most corporate managements and boards of directors list *improving shareholder value* among their top goals. Yet, given the fact that all shareholders are not the same in their exercise of economic (and political) power, managements and boards must make important decisions about *which shareholders* should be those for whom the company designs its strategies to achieve improved value. While corporations may attract traders (such as *momentum traders,* discussed in Chapter 5) for certain periods of time, they should not gear their investment strategy to satisfy these traders lest they impair their viability to generate sustained investor value. Nor should the task before boards and managers be confused or even sidetracked by the so-called stakeholder statutes (discussed in Chapter 4) which permit boards of directors to consider not only shareholders but other *stakeholders* of the corporation, such as customers, suppliers, and the community, as they fashion corporate policy. Corporations can rightly center their efforts on creating sustained shareholder (as opposed to *stakeholder*) returns and, in the process of building wealth by creating intrinsic value for the in-depth investor, they may well satisfy most of their responsibilities to these other key constituencies of the corporation. Indeed, as will be discussed in Chapter 2, designing corporate strategies to incorporate the best interests of many of these constituents can synergistically improve intrinsic shareholder value.

This book is not only meant to assist corporations to understand their shareholder base, but also to help institutional investors clarify how their behavior as investors may be interpreted by corporations. Figure 1–2 is a simplified view of the various levels of shareholders according to their investment and voting strategies. A *level 1* shareholder is typified by Warren Buffett, chief investment officer of Berkshire Hathaway and a major "relationship investor." Buffett is renowned for his investment strategy of taking large positions in a relatively few number of stocks, holding

FIGURE 1-2

Levels of Shareholder Participation

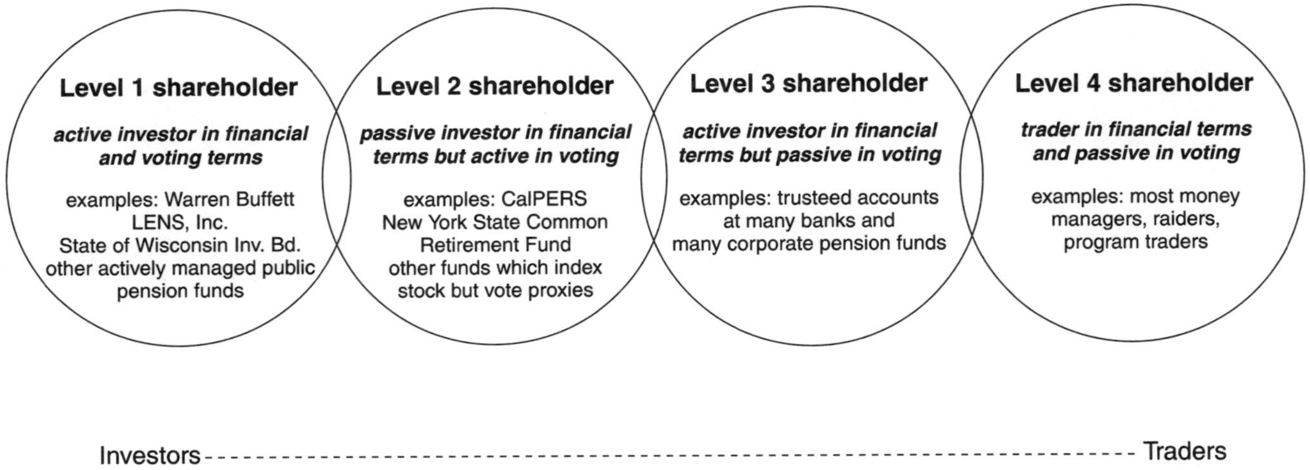

Level 1 shareholder

active investor in financial and voting terms

examples: Warren Buffett
LENS, Inc.
State of Wisconsin Inv. Bd.
other actively managed public pension funds

Level 2 shareholder

passive investor in financial terms but active in voting

examples: CalPERS
New York State Common Retirement Fund
other funds which index stock but vote proxies

Level 3 shareholder

active investor in financial terms but passive in voting

examples: trusteed accounts at many banks and many corporate pension funds

Level 4 shareholder

trader in financial terms and passive in voting

examples: most money managers, raiders, program traders

Investors - Traders them for long periods of time, and actively monitoring his investment. (See Box 1–2 for more on Buffett.)

The LENS fund and the State of Wisconsin Investment Board are also examples of *relationship investors* who pursue an active investment and voting strategy and therefore may be classified as level 1 shareholders. The LENS fund began in 1992 with the purpose of acting as an active "money manager" in what may be regarded as the first "corporate governance fund." The LENS investment strategy of active management is grounded in what Robert A.G. Monks and Nell Minow now believe to be well-established principles of "value" investing:

> We invest in companies that have unrealized value, and then we use the wide variety of initiatives available to shareholders to encourage a company's managers and directors to make the necessary changes to realize that value. We invest in companies that have strong assets undervalued by the market. . . .
>
> Andrew Carnegie once said that the best investment strategy is to put all your eggs in one basket and then watch the basket. Our strategy is to watch not just the basket but the eggs; and we make sure that the eggs understand that they are being watched. We have found that boards of directors, like sub-atomic particles, behave differently when they know they are being observed. Our initiatives are designed to create this difference. Our experience has shown that shareholder involvement can add value. . . .[4]

Unlike the California Public Employees' Retirement System (CalPERS) and the other major public pension funds, LENS invests in only a small number of companies and becomes much more involved with its portfolio companies. LENS is engaged in *relational investing,* whereby an investor seeks to develop an in-depth relationship with that investor's portfolio companies. During its first two years of operations, LENS invested in seven companies: Sears Roebuck, American Express, Westinghouse, Scott Paper, Borden, Stone & Webster, and Eastman Kodak. The fund also evaluates companies for future investment potential and has formed its own group of "focus companies," which include candidates outside the United States. Nell Minow has often pointed out that the CEOs in virtually all the companies in the LENS portfolio resigned sometime following LENS' taking a position in the company and frequently amid considerable media attention; she is quick to add that LENS was surely not responsible for the CEOs' departures. However, intense scrutiny from the institutional investor community can rapidly spread to involve boards

BOX 1–2

Warren Buffett: The Relationship Investing Guru

Warren Buffett is Chairman of the Board of Berkshire Hathaway Inc., a holding company owning subsidiaries engaged in a number of diverse business activities, including selling insurance, candy, encyclopedias, home cleaning systems, home furnishings, newspapers, shoes, and uniforms.

While Buffett is known for making wise acquisitions of relatively small, well-run enterprises, his major notoriety comes from his investment style, which is to choose a limited number of good, long-term investments in stocks of other companies. The Berkshire Hathaway 1994 annual report lists the company's ownership stake in the following companies: American Express (5.5 percent), Capital Cities/ABC, Inc. (13.0 percent), The Coca-Cola Company (7.8 percent), Federal Home Loan Mortgage Corp. (6.3 percent), Gannett Co., Inc. (4.9 percent), GEICO Corp. (50.2 percent), The Gillette Company (10.8 percent), PNC Bank Corp. (8.3 percent), The Washington Post Company (15.2 percent), and Wells Fargo & Company (13.3 percent).

At the end of 1994, every single stock in the Berkshire Hathaway portfolio had risen in value and, together, the cost of all stocks purchased was $4.6 billion and the market value was $14 billion, for a book profit of $9.4 billion.

Many of these stocks have been in the company's portfolio for decades. Buffett, in the company's 1994 annual report (p.16) writes:

> Our investments continue to be few in number and simple in concept: The truly big investment idea can usually be explained in a short paragraph. We like a business with enduring competitive advantages that is run by able and owner-oriented people. . . .We try to *price*, rather than *time*, purchases. In our view, it is folly to forego buying shares in an outstanding business whose long-term future is predictable, because of short-term worries about an economy or a stock market that we know to be unpredictable. Why scrap an informed decision because of an uninformed guess?

The annual report discusses the company's acquisition strategy for new businesses to operate in addition to the diverse group of candy, home cleaning and furnishings, shoe companies, and so on.

Under the heading *Acquisition Criteria* (p. 21), Buffett writes to his shareholders:

> We are eager to hear about businesses that meet all of the following criteria:
> (1) Large purchases (at least $10 million of after-tax earnings),

(continued)

Warren Buffett—Continued

(2) Demonstrated consistent earning power (future projections are of no interest to us, nor are "turnaround" situations),

(3) Businesses earning good returns on equity while employing little or no debt,

(4) Management in place (we can't supply it),

(5) Simple businesses (if there's lots of technology, we won't understand it),

(6) An offering price (we don't want to waste our time or that of the seller by talking, even preliminarily, about a transaction when price is unknown).

We will not engage in unfriendly takeovers. . . . Charlie [Charles Munger, Vice Chairman of the Board and Buffett's colleague in his business decisions] and I frequently get approached about acquisitions that don't come close to meeting our tests: We've found that if you advertise an interest in buying collies, a lot of people will call hoping to sell you their cocker spaniels. . . . Besides being interested in the purchase of businesses as described above, we are also interested in the negotiated purchase of large, but not controlling, blocks of stock comparable to those we hold in Capital Cities, Salomon, Gillette, USAir and Champion.

Fortune, in its March 4, 1996 list of "America's Most Admired Companies," rates Berkshire Hathaway as number 17, with a rating of 7.97 out of a possible score of 10. When attributes of successful companies are broken down into various categories, Berkshire Hathaway rates at the top or near the top in four out of eight categories:

Use of Corporate Assets	1st of all the companies
Value as a Long-Term Investment	2nd
Financial Soundness	3rd
Quality of Management	3rd

In the *Business Week,* April 22, 1996, "Special Report on Executive Compensation," companies were rated to see how pay matches up to performance. One measurement system relates to how good a job the Chairman/CEO did for shareholders. Warren Buffett rates highest in terms of executives who gave shareholders the most for their executive compensation.

(continued)

of directors who may make changes in top management if faced with a Chairman/CEO who remains deaf to investors' concerns over performance. LENS' primary focus in companies it is involved in continues to be

Warren Buffett—Concluded

From 1993 to 1995 Buffett's total pay (salary, bonus, and long-term compensation paid for the entire three-year period) was $942,000. Meanwhile, during the 1993–95 period, shareholder return (as measured by stock price changes plus dividend reinvestment) was 173 percent. This earned the highest place on the relative index of shareholder return for compensation (290 index points). By comparison, William Gates, CEO of Microsoft, earned fifth highest place on the list of executives who gave their shareholders the most for their pay. Gates earned $1.3 million over the three-year period, while shareholder value increased 106 percent, for an index rating of 159.

For the second year in a row, Warren Buffett earned the distinction of being the CEO in *Business Week's* survey of executives who provide shareholders with the greatest returns relative to their compensation. According to the April 22, 1996 issue of *Business Week*, while his $100,000 annual salary is paltry by CEO standards, his fortune rises and falls on the performance of Berkshire Hathaway stock—he owns 40.2 percent of the company, a stake now worth $16.5 billion.

During early May 1996, Berkshire Hathaway made an offering of Class B shares, "Baby Berks." Many of the details of the transaction are consistent with Buffett's investment philosophy. The offering was priced high—at $1,110 per share—consistent with the approach taken by Buffett as he has always resisted splitting the price of Berkshire Hathaway just to please the market or make the shares "more marketable." The Baby Berk Class B offering was also managed on Wall Street in an unusual way—*to reduce volatility in the stock,* not to increase activity following the offering. Typically underwriters hold back the supply of stock to ensure enough demand to push the price up 10 to 15 percent when trading starts. Buffett increased the size of the offering several times—to over 500,000 shares from the original 100,000 contemplated—to give the public the ability to buy the stock at the offering price, keeping it from becoming a "hot deal" that quickly soars. In addition, the slim fee to the underwriter, Salomon Brothers Inc., of $7.8 million, or about 1.5 percent of proceeds, was uncharacteristically small for Wall Street, but clearly reflected Buffett's shrewd investment acumen.

the board, and its initiatives have been directed toward ensuring that each company's board of directors devotes the time, the energy, and the independent analysis necessary to create long-term shareholder value.

In comparison to the active relational investment strategy of LENS, which is directed at a small number of companies, most of the large public pension funds like the New York State Common Retirement Fund, the state funds of Connecticut and Pennsylvania, and CalPERS are substantially indexed. Since they do not generally sell stocks in their indexed funds and maintain that they are invested for the long term, these institutions get involved in companies mainly through the *value added* of their proxy voting and, more recently, through their personal attention to a small list of underperforming companies culled from their portfolios, which might contain in excess of 2,000 stocks. The State of Wisconsin Investment Board is a notable exception, since it pursues both active investing and voting strategies.

Thus, on the spectrum of investing styles, CalPERS is a *level 2* shareholder since it pursues a passive investment strategy and an active voting strategy. An important development in the institutional investor movement may have been signaled by Richard Koppes (General Counsel, CalPERS) when he said that, although the fund is largely indexed at this time, it might consider taking a more relational investing approach whereby it might invest in a small number of stocks with the intention of becoming more actively involved—thus shifting a portion of its assets to pursue an approach more like LENS' strategy. Thus, although the bulk of its equity portfolio may be in level 2 shareholdings, if CalPERS does place a small portion of its funds in a nonindexed investment portfolio which it will actively monitor, that portion of CalPERS' portfolio investment would then be reclassified as a level 1 shareholder investment in what is otherwise a level 2 shareholder portfolio. Most nonindexed corporate pension funds and bank investment departments would qualify as level 3 investors, since they actively manage money but generally do not become involved in governance issues. On the final end of the spectrum, a money manager with an aggressive trading strategy and no interest in voting might be regarded as a level 4 shareholder. Program traders (who buy and sell according to computer programs of stock price movements regardless of the intrinsic value of the underlying stocks) are prime examples of level 4 shareholders. A pension fund that delegated its investments and voting authority to such a money manager would also be a level 4 shareholder.

While not legal distinctions, these classifications represent the intensity with which a shareholder becomes involved in the success of the corporation. Corporations recognizing this framework will be in a better position to tailor their shareholder value programs to suit the shareholders who are most important to them, since they cannot hope to satisfy all of them at the same time—*nor should they try.* This categorization should also help corporations decide among such strategic choices as whether to increase immediate dividend payout (i.e., appeal to level 3 and 4 shareholders), or plow back excess cash into research and development (appeal to level 1 shareholders). Moreover, at one time in its development a corporation might advocate an acquisition program geared to attracting level 4 shareholders looking for immediate price appreciation. But when that same corporation restructures, it might shift its shareholder value focus to appeal to more growth oriented level 1 shareholders willing to tolerate a drop in this quarter's earnings to allow the corporation to invest to develop its intellectual and capital asset base.

Much like a widespread psychological testing matrix of personality traits, where individuals are rated according to their personality attributes, classifying shareholders along a level 1 to 4 spectrum can lead to better understood objectives and definitions of mutual responsibilities for investment and corporate governance behavior on the part of both corporations and institutional investors. Not only should a corporation which wants to attract investors of the level 1 shareholder variety fashion its strategies accordingly, but if an institutional investor wants to be considered a level 1 shareholder and communicate to the corporation on that basis, it should assume responsibility for active investment and voting. This implies that the investor should not abrogate his fiduciary responsibility (even if he does not strictly violate fiduciary trust law) to delegate investment and voting functions to outside managers.

The typology of shareholders presented here clearly goes beyond any letter of the law to consider both economic and political forces. Moreover, a more detailed knowledge of the forces behind the 21st century corporate model can lead to a better understanding of the makeup of corporations, what corporations and shareholders want from each other, and how both sides can achieve their goals.

THE ECONOMIC CLOUT OF U.S. INSTITUTIONAL INVESTORS

Corporations seeking to create shareholder value should become fully acquainted with the highly varied U.S. institutional investor base, which dominates not only U.S. markets, but increasingly global financial markets as well. By mid-1995, U.S. institutional investors held assets of $10.2 trillion (Figure 1–3), or nearly 22 percent of all U.S. financial assets. While their holdings of the total equity market have remained at approximately 50

FIGURE 1-3

Institutional Investor Growth: 1980–2Q 1995

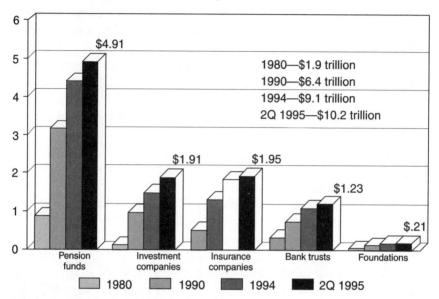

Source: *The Brancato Report on Institutional Investment* 3, ed. 1 (January 1996).

percent, by the end of 1995 their percentage ownership in the largest 1,000 U.S. corporations had increased to 57.2 percent, up from 46.6 percent in 1987 (Figure 1–4).

Growth in institutional investment during the past 25 years has been extraordinary. Total institutional investor assets nearly tripled in one decade, from $672.6 billion in 1970 to $1.9 trillion in 1980. The next decade brought *more* than a tripling in assets, to $6.3 trillion in 1990. There was an additional, staggering increase of more than 50 percent in the next four years, to $9.3 trillion at the end of the third quarter of 1994; then, with a booming stock market in 1995, a further increase to $10.2 trillion by the end of the second quarter of 1995. Annual institutional investor growth rates were fastest at 14.9 percent per year during the first half of the 1980s, then leveled off to a still respectable 10.8 percent per year during the second half of the 1980s. Aided by the boom in the stock market, assets grew 13.3 percent from 1990 to 1993, slowed to only a 2.1 percent growth during 1994, then rose 9.7 percent in the first six months of 1995 over the 1994 year-end figure.

FIGURE 1-4

Institutional Ownership in the Top 1,000 Corporations: 1987–1995

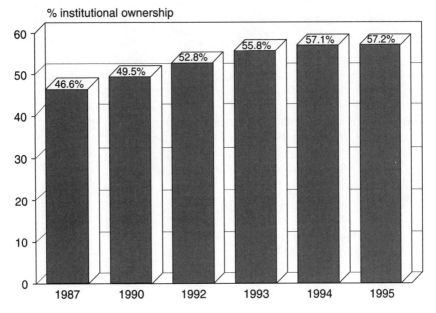

% institutional ownership

Source: *The Brancato Report on Institutional Investment*, 3, ed. 1 (January 1996).

The term *institutional investor* refers to an investor with money under professional management in an organization that invests on behalf of a group of individuals, another organization, or a group of organizations. Unfortunately, it is difficult to categorize every variety of funds that flow from individuals into various poolings such as venture capital funds, partnerships, and private market transactions. Therefore, throughout this book, institutional investors will be grouped into a few primary categories: public and private pension funds, mutual funds, insurance companies, and banks. The main categories of institutional investors and their key investment and governance characteristics are described in Box 1–3.

Institutional investors have widely differing investment objectives, trading and turnover patterns, and participation rates in corporate governance. Pension funds are the single largest category of institutional investor. Their growth was clearly aided by U.S. regulatory policy. Corporate pension funds operate under federal regulations established by the Employee Retirement Income Security Act (ERISA) of 1974, administered by the

BOX 1-3

Types of U.S. Institutional Investors

Public Employee Pension Funds

These "public funds" represent various state and federal agencies and have tended to be the more activist of the pension funds. They have made their demands known and pursued their goals either individually or through shareholder groups such as the Council of Institutional Investors. Most of the public funds delegate significant investment authority to other fiduciaries, such as banks or money managers. Although they delegate investment authority, they may still retain voting authority or impose voting standards on their delegated managers. Some, like the State of Wisconsin Investment Board, are level 1 investors since they choose to retain all of their investing and voting authority. Even among those funds that adopt passive investment strategies and place large amounts of their portfolios in indexed funds, some, like CalPERS, have made specific companies in their indexed portfolios the focus of their activism. Recently, CalPERS announced that it intends to take large positions in companies and pursue a kind of activist role with them called "relationship investing"—level 1 investing.

Corporate Pension Funds

Corporate pension funds, the pension funds of publicly traded corporations, are known as "private-trusteed funds" and are those in the pension systems of major corporations such as General Motors, Mobil Oil, and General Electric. These corporate pension funds have generally not been shareholder activists, in large part because of their obvious discomfort at taking aim at managements of other corporations. Private corporate pension funds also tend to delegate a large proportion of their investment and voting fiduciary responsibility to other institutions, such as banks and money managers, which are even more reluctant to become involved in controversy. One corporation, Campbell Soup, has publicly stated that it intends to vote the stock in its corporate pension fund in accordance with a list of its own corporate governance standards. General Motors has also taken a corporate governance stance, although not with regard to voting the stock of its pension fund. In 1994 John G. Smale, Chairman of the Board of General Motors, announced that the company had adopted a slate of corporate governance guidelines.

(continued)

Types—Concluded

Mutual Funds

Mutual funds and other investment companies are the fastest-growing segment of the institutional investor market. They have, to date, had relatively little incentive to actively participate in corporate governance, unless they were voting in the context of a takeover, where their vote would carry with it a direct economic value. Some have kept away from controversial issues, lest they alienate those who allocate corporate pension fund money to them to manage. Managers of these types of institutions tend to ignore proxy voting methods of exerting pressure on companies. Instead, if they think the company is not performing well on the "fundamentals" (i.e., on the intrinsic value of the stock), they tend to sell their stock, also called "doing the Wall Street walk" or "voting with their feet" by selling their shares. Recently, however, several large fund managers (Fidelity and Alliance Capital) have become more involved in shareholder activism.

Insurance Companies

Insurance companies tend to invest a very small percentage of their assets in equities. Prudential, one of the largest, actively manages its entire equity portfolio (i.e., retains all authority for its equity investment decisions) while giving its fundamental security analysts free rein over proxy voting. But because most of their assets are invested in bonds, insurance companies tend to participate in less obvious ways in corporate governance. Rather than exerting pressure as shareholders, insurance companies have had extraordinary influence as bondholders over the corporate governance decisions of companies that are restructuring or facing or emerging from bankruptcy.

Bank Trusts

Bank trust departments occupy a position in capital markets similar to that of mutual funds and investment companies. With significant fiduciary authority delegated to them, they manage funds far in excess of what their own asset data would suggest. When other fiduciaries delegate investment authority to banks, they tend to delegate approximately 70 percent of the voting authority as well. Recently, a press for improved portfolio returns has led a very small number of banks to begin to participate more actively in corporate governance.

Department of Labor's Pension and Welfare Benefits Administration. ERISA pension funds are modeled on trust law, whereby a fiduciary must act for the "exclusive benefit" of pension plan participants and beneficiaries. This system is designed to prevent pension plan sponsors from investing undue amounts in risky, illiquid, or self-dealing transactions. Although not the original intention, in providing this framework for confidence, ERISA inspired the investment of vast sums in U.S. corporate pension systems. While ERISA applies only to private corporate pension plans, through a series of state laws most public pension funds have by reference and regulation become covered by the same ERISA principles and must adhere to the "prudent person" standards of fiduciary conduct. Public employee pension funds have also enjoyed substantial growth, especially within the last 15 years.

By the first half of 1995, pension funds accounted for 48.1 percent of total institutional investor assets. They also accounted for the largest dollar increase of any type of institution between 1980 and 1995. Pension fund assets rose from $860 billion in 1980 to $4.9 trillion by mid-1995, representing more than a five-fold increase. Since 1985, average private trusteed (corporate) pension fund growth has been outpaced by growth in the public pension fund sector, although proceeding from a smaller base. Most recent data show that private trusteed funds (corporate and Taft Hartley) have declined to 26.6 percent of total institutional investor assets. The public pension funds, otherwise known as state and local funds, have steadily increased their share of total institutional investor assets to 12.9 percent by the end of the second quarter of 1995. (The remaining 8.6 percent of total institutional investor assets ascribed to pension funds is held in private insured pension fund accounts generally placed with insurance companies or other fixed annuity fiduciaries.)

In 1995, all institutional investors accounted for 47.5 percent of total equity. Pension funds in the aggregate accounted for 25.4 percent of total equity: private trusteed pension funds accounted for 14.6 percent, public state and local funds accounted for 8.2 percent, and private insured funds accounted for the remaining 2.6 percent. The relative importance of various types of pension funds, based on assets and percentage of equity holdings, is shown in Table 1-1.

Key to understanding how various types of U.S. institutional investors behave, is the fact that they may not manage all their assets—they may allocate a large portion of these assets to other institutions to manage on their behalf. This gives rise to substantial differences between money held

TABLE 1-1

Pension Fund Assets and Equity Holdings

	% of Total 1995 Institutional Investor Assets	% of Total 1995 Outstanding U.S. Equity
All pension funds	48.1%	25.4%
	% of Total Pension Fund Assets	% of Total Pension Fund Equity
Private trusteed	55.3%	57.5%
Public state/local	26.8	32.4
Private insured	17.9	10.1
	100.0%	100.0%

Note: Data are as of June 30, 1995.
Source: *The Brancato Report on Institutional Investment*, 3, ed. 1 (January 1996).

FIGURE 1-5

Holdings versus Management of Assets: 1994

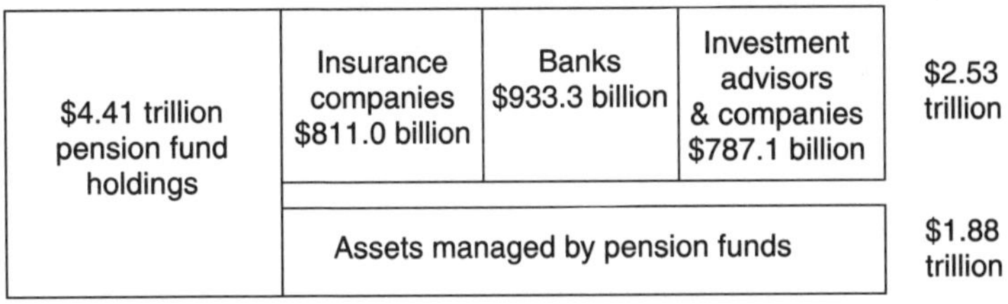

$4.41 trillion pension fund holdings	Insurance companies $811.0 billion	Banks $933.3 billion	Investment advisors & companies $787.1 billion	$2.53 trillion
	Assets managed by pension funds			$1.88 trillion

Source: *The Brancato Report on Institutional Investment*, 3, ed. 1 (January 1996).

by institutions as prime fiduciaries and money actually managed by these institutions. For example, Figure 1–5 shows that while pension funds held a total of $4.41 trillion in assets in 1994, they allocated significant portions of these assets for *management* to insurance companies ($811 billion), banks ($933 billion), and external investment advisors ($787 billion). In 1994, therefore, pension funds actually managed only $1.88 trillion out of their $4.41 trillion in assets, while a total of $2.53 trillion was delegated to other institutions to manage. As Table 1–2 shows, pension funds *held* 47.4

TABLE 1-2

Institutional Investor Holdings versus Management: 1994

Institution	Assets Held	Assets Managed
Pension funds	47.4%	20.2%
Private trusteed	26.3	15.5
Private insured	8.4	0.0
State & local	12.6	4.7
External investment advisors	0.0	8.2
Investment companies	18.6	24.5
Insurance companies	20.0	27.3
Banks	11.9	19.4
Foundations	2.1	0.4
Total	100.0%	100.0%

Source: *The Brancato Report on Institutional Investment*, 3, ed. 1 (January 1996).

percent of 1994 institutional investor assets but *actually managed* only 20.2 percent of institutional assets. Money allocated to banks to manage, primarily from pension funds, increases their influence in the markets: In 1994 banks held 11.9 percent of assets as institutional investors themselves but managed 19.4 percent of all 1994 institutional investor assets. Similarly, insurance companies held 20.0 percent of institutional assets in 1994 while their managed assets amounted to 27.3 percent. In terms of aggregate managed assets, therefore, the key groups to focus on when planning a corporate strategy to attract U.S. institutional investor capital are not only pension funds, but other intermediaries such as investment companies, insurance companies, and banks.

INSTITUTIONAL INVESTOR TRADING PATTERNS

When the money actually managed by each type of institutional investor is considered (as opposed to the total assets under their control), significant differences in patterns of holding and trading stock are uncovered. All institutions managing their own money experienced an average portfolio turnover of 42.6 percent for the year ended September 30, 1995. (Turnover percentages relate to the amount of the portfolio traded during a year, e.g.,

TABLE 1-3

Average Turnover Rates by Type of Institution: 1993-1995

Type*	1993	1994	1995
Corporate pension funds	33.2%	19.9%	24.8%
Public pension funds	13.3	20.9	20.7
Mutual fund managers	48.2	50.5	42.3
Money managers	56.7	55.7	59.2
Insurance companies	53.6	44.7	46.4
Banks	24.3	29.5	25.3
Weighted average for all institutions	41.5%	43.6%	42.6%

Notes: Data calculated using Georgeson & Company, Inc. database as of September 30th of each year.
* Weighted by value of portfolio.
Source: *The Brancato Report on Institutional Investment*, 3, ed. 2 (May 1996).

a 50 percent turnover rate would mean that half the portfolio traded that year.) Table 1–3 shows corporate pension funds that managed their own equity portfolios had much lower 1995 turnover (24.8 percent) than all institutions. Public pension funds had the lowest turnover (20.7 percent), and money managers averaged the highest turnover (59.2 percent).

The lower turnover within the portfolios of public pension funds is primarily a result of the higher level of funds they index. Indexation is most pursued by public pension funds, with 66.8 percent of their portfolios (Table 1-4) under management allocated to indexation. Institutional investors such as pension funds pursue indexation because they believe they cannot beat the market averages by a margin sufficient to cover the higher transaction costs of trading stock in a more active portfolio. Indeed, this reasoning proved sound during 1995, as stock price returns, including reinvested dividends from the Standard and Poor's 500 index, were 37.5 percent compared to the Lipper Analytical Services calculation of average stock mutual fund return of only 30.2 percent. By comparison, corporate pension funds index a significantly lower amount of the total equity they manage—13.2 percent for corporate pension funds versus 66.8 percent for public pension funds. Even these aggregate data show significant variation in the overall investment strategies pursued by institutional investors. (A more

TABLE 1-4

Equity Indexation by Type of Institution: September 30, 1995

Type	Indexed Equities (millions)	Total Equities (millions)	Percent of Equity Portfolio
Corporate pension funds	$ 11,074	$ 83,840	13.2%
Public pension funds	156,489	234,385	66.8
Mutual fund managers	Negligible*	523,341	Negligible*
Money managers	12,336	1,246,412	1.0
Insurance companies	8,956	212,722	4.2
Banks	281,394	855,619	32.9
All institutions	$470,249	$3,156,319	14.9%

Notes: Data calculated using Georgeson & Company, Inc. database.
* May pursue indexation as part of a "balanced" portfolio strategy.
Source: *The Brancato Report on Institutional Investment,* 3, ed. 2 (May 1996).

detailed analysis of each subsegment of their portfolios is shown in Chapter 5, so that corporations can better understand the dynamics *within* the specific portfolios of their investors and not merely on an aggregate level.) These data show that institutional investors are not a monolithic group and should not be treated as such.

Moreover, the charge that public pension funds are selling out corporations in the short term is entirely too simplistic and not substantiated by the data regarding the money they manage directly, although the extent to which they delegate this money to external money managers clearly has negative potential for high degrees of overall trading and turnover. This makes it all the more important, as will be demonstrated in Chapter 5, for corporations to consider marketing their stock specifically to those investors who share their investment objectives. If successful, this approach will stabilize their shareholder base, putting less in the hands of high-turnover investors. In turn, this should minimize corporate stock price volatility and help the market realize the inherent fundamental value of the company.

THE MYTHS OF SHORT-TERMISM

During the last decade, two well-known myths regarding short-termism have blurred the distinctions between investors and traders and distracted market participants from more productive discussions about building shareholder value. Myth Number 1 says that institutional investors buy and sell stock for the short term. Myth Number 2 says that corporations invest only to please short-term shareholders. Together, both myths have diverted professionals from focusing on intrinsic shareholder value and critical corporate performance issues.

Shareholder Short-Termism

The charge that shareholders are in the markets for short-term gain was first hurled by CEOs at all types of institutional investors during the 1980s takeover wave. Then, in the early 1990s, it was used by many as an excuse for a deteriorating U.S. corporate competitive position. The myth that shareholders act only in the short term was also espoused by noted academics such as Professor Michael Porter from Harvard Business School as well as by Michael T. Jacobs, Assistant Secretary and Director of Corporate Finance of the U.S. Treasury. In 1991, Jacobs summed up the key elements of short-termism in his book *Short-Term America: The Causes and Cures of Our Business Myopia:*

> Shareholders trade stocks so often and hold such broadly diversified portfolios that they cannot possibly keep up with the business activities of the companies they own. Because most U.S. investors are detached from the businesses they fund, they rely on outward manifestations of what is really going on within the company; namely, quarterly earnings and other accounting measures of performance. . .When they are dissatisfied with corporate performance shareholders sell stock. . . .[5]

This is a prime example of generalities that ignore the varied investment objectives among types of institutional investors, and indeed, among various segments within the same institution's portfolio. Data in this chapter contradict this monolithic view of shareholders and confirm that trading and turnover patterns vary by type of institutional investor, by investment objective, and by the investment segment within each portfolio. One must, therefore, reject the generalization that institutional investors are only short-term oriented. Clearly, some of them are and some of them are not.

During the 1980s, corporations under siege from raiders saw blocks of stock move from institutional investor hands to arbitrageurs (who hoped to trade rapidly on the spread between the merger bid price and the current open market price of the stock of a company under threat of a hostile bidder). Significant blocks of stock did move into the hands of arbitrageurs for a variety of reasons: (1) premiums were large and irresistible; (2) principal institutional fiduciaries such as the heads of public and private pension funds sold stock rather than risk being sued for breach of fiduciary responsibility since they were concerned that their fiduciary obligations required the tendering of shares at a "bird in the hand" premium; and (3) even those institutional investors with long-term payout requirements enabling them to take a long-term and more in-depth market outlook may have delegated their investments to other fiduciaries more intent on earning shorter-term profits (or feeling pressure themselves not to be replaced by the pension fund with another, higher performing money manager). The debate over whether fiduciaries were compelled to tender their stock (hand them in to the bidding company) in a takeover situation became so confusing to fiduciaries that the Department of Labor (DOL) and the Treasury Department felt compelled to clarify (the DOL regulates private pension funds, while the Treasury oversees the tax exempt status of both private and public funds) that fiduciaries were not required to tender their shares if they believed that shareholder value over the longer-term would be greater if the shares were retained.[6]

The 1980s takeover wave brought sharply into focus the various segments of the shareholder universe. The greenmailers (traders who were level 4 shareholders) bought a block of stock and threatened to launch a takeover unless they were quickly bought out at a premium. The raiders launched the takeover bids, funded initially by *high yield* or *junk* bonds (bonds which paid high yields or returns based on a higher risk profile). In a few cases, some of the raiders said they fully intended to run the target companies (in that case they would have been level 1 shareholders), but many more (level 4 shareholders) intended to buy companies and immediately sell off their assets for a profit. Many embattled managements under siege by hostile bidders blamed the large pension funds, and in particular the public pension funds who had, in 1984, formed the Council of Institutional Investors to oppose the payment of greenmail to financiers such as Saul Steinberg and Carl Ichan. (The rise of institutional investor activism will be discussed in Chapter 3.) Although the public pension funds within the Council had not initiated the hostile bidding, many corporations tended to confuse their actions to protect their interests (institutions rejected the payment of greenmail to one shareholder because it diluted the value of the remaining shares) with the actions of raiders and other financiers who initiated the hostile bidding. All were labeled enemies to management, and a gap between public pension funds and corporations opened which remains to this day. It was only after the dust settled over the wreckage of many corporations that observers began to lament the misalignment of the interests of institutional investors (mainly pension funds) and corporate managements. In 1993, speaking at a Columbia Institutional Investor Project conference in New York City, Robert Monks, a former Department of Labor regulator who subsequently became a shareholder activist, noted how the interests of the corporation and those of the large public pension fund should converge in a positive "relationship."

> "Relationship investors" become informed and interested partners insisting on competitiveness—meaning long-term superior returns. The long-term perspective reflects the fact that their fate is inextricably linked with the enterprise in which they invest. Investors like pension funds are not just permanent investors, they are permanent consumers, employees, and neighbors, and that makes them permanent partners. A pension fund with a significant stake in the company has no interest in short-term cost cutting that increases pollution, reduces research and development to undermine future productivity or eliminate jobs. They will feel the adverse effects of "savings" like these in excess of any short-term benefits in dividends or share price appreciation.[7]

Corporate Short-Term Investment

Short-termism Myth Number 2 is that corporations arrange their investments to cater to the short-term mentality of the markets to satisfy Myth Number 1. The most vocal advocate of Myth Number 2 was Harvard Professor Michael Porter, who headed up a project entitled *Time Horizons for Business,* sponsored by the private-sector Council on Competitiveness and the Harvard Business School. In June 1992, Porter wrote a summary report of this project entitled *Capital Choices: Changing the Way America Invests in Industry,* which was published by the Harvard Business School. Porter argued that the capital investment and allocation process in the United States was flawed, that the German and Japanese processes are superior, and that, consequently, the United States is at a competitive disadvantage and should reform its system. Porter's model of the institutional investor was, however, based on a simplistic and monolithic view of the institutional investor. It produced generalities about the behavior of shareholders, which continued the polarization between corporations and shareholders begun during the 1980s takeover period. Moreover, Porter's analysis was unfortunately made on the brink of a spectacular reversal in fortunes for the Japanese and German economies as well as a recovery in the competitiveness position of U.S. businesses.

During the early 1990s, the federally legislated U.S. Competitiveness Policy Council (CPC)[8] initiated a major inquiry into ways to improve the ability of U.S. corporations to compete in world markets. In 1992, the same year that Porter wrote his *Capital Choices,* the CPC's Subcouncil on Corporate Governance and Financial Markets heard publicly from many executives throughout the country who soundly rejected the simplistic notion that financial markets were only short-term oriented. The members of the Subcouncil also rejected the notion that any inability to raise capital for long-term planning purposes was attributable to short-termism.

> The financial markets, per se, are not the cause of our competitiveness problems. At times, they are used as excuses for poor performance. . . .
>
> . . . many Subcouncil members were not persuaded that we have a pervasive underinvestment or capital allocation problem and did not, in general, find Porter's policy prescriptions persuasive . . .[9]

The Subcouncil noted that credibility was the critical factor necessary for businesses to attract needed investment and found that "while rejecting facile arguments about 'short-term' America, we recognize that U.S. businesses operate in a culture that does not stress physical or institutional preservation." The Subcouncil recommended that policymakers examine ways to improve the tangible and intangible investment environment and that corporations and accountants work on measures to capture improvements in corporate performance attributable to making the kinds of intangible and tangible investments that will ensure future corporate growth and success.

The Subcouncil finally put to rest the investment time horizon question:

> Many Subcouncil members believe the issue is not one of time horizons for investment. Rather the issue is the nature of the types of investments needed to enhance competitiveness, regardless of how long investment money is committed. There are many types of corporations which invest along different time frames: what is short term for the electric utility is long term for the toy industry. There are also many types of investors who invest with different time horizons and objectives; some index and hold for years, while others are more quantitatively oriented and trade more frequently. . . . All these participants combine to produce highly liquid and efficient markets.
>
> Nor is the issue "transient" or fragmented shareholder ownership. Owners come from all investment schools and behave with more or less impact on the corporate governance process. Our system has many large, long-term owners, some active and some passive. Even passive investors with small

blocks of shares, if they are vocal, can have an impact on the corporate governance process. The key is whether investors—regardless of their make-up or time horizons—have the means to monitor and communicate, as well as the will to act to effect changes either in the direction of corporate investment or in the corporate governance/strategic planning process or both.

Thus, the concept of short-termism ignores the complexity of the financial market system, the varying investment strategies of each type of investor, and the varying time frames for corporate investment and strategic planning.[10]

MEASURING SHAREHOLDER VALUE

Regulators, corporate finance officers, and public and private pension funds continue to debate what constitutes shareholder value. Numerical methods of determining shareholder value include: (1) calculating *cumulative shareholder returns* as the sum of returns to shareholders assuming reinvestment of dividends over a specified period of time, usually five years; (2) determining *excess returns* over and above a market index such as the S&P 500; and (3) calculating a variety of balance sheet and income statement ratios such as *economic value added* (EVA) and *market value added* (MVA). All three methods are based on historical data and behavior. A major new approach to determining shareholder value is under development as new measures of corporate performance are being designed to capture the potential to create shareholder value, not merely the historic accounting basis for such value. The first three methods will be discussed in the remainder of this chapter and the next chapter will be devoted primarily to the future-oriented new performance measurement approach to determining shareholder value.

Cumulative shareholder returns are now commonly calculated according to regulatory prescriptions set forth by the U.S. Securities and Exchange Commission (SEC). Revising its proxy reform regulations in October 1992, the SEC asked that companies disclose their relative shareholder returns by requiring a graphic representation of the increase (or decrease) in stock price plus reinvested dividends as the basis for calculating shareholder returns. Companies are then required to compare this trendline to a broad market index (such as the Standard and Poor's 500) and then to a more narrow index of comparable companies in the same industry. Only trendline comparisons are required; no calculations of the differential between company and index returns (excess returns) is required.

A second method of describing shareholder value—the excess returns method—centers around price fluctuations in stock and originated primarily from quantitative calculations made by examining an event such as a merger announcement, tracking the stock price prior to and following the event, then comparing the price fluctuation to changes in some overall indicator of stock market pricing such as the Standard and Poor's 500 index of stocks. If the event triggered a price movement beyond movement in the basic market index, there were "excess returns." CalPERS commissioned a study from Wilshire Associates to measure the six-month price and "excess returns," which included not only price but dividend reinvestment, derived from CalPERS' intervention in corporate governance. An initial Wilshire study done over a six-month time frame was criticized as being too short for a fund that takes a future-oriented investment approach and is largely indexed. In a subsequent study, Wilshire extended the study period to five years from each intervention.[11] Shareholder activist groups such as the Council of Institutional Investors (CII) have basically adopted this excess return/price appreciation approach to measuring shareholder value in compiling their "hit lists" of corporate underperformers who will be targeted for corporate governance initiatives.

Economic Value Added (EVA) is a third method of looking at shareholder value. One need only consult the "Bible" of security analysts, Graham and Dodd's classic book *Security Analysis,*[12] to find a variety of ratios routinely calculated by security analysts to reflect various aspects of shareholder value: earnings per share; return on equity; return on assets; pretax profit margins; cash flow; and so on. Consulting firms such as Stern Stewart have combined some of the basic concepts behind the Graham and Dodd ratios in two measures: Economic Value Added (EVA) and Market Value Added (MVA). Economic Value Added shows the net cash return on equity capital and is measured by taking a company's after tax operating profit, deducting its weighted cost of capital, then multiplying the result by the company's total capital. In a 1993 *Fortune* story on EVA, representatives from Stern Stewart asserted that a positive EVA will correlate with a strong stock price because equity capital can been seen to be generating returns.[13] Stern Stewart, in a more recent article in *Fortune,* has begun to tout another indicator, Market Value Added (MVA), which it claims represents a better indicator of whether a company is creating value. MVA is calculated by taking the company's total capital raised from debt and equity, adding back retained earnings, making adjustments for research and development (R&D) spending, then comparing this number representing the total capital in the business with the current value of the company's stock and debt. The difference between total market value (the amount investors now have) and the total invested capital (the amount investors have put into the company) is the MVA and shows how much wealth has been created (or destroyed) over the life of the company.[14] Application of these measures is designed to help managements value alternative projects and make value-creating decisions.

The problem with EVA and MVA analysis is that it is still largely based on the historical ratio analysis of the Graham and Dodd school, which is, in turn, based on traditional accounting numbers and the entire history of the company. While these measures are easy to devise and understand and may give some notion of how a company behaved in the past, major shifts in markets, changes in interest rates, and the investing climate will quickly render these historical data obsolete. Worse still, much like rearranging the deck chairs on the Titanic, preoccupation with these historic data may distract managers from the kind of forward looking strategic assessments needed to create and enhance future investor value.

More creative approaches to measuring shareholder value are now being developed which are geared to capturing the *potential for adding investor value*. These measures, which signal a major revolution in conceptualizing shareholder value, are referred to as *strategic corporate performance measures* and are described in the next chapter.

ENDNOTES

1. Robert A.G. Monks and Nell Minow, *Corporate Governance* (Cambridge, Massachusetts: Blackwell Publishers, 1995), pp. 99–100; quoting from Edward J. Epstein, *Who Owns the Corporation?* Twentieth Century Fund Paper (New York: Priority Press Publications, 1986).

2. John C. Wilcox, "What Types of Institutional Investors Would Your Company Like to Attract?," mimeographed notes from presentation at The Conference Board Seminars, *Access to U.S. Capital Markets: What Companies Should Know About U.S. Markets and Institutional Investors,* Melbourne and Sydney, June 15–16, 1995. p. 4.

3. Robert J. Eaton, Prepared Remarks, Economic Club of Detroit, Detroit, Michigan, March 18, 1996, pp. 6–7.

4. LENS, Inc., Annual Report, period ending July 31, 1994, p. 4.

5. Michael T. Jacobs, *Short-Term America: The Causes and Cures of Our Business Myopia* (Boston: Harvard Business School Press, 1991), p. 10.

6. U.S. Department of Labor and U.S. Treasury Department, Joint Press Release and Joint Statement of Role of ERISA Plans in Takeovers, January 31, 1989.

7. Robert A.G. Monks, "Relational Investing," remarks to The Relational Investing Conference, Columbia Institutional Investor Project, New York City, May 6, 1993, p. 8.

8. The Competitiveness Policy Council was established pursuant to the 1988 Omnibus Trade Act and its amendments. The Council is composed of 12 individuals, 4 selected by the President, 4 by the Senate, and 4 by the House of Representatives. It is not to be confused either with several private sector efforts with similar names or with the special effort of former vice president Daniel Quayle.

9. Competitiveness Policy Council, Subcouncil on Corporate Governance and Financial Markets, *The Will To Act,* Competitiveness Policy Council, Washington D.C., December 7, 1992, cover and p. 5.

10. Subcouncil on Corporate Governance and Financial Markets, p. 5.

11. Stephen L. Nesbitt, *Long-Term Rewards From Corporate Governance,* Wilshire Associates Incorporated, January 4, 1994.

12. Sidney Cottle, Roger F. Murray, and Frank E. Block, *Greham and Dodd's Security Analysis* (New York: McGraw-Hill, 1988).

13. Shawn Tully, "The Real Key to Creating Wealth," *Fortune,* September 20, 1993, p. 38.

14. Anne B. Fisher, "Creating Stockholder Wealth," *Fortune,* December 11, 1995, pp. 105–6.

2

STRATEGIC CORPORATE PERFORMANCE MEASURES: NEW WAYS TO ENHANCE INVESTOR VALUE

For many years, *Fortune* magazine has compiled a list of "America's Most Admired Companies." The 1996 list is a product of the responses of 11,000 executives, directors, and financial analysts asked to rate companies according to eight characteristics (the following is a list of those eight in order of importance given by respondents):

1. Quality of management.
2. Quality of products or services.
3. Ability to attract, develop, and keep talented people.
4. Value as a long-term investment.
5. Use of corporate assets.
6. Financial soundness.
7. Innovativeness.
8. Community and environmental responsibility.

After *Fortune* compiled its list it investigated how cumulative shareholder returns for this year's top 10 companies compared with returns for companies in the Standard & Poor's 500 index. Not suprisingly, most of the companies in the 1996 *Fortune* list outperformed the S&P 500 in 1995 and for the period 1985–1995 (see Table 2–1). Conversely, those companies ranked least admired tended to produce returns to shareholders below the S&P 500 (see Table 2–2).

Embedded in the rankings are assumptions about eight characteristics of good management. Only some (e.g., financial soundness) can be directly related to the traditional balance sheet, income statement, and accounting measures used by most businesses. An increasing number are what have become known as *intangibles.*

> Each year we hear of more companies that have made an explicit corporate goal of improving their performance in *Fortune's* annual survey of corporate reputations. . . . One reason companies fret over their reputations is financial. Good name is to strong financial performance as chicken is to egg. It's not always clear which begets which, but it's awfully hard to have one without the other. . . . There was virtually no relationship between the size of a company's assets and the sheen on its reputation. But financial performance, including measures like total return and earnings growth, correlates strongly with reputation. . . .

TABLE 2–1

Fortune's Most Admired Companies: Total Cumulative Returns to Shareholders Compared to the S&P 500

Company	Total Return to Shareholders: 1985–1995 (compound annual rate)	Total Return to Shareholders: 1995
Coca-Cola	29.3%	46.1%
Procter & Gamble	20.0	36.7
Rubbermaid	13.0	-9.8
Johnson & Johnson	23.1	59.1
Intel	27.9	78.2
Merck	27.1	76.8
Microsoft	N/A	43.6
Mirage Resorts	22.2	68.3
Hewlett-Packard	17.4	69.4
Motorola	20.7	-1.1
S&P 500	14.9	37.5

Source: Anne B. Fisher, "America's Most Admired Companies: Corporate Reputations," *Fortune,* March 6, 1996, p. 98.

TABLE 2-2

Fortune's Least Admired Companies: Total Cumulative Returns to Shareholders
Compared to the S&P 500

Company	Total Return to Shareholders: 1985–1995 (compound annual rate)	Total Return to Shareholders: 1995
TWA	N/A	1,176.9%
Morrison Knudsen	−12.5%	−64.2
Kmart	− 0.8	−42.3
USAir Group	− 8.9	211.8
A&P	2.4	28.0
Continental Airlines	N/A	370.3
Amerco	N/A	20.9
Salomon	− 0.1	−4.0
Woolworth	1.8	−12.5
Standard Commercial	1.2	−14.4
S&P 500	14.9	37.5

Source: Anne B. Fisher, "America's Most Admired Companies: Corporate Reputations," *Fortune,* March 6, 1996, p. 98.

But reputation entails much more than just minting money. As measured
in the survey, half of it comes from intangibles like the way a company treats
its employees, how much it spends on research and development, and the
strength of its management team. These abstractions count more than you
might think.[1]

Senior executives in a number of major corporations in the United
States and abroad are exploring new strategic performance measures to help
them track these "intangibles," better manage their businesses, and ultimately enhance their future corporate performance. They are searching for
ways to evaluate their strategic investments in physical and human capital
and to communicate their *potential for creating investor value* to the
financial markets. In order to appeal to the investors in the marketplace
(level 1 shareholders as described in Chapter 1) as opposed to the traders
in the marketplace (level 4 shareholders), these companies are searching
for and finding new ways to track, value, and enhance the strategic intangibles in their businesses. These intangibles, such as investments in intellectual capital and processes to improve customer satisfaction, workplace

practices, and innovation, will position the corporation to achieve future sustained success and, therefore, a sustained flow of investor value.

The strategic performance measurement movement grows out of prior quality and strategic planning initiatives, but promises to be far more dynamic and forward looking. A key problem with the three types of shareholder value measures discussed in Chapter 1 is that they largely depend on historic accounting-based measures, which may not necessarily provide a good indication of where a corporation is heading in the future. Also, these accounting-based measures do not show whether a company has a clear set of goals (beyond simply making more profit) or whether it is strategically positioned to achieve those goals.

The new strategic performance measurement approach looks at an organization much like the Department of Defense (DOD) might evaluate a mission such as launching Desert Storm. The DOD asks a number of key questions and arranges information in a goal-oriented tactical planning matrix (which will be discussed in more detail later in this chapter). Although developed in a military context, the same approach and key questions can be of use in a business context:

Military context:
   1. What is our mission?
   2. Who is the enemy, and what is their capability?
   3. What do we need to achieve our goal, e.g., what mix of aircraft carriers, land-based vehicles, missiles, etc.?

Business context:
   1. What is our business goal, e.g., what is our market and which "customers" do we need to satisfy?
   2. Who is our competition, and what is their capability?
   3. What do we need to achieve our goal, e.g., what mix of technology, intellectual assets, research and development, etc.?

Military and business context:
   4. What are our current resources?
   5. What is our capability ratio, e.g., the ratio of what we need to what we have?
   6. How best can we deploy our current resources to maximize the possibility that we will achieve our goal, e.g., where do we add strength and where is strength already sufficient?

INVESTMENTS IN INTANGIBLES ARE KEY TO U.S. ECONOMIC DEVELOPMENT

In 1992, the federally legislated Competitiveness Policy Council established a Subcouncil on Corporate Governance and Financial Markets, which concluded that U.S. competitiveness problems will persist unless the country takes steps to improve its present corporate performance evaluation system. In its December 1992 report, *The Will To Act,* the Subcouncil found:

> Competitive realities demand new performance measurement systems, and should precipitate a "revolution" in the use of non-financial measurements of corporate performance. . . .
>
> Qualitative indicators of corporate performance—quality of products, customer satisfaction, employee training, and strategic direction—are now routinely discussed internally in well-managed and successful corporations. They are discussed with a select group of "fundamental" security analysts who develop qualitative opinions based on personal dialogue with company officials. However, a more systematic development of these measures is called for. . . .[2]

The Subcouncil found that nonfinancial measures should be developed as a supplement to traditional financial measures. Three major advantages of using nonfinancial concepts to measure corporate performance were cited:

1. Current accounting systems do not square with economic reality and are not doing the job of accurately measuring performance in this broader context.
2. Nonfinancial measurements tell much more about the "true value" and "strategic positioning" of the corporation than many of the more traditional financial measurements.
3. Strategic performance measurements will greatly assist institutional investors who invest for the long term and can encourage investors to stay with a company, when sole reliance on financial measurements might suggest otherwise.[3]

The full membership of the Competitiveness Policy Council decided to follow up the report of the Subcouncil on Corporate Governance and Financial Markets by forming another Subcouncil. In September 1995, this Subcouncil on Capital Allocation released its report, entitled *Lifting All Boats: Increasing the Payoff from Private Investment in The U.S. Economy.* This report noted that American companies appear to invest at lower rates than their foreign counterparts in important intangible assets, such as research and development (R&D), workforce training, new products and new markets, supplier relationships, and establishment of brand names and distribution channels. It also found that, at a time when the knowledge intensity of competition makes R&D investment critical, the rate of corporate R&D investment as a percentage of gross domestic product has been flat or slightly declining in the United States.[4] Both Subcouncils agreed on several key factors relating to U.S. competitiveness: financial markets per se are not the problem; U.S. markets are highly efficient even though they may contain significant distortions in the allocation of private capital; and market imperfections coupled with a lack of information on how to measure the value of intangible investments contribute to the problem of insufficient tangible and intangible business investment. Moreover, the Subcouncil on Capital Allocation recommended that the SEC and the Financial Accounting Standards Board (FASB) undertake a project to develop generally accepted principles for measuring salient categories of nonfinancial information.

MANAGING FOR SUCCESS

How does a company measure intangible assets? A major study[5] to address this issue was undertaken by the author at The Conference Board, a global business membership and research organization. The study was conducted through the formation of an International Working Group of corporations, institutional investors, and regulatory advisors which met during 1994 and 1995 to hear presentations from and discuss the experiences of 10 case study companies engaged in various stages of strategic performance measurement (see Box 2–1 for a list of The Conference Board's case study companies as well as other companies reported to be investigating similar measures).

Conference Board Case study companies agree that they can improve their performance by developing a relatively short list of key performance indicators and relating those to the underlying strategic objectives of the business. According to Dr. Ivor S. Francis, Director of The Deming Center International in Australia (founded by the renowned Edward Deming), new performance measures are intended to capture not only the value of current assets, but the ability of those assets to produce wealth in the future. Dr. Francis maintains that *measurement* of performance is only a means to an end, which is *enhancement* of performance. Moreover, performance cannot be enhanced unless the synergy between the various parts of the corporate

BOX 2-1

Companies Engaged in Developing Strategic Performance Measures

The Conference Board's Strategic Performance Measurement Case Study Companies

- Chase Manhattan Bank
- First Chicago Trust of New York
- GenCorp Inc.
- Kellogg's (Australia) Pty. Ltd.
- Kleinwort Benson Investment Management Ltd. (UK)
- Pfizer Inc
- Pitney Bowes, Inc.
- Polaroid Corporation
- Toyota Motor Corporation
- USG

Other Companies Using Strategic Performance Measures

- Allstate
- The Bank of Montreal
- Dow Chemical
- General Electric
- General Motors
- IBM (U.K.)
- John Lewis Partnership (UK)
- Merck & Co.
- The Royal Bank of Canada
- Skandia AFS
- Tenneco
- Unipart Group of Companies Ltd. (U.K.)
- Whirlpool

system as a whole is recognized and improved. It is impossible to prove the value of any particular improvement, whether it occurs in the area of human resources or corporate governance, unless it is accompanied by true, systemic improvement in information about how the company works (comprehensive measures) and action taken to improve those measures in totality. Dr. Francis told The Conference Board's International Working Group:

> Traditional measures of accounting are inadequate to understand how a company creates value. Companies may spend vast sums accounting for present fixed assets which may represent but a small proportion of the present financial value of the company; at the same time, the company's accountants may ignore those intangible assets which determine the production of future wealth. Measuring performance must entail measurement of the potential for performance, not last year's performance, but the potential for performance in the future. This involves accounting for capability, in order systematically to understand a company's value adding activities, then using this performance measurement system as a tool for constructive oversight.[6]

Joseph F. Spadaford, President of First Chicago Trust of New York, has been involved for many years with nonfinancial or key performance measures both at First Chicago Trust and, prior to that, at Citibank. He defines a nonfinancial or key performance measure as *an outcome-based metric that provides direct feedback on process execution and indicative feedback about key performance results.* To Spadaford, the strategic performance measures are "internal measures" which indicate "something about how the process is working" and give "clues about how results might come out based on the process execution." Key performance measures are intended to *augment* rather than *replace* entirely what are generally known as financial measures. But more importantly, they are measures that focus the company on the elements needed to achieve its strategic goals.

Figure 2–1 shows how typical strategic performance measures are converted, through a company's process of strategic achievement, into more recognizable financial outputs such as sales and profits.

Companies choose varying numbers of key measures to track and enhance their success. For Jack Welch of General Electric Inc., there are three key measures to track:

> The three most important things you need to measure in a business are customer satisfaction, employee satisfaction and cash flow.
>
> If you are growing customer satisfaction, your global market share is sure to grow too. Employee satisfaction gets you productivity, quality, pride and creativity. Cash flow is the pulse—the vital sign of life in a company.

FIGURE 2-1

The Performance Measurement Process

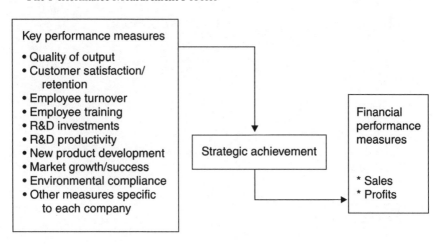

We are trying to differentiate GE competitively by raising as much intellectual and creative capital from our work force as we possibly can. That is a lot tougher than raising financial capital, which a strong company can find in any market in the world.[7]

A Chase Manhattan Bank vice president reporting to The Conference Board's International Working Group also says the three most important measures in a business are customer satisfaction, employee satisfaction, and cash flow. If companies achieve success with these three, all other measures, including returns to shareholders, will be positive. When asked by the CEO to produce a list of the company's 20 most critical success factors, the managers at the U.K. investment firm Kleinwort Benson at first came up with 150 different measures deemed absolutely critical to the performance of the business. The process of simplifying and distilling measures to a maximum of 20 became part of the performance measurement process itself, as managers sharpened their vision of the company and arrived at a consensus of how to realize that vision (see Box 2–2 for a list of the 20 key performance measures used by Kleinwort Benson).

According to Mark Green, Director of Strategic Information Services, Pitney Bowes has established a "5 up" success indicator system which it attributes to IBM. These are the five things that help a company focus on

BOX 2–2

20 Key Performance Measures Used by Kleinwort Benson Investment Management Holdings Limited, U.K.

A. *Growth*
   Operating profitability
   Business volumes
   Value of client assets

B. *Client satisfaction*
   Client retention
   Client satisfaction survey ratings
   Client satisfaction index
   Client service standards
   Investment performance

C. *Marketing and sales*
   Audience perception
   Recognition of client needs/opportunities
   Innovation index
   Sales pipeline
   Product movements

D. *Business management*
   Staff retention
   Staff satisfaction
   Training progress
   Project progress
   Internal customer relations
   Credit quality
   Balance sheet

the business: "the theory is that, if you can keep focus on the first four, the financial results will take care of themselves":

- Employees.
- Customer satisfaction and loyalty.
- The competition.
- Postal service requirements.
- Financial results.

D. Michael Steuert, Senior Vice President and Chief Financial Officer of GenCorp Inc., reports a different set of five key measures tailored to businesses in the fields of aerospace, automotive parts, and polymer products where safety and quality play critical roles. GenCorp's key measures are:

- Customer satisfaction index.
- OSHA recordables.
- Quality cost and loss.
- Productivity index.
- Through-put cycle.

For GenCorp, OSHA (Occupational Safety and Health Administration) recordables reflect safety within the company, and the through-put cycle measures the elimination of waste, a key measure in terms of environmental control and the efficiency with which product is utilized. Some companies, like Polaroid, have not set a specific number of performance measures; rather, they view the performance measurement process as a "strategic navigation" process which changes the roles of the senior managers to allow them to focus more on longer range performance. According to John Driscoll, Senior Executive, Strategic Planning and Corporate Development at Polaroid, the company first established an economic set of goals for the company to deliver shareholder values, then developed a group of nonfinancial metrics that "have to do with skills, performance, and with all those things that ensure whether or not the company is going to achieve its economic goals."

NAMING THE NEW MEASURES

Virtually all of The Conference Board's case study companies report they debated what to call newly developed performance measures. Many started by naming them *nonfinancial, intermediate, nontraditional,* or *soft* measures. D. Michael Steuert of GenCorp originally referred to nonfinancial measures as intermediate in contrast to financial measures, which were the *final financial outcomes.* Kevin Kinnaw, Manager of National Manufacturing Relations at Toyota Motor Sales, USA, says that nonfinancial measures are "the long-term measures such as customer satisfaction and retention. The more short-term measures would be, of course, the financial."

Not far into their performance measurement processes, however, many companies abandoned these names in favor of *key strategic performance measures; nonfinancial* was found lacking in precision since several measures were clearly financial. Moreover, all the measures were found to relate, at least in a longer-term context, to tangible financial results. In that respect, they might be viewed as intermediate, but that did not capture the fact that the measures were seen as fundamental drivers of success. Use of the word *nontraditional* also proved to be less than optimal, because many companies believed that placing these measures in a *traditional* or *modern* context was not only confusing but also irrelevant to the process of measuring and enhancing performance in the present and for the future. Dr. Ivor Francis rejects the term *soft measures,* arguing that intellectual capital is not merely a soft or intangible asset:

> Many of those assets which were thought to be intangible are not so intangible after all. Those intellectual assets that actually run the company, breathing life into otherwise idle assets, are all the functions or activities, the things people do, and they have characteristics—capabilities—which can be quantified and estimated, as can their impact on the creation of value.[8]

Steuert from GenCorp ultimately arrived at an acceptable definition; he speaks of these strategic performance measures:

> We put these in a package together with financial measures. Nonfinancials is a misnomer because there are financials embedded in all the measures we look at, but they are certainly not traditional financial measures. We do not call them nonfinancial measures. We just call them key measures. At one time we went from nonfinancial to nontraditional, and that was a problem because we wanted them to be our traditional measures. So we just went to key measures.[9]

Increasingly, therefore, companies are referring to these performance measures as *key strategic performance measures* rather than *nonfinancial, intermediate, nontraditional, intangible,* or *soft* measures.

RATIONALE FOR DEVELOPING KEY MEASURES

Companies are developing key strategic measures of performance for a variety of reasons. According to one CEO, historical and purely financial performance measures provide an inadequate and insensitive tool for decision making. Companies agree that traditional accounting and financial measures were developed to meet regulatory and financial reporting requirements rather than to run businesses—they are better used to report on the stewardship of money entrusted to managements' care than to chart the strategic direction of the business.

A commonly reported goal is to create a broader set of measures which captures a broader concept of value creation in the business. A number of companies report the need to develop performance measurement systems that track not only value but also *those factors which lead to its creation.*

According to Ken Coppock, Director of Corporate Management Accounting of the U.K. Cable and Wireless Company:

> We are not satisfied with our performance indicators—particularly the level of information we have on the business units. They are too financially oriented and don't tell you much about management performance or quality performance.
>
> The big problem is that if you look at the Group from the financial perspective we are performing right on target. But then there is a whole raft of other issues around which we have no view at all, like product development or customer satisfaction. We have numbers on these things but no idea of our effectiveness.[10]

The Conference Board case study companies say they are developing key measures of performance because traditional, accounting-based measures:

- Are too historical.
- Lack predictive power.
- Reward the wrong behavior.
- Are focused on inputs and not on outputs.
- Do not capture key business changes until it is too late.
- Reflect functions, not cross-functional processes, within a company.
- Give inadequate consideration to difficult-to-quantify items such as intellectual capital.

Companies may resist developing key performance measures because financial and accounting measures, which rely on a clearly defined set of standards, are generally powerful and familiar to managements. By comparison, certain key nonfinancial measures, some of which may in fact already be in use in the business, may have been developed on a piecemeal basis and may lack consistency. As companies make a greater commitment to and gain more experience with key performance measurement techniques, they develop their own internal benchmarking systems to track and enhance their progress.

HOW TO DEVELOP STRATEGIC PERFORMANCE MEASURES

Conference Board case study companies use a variety of systematic approaches to develop key performance measurement systems. There are, however, common factors among them. Each system begins with defining the vision or goals of the company. Next, there is a meshing of key performance indicators within a strategic evaluation format where managers rate the significant factors pertaining to achieving each strategic objective. Finally, managers coordinate the processes to develop, track, and relate those measures back to the overall strategic vision on a continuous basis.

Start with a Clean Slate

When initiating a key performance measurement system, companies generally start by completely ignoring all the performance measures they have routinely tracked. They may later return to some of these measures to build upon data which is readily accessible rather than initiate entirely new information systems. Companies, however, report better success when they "remove the blinders" and "start with a blank sheet of paper."

Companies say it is important to remember three critical factors:

- Do not mistake data for information.
- You are what you measure.
- What gets measured gets managed.

It is important to avoid measuring things just because they have always been measured. Generating too much information of the wrong sort is a common complaint. Managers recommend measuring only things that are *actionable and will lead to enhanced performance.* CEO Colin Maltby reports: "In Kleinwort Benson's experience, it's much easier to measure sales activity than it is to measure the effectiveness of marketing. That fact led to some biases and distortions in our behavior, which I think had the characteristic of focusing us more on short-term sales activity than was desirable."

The Importance of a Clear Vision

Restructuring provided an extra impetus for certain case study companies to develop new performance measures because they were more cognizant of their need to redefine their vision. Harvard Professor Robert Eccles developed a business model that provides a generic framework for defining a company's vision (see Figure 2–2).

FIGURE 2–2

The Business Model

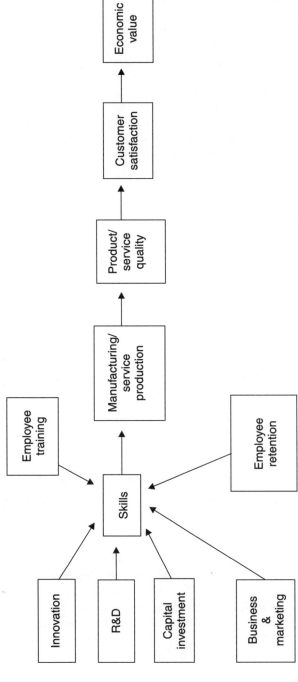

- Innovation
- R&D
- Capital investment
- Business & marketing
- Employee training
- Employee retention
- Skills
- Manufacturing/ service production
- Product/ service quality
- Customer satisfaction
- Economic value

Source: Robert G. Eccles, Presentation to National Invesor Relations Institute, Palm Springs, California, November 1994.

Several companies, including Kleinwort Benson, found using this type of generic business model helpful to focus management on the key elements in the business, although Maltby, speaking to The Conference Board's International Working Group, does suggest some improvements:

> We did find it useful, and the recommendation I would make would be to conduct the discussion in a more explicit manner with a broader group of people. Essentially, the exercise we went through was that a relatively small group on a project team worked on the business model, and then interrogated the senior members of operating management on the measures they used, and then mapped the two. What we should have done was to have a debate about the model explicitly with the members of the management team.
>
> But, it was useful in identifying gaps. The existing measures of operational performance, both those which we used at the board level across the business and those that the operational management used in a fragmented way, tended to be unevenly spread across what the model suggested to us were the sources of value creation in the business. Had we not used the model, we would have fallen further into the trap of focusing excessively on what we could already measure, rather than upon what was truly important but difficult to track.[11]

Another case study company executive notes that the company's two-year-old performance measurement process, spearheaded by the chairman and the president, depended on developing a vision.

> We needed a compelling vision for the corporation. This process did not occur overnight. It took several months, a multitude of meetings, including holding focus groups with employees at all levels throughout the corporation, and having extensive dialog with them. Finally, the vision was determined to be three things: to be provider of choice, employer of choice, and investment of choice.[12]

Be Prepared to Devote Time and Resources

Polaroid underwent an intensive process that culminated in a new corporate vision incorporating both an internal and external business model framework (see Box 2–3). Jack Driscoll describes the process:

> In 1991–1992, we asked ourselves whether we had the growth potential to give the shareholders the return they would expect from us. From the fall of 1991 to the fall of 1992, we began a process in which we asked the officers and the senior managers to engage in a strategic visioning process.
>
> Some talked about the difficulty in implementing change processes and getting the people in the company engaged and behind them. We recognized this potential problem at the start; we picked not only the officers of the

BOX 2-3

Polaroid's Strategic Visioning Process

In 1991–1992, officers and senior managers engaged in a Strategic Visioning Process. Working with outside consultants, participants looked at:

1. Polaroid's current condition:
   - The economic condition of the company—how do we achieve the return on investment demanded by our shareholders?
   - The internal condition of the company—how do we identify the critical behaviors and systems necessary to achieve economic objectives, including:
     — core competence
     — cultural environment
     — management processes
     — organizational architecture
     — personal characteristics

2. The external vision:
   - defines the areas of growth to produce shareholder returns.

3. The internal vision (nonfinancial metrics):
   - Create a redefined corporate structure to achieve specific goals.
   - Create an "at cause" sense of responsibility throughout the corporation.
   - Develop an ongoing "strategic navigation" process.
   - Establish a performance management process that achieves specific goals.
   - Practice commitment to a "best leadership" set of traits and practices.
   - Achieve the technical and business skill mix required to accomplish our economic vision.

Source: John Driscoll, Presentation to The Conference Board's International Working Group on New Performance Measures, Polaroid Corporation, November 15, 1994.

company, but 60 senior people in the company to form an extended strategy team. We drew a contract with them stipulating we would take a significant part of their time over the next year away from their jobs, to have them participate in a strategy exercise with the ultimate intent of restructuring the corporation for future growth.[13]

Link Measures Back to Strategic Vision and Goals

Companies report that a systematic process to institute key performance measurements takes a broadly based effort, time, and commitment. Some companies have attempted to make operational changes in areas such as customer satisfaction and retention, but other companies report that efforts are best rewarded when there is a systematic, overall approach which is constantly linked back to achieving the company's strategic goals.

Companies report that the process of deciding what they want to measure may lead them into a comprehensive planning process with beneficial results. Many note that past planning exercises have failed because the plan is considered a "one shot" document. It is critical to avoid this common pitfall by first choosing the measures considered important, then mapping them back against the key strategic goals of the business identified in the initial analysis of the corporate purpose and values. The company will then inevitably discover gaps in information to track the key measures of performance. These gaps may be filled with new or revised information systems.

Perhaps the most important message the case study companies delivered was that whatever measures are tracked should link back to the strategic vision and plan. Mark Green of Pitney Bowes put in an information system to track key performance indicators which contains an alarm system to warn when indicators deviate from strategic plan goals. Key information is updated as needed and depending on the type of information. Customer satisfaction information is collected by survey and updated less frequently than certain operational indicators such as "flash written business," which is the amount of business that is written and translated into an actual installation. "Other information such as this (backlog, inventory, etc.) is updated daily, to know how much business you're looking at on a daily basis instead of at the end of the month." Green says:

> Key indicators are strategic plan milestones. One of the nicest features of the system is this alarm button. We have objectives set for each measure. We have goals and a system to track our actual progress versus our goal. When progress is out of line for a particular measure by more than plus or minus 5 percent, it will be alarmed.
>
> If you are a key executive, and you do not want to look at 400 measures within the system but you want to know what is in alarm status, you just flick on this, and you will see the things that are out of alignment. That will help you focus on what is important.[14]

Determine a Method to Track Measures

D. Michael Steuert of GenCorp reports going through an extensive process not only to develop nonfinancial measures but to track them in a quantifiable manner. The company has developed various series of indexes pertaining to customer satisfaction, OSHA recordables, quality cost and loss, productivity, and through-put cycles. "Control charts" are of considerable use in measuring and tracking performance:

> As we look at nonfinancial measures, we need some way to track them and to see that we are really making improvements. To do that, our quality people came up with a fairly simple statistical product called control charts that will allow us to track those measures and see from year to year if we are making fundamental improvements. Are we making statistically significant improvements in those ratios?
>
> These control charts set upper and lower limits which identify the variability of 95 percent of the occurrences. If you move outside the limit, you know something fundamentally has happened where there is a major change in what you are doing. So we can track how we have performed, how we are going to perform, and if we are really making statistically significant improvements in these nonfinancial measures.[15]

Pitney Bowes uses a "lift analysis" to track the progress of measures, while Kellogg's Australia uses an opportunity ratio that tracks the ratio of capability to potential success for measures.

Initiate from the Top and Involve Managers and Employees

Most case study companies believe that the performance measurement process works best if it starts from the top, spreads to senior management, to middle management, and then to employees. The process starts with:

- Training senior managers how to approach the visioning process.
- Laying a foundation for successful performance measurement.
- Developing a shared vision of the corporation's criteria of success.
- Communicating that vision throughout the organization.
- Obtaining feedback on the vision and the measures to get there.
- Getting the organization aligned behind the new goals.

The Polaroid process emanated from the CEO, who asked: "Have I got a business, a set of employees, and a set of management processes that can deliver the growth and profitability that translates into shareholder value at least over the next decade?" Polaroid's "strategic architecture process" is shown in Figure 2–3, beginning with how the company first trained its 60 to 80 senior executives to approach the issue, then laid a foundation for senior managers to learn to develop a shared sense of values. Driscoll describes the process as follows:

> In order to get a group of executives to grapple with the issue of how to restructure the company for growth, we first put all 60 people through a behavioral training exercise. We trained them for about a week to learn to develop a shared sense of values, such that we could have an open and honest dialogue about not only the state of the company, but what we needed to do to grow the company to meet shareholder perspectives. This was very important, because if you don't create an honest and open environment, you never get a robust strategy. We spent about six weeks on training before we even began the process.
>
> Then, in groups of 12 or 15, we had a series of meetings, during which we agreed on the values that we shared, the purpose of the company's existence, and the operating principles. At this point in the process, we had not yet discussed strategy or the current condition regarding our performance as a company. But we had joined 60 to 80 people with an agreement about the type of behavioral principles each one of us needed to employ, and an agreement on where we were headed.[16]

One senior vice president of a case study banking company describes how the performance measurement process emanated from the chairman and the president, spread through the 25 most senior managers, then through the next 200 managers, and ultimately throughout all 34,000 employees in the organization. "A lot of time, effort, and energy was spent in this communication process, in this kind of feedback process, and in this iteration process which was very new and different for our culture."

According to Colin Maltby, it is crucial to identify key indicators to make sure they correspond with the agreed upon corporate purpose, and see that they are accepted throughout the company. He says:

> A very important element has been continuously to feed back to senior and middle management the relationship between the performance indicators we are talking about and the underlying statements of corporate purpose and value in which they participated.[17]

Most companies did not initially enlist the support of the board of directors in their key performance measurement processes. Executives report they would rather develop the process within the management

FIGURE 2-3

Elements of Polaroid's Strategic Architecture

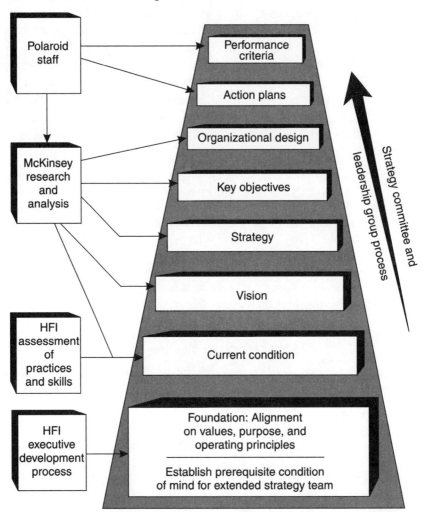

structure of the company, then present it to the board, assuming it works. Managers who were undertaking what they considered to be a new area of activity generally seemed quite reluctant to solicit support from boards of directors prior to embarking on a performance measurement project whose outcome they could not necessarily predict.

Work from the Familiar, if Possible

First Chicago Trust's Joseph Spadaford recommends tailoring some measures to be more recognizable by current management. Other case study companies make the same point. For example, Kleinwort Benson CEO Colin Maltby also advocates involving managers in the process and trying to provide them with measurements based, as far as possible, on things that are "familiar to them." Companies report striving to attain a balance between developing cost-effective measures, based on readily available data, and falling into the trap of relying on noncritical measures in the system because they are familiar. Mark Green of Pitney Bowes discusses this trade-off:

> We knew that the measures which were most critical were unavailable. Rather than spend three years to get the information that was most strategic, and most critical, we determined that, within three months, we would develop important, reliable, on-line information for which you don't have to rekey or have people create spreadsheets. Maybe we will hit 80 percent of those measures.
>
> As a matter of fact, we did hit about 85 percent of the key measures. Also, there were some things that were mechanized already, but were not very reliable. We got rid of those.[18]

Choose Performance Measures Wisely

For Polaroid, key drivers of success must be the key to the business planning cycle and must be "SMART" goals:

- Specific
- Measurable
- Attainable
- Result Oriented
- Time Bound

Joseph Spadaford offers the following advice on developing performance measures:

- *Identify measures that are accomplishment-based.* Measures should reflect what the company is trying to accomplish, and the measures chosen should tell you most about that accomplishment—this is where the rubber meets the road. Think about measures in terms of outcomes and accomplishments that are expected (see Box 2–4, "Measurement Guidelines: First Chicago Trust of New York").

- *Limit the number of measures.* You can measure so many things that you will be spending too much time measuring and not enough time doing.
- *Seek the level of precision sufficient for the purposes of the measurement.* This is one of the biggest problems. Until recently, everyone wanted to achieve the six-sigma level or 99.999 pure result. That is not necessary in most cases. If you are an airline company, and we are talking about flight safety, yes; but in most cases, the level of precision does not give you the payback that you need.
- *Use a family of measures rather than looking for a single, global measure.* Picking two or three measures that give you feedback on some important area of performance is far more useful than

---

BOX 2–4

Performance Measurement Guidelines at First Chicago Trust of New York

- Identify measures that are accomplishment-based.
- Limit the number of measures used.
- Seek a level of precision sufficient for the purposes of the measurement.
- Develop group of team-oriented measures, not measures of individual employee performance.
- Use a family of measures rather than try to force one measure to serve as the ultimate indicator.
- Continually raise the standards.
- Develop some averages to track measures.
- Review and change measures, if necessary, when strategies change.

Source: Joseph Spadaford, Presentation to The Conference Board's International Working Group on Key Performance Measures, New York, New York, June 14, 1994. See also: Joseph H. Boyett and Henry P. Cown, *Maximum Performance Management* (London: Glenbridge Publishing Ltd., 1988).

picking one, because one measure might miss something critical in understanding performance.

- *Develop group or team-oriented measures and do not combine them with measures of individual employee performance.* There is a place for employee performance measurement, but if you are trying to change and continuously improve companies, it seems better to get measures related to a team trying to make change happen rather than an individual. Having said that, somebody must be accountable to make sure the team is on track and making headway.

- *Constantly raise the bar.* Based on the ultimate strategic purpose of the measure, make sure the goals and standards are adjusted as capabilities improve.

- *Do not be afraid to change.* The business strategy may beg for new metrics. Do not get so hardwired into your measures that you fail to perceive the need to change them.

- *Develop some average scores of how well the measures have done.* These can tell, at a glance, almost like a financial statement, how quality is operating in a particular unit at any given time. This will enable a company to make the measurement process as familiar as possible to managers used to reviewing financials.[19]

Mistakes to Avoid

Having worked through various stages of devising and implementing strategic performance measurement processes, most companies admit they made mistakes or, at the least, recommend improvements. Mistakes fall into the following categories:

- *Measuring the wrong things right.* In an effort to hone their ability to measure, some managers directed flawless efforts at measurement but were less successful in discovering what factors best related to the company's overall strategic goals. Spadaford describes this is as "rather like making sure the dining facilities on the Titanic are world-class." He recommends: "Think about what you are measuring to ensure the measure relates to the overall strategic goal."

- *Experiencing a breakdown of the process.* Unforeseen negative events may sidetrack the measurement process, as people focus on the crisis at hand and give up on the process. Spadaford notes: "Sometimes when there is a negative event, management focuses on the event and does not think about the need to change the underlying process. It is important to steer energy into a process improvement approach."
- *Experiencing antagonisms among managers.* As functional lines of authority are broken down, cross-functional conflicts can emerge. In the Kellogg's Australia case study, top management started to realize certain risks when internal measures of performance were put in place. One director (of manufacturing, for example) was not delivering the expected results to another director (of finance, for example). There was now on the table information that proved that the internal service level was far from optimal. Although the company was successful, when one considered its potential, there was a tremendous gap between what was being done and what could be.

Dr. Francis refers to difficulties experienced by Kellogg's chief executive:

> Managers didn't know how to handle the situation or how to improve it. So they started to avoid it. They then started complaining about the performance measurement approach, which became the problem. They started blaming it for taking time away from their business. They said it was complicated. So they started to blame this change program as the source of the conflict. The managers and others in the company finally said, "It's not your fault or the system's fault; it's our fault, and we have to solve it. The genie is out of the bottle. The information is out. We've got to do something about it, and we have to fix the processes."[20]

- *Not having someone accountable.* Case study presenters generally agree that someone must be accountable in order for things to improve. This may be difficult to achieve in a team environment, but someone must make the measurement process their personal charge. The Deming Centre International developed an accountability matrix for Kellogg's Australia to avoid the "everybody is in charge or nobody is in charge" syndrome. In the analysis process, four divisions or "owners" initially indicated they had accountability or ownership over providing capacity. According to Dr. Francis:

Frequently, you will find at the first that you have four or five people in charge of some function with no owners. For example, in this case, providing capacity actually reflects a number of activities, including engineering, technology, human resources, and R&D. There are, in fact, four legitimate owners: the directors of human resources, product development, engineering, and information services.[21]

- *Not measuring certain activities.* In some companies, people resist having their activities subject to measurement on grounds they are "too professional." Spadaford says: "You should be able to measure what everybody does, in some way. If not, how can you be sure everyone is contributing to the company's strategic goals?"

TACTICAL PLANNING: BEYOND THE BALANCED BUSINESS SCORECARD

The Balanced Business Scorecard was developed by Robert S. Kaplan and David P. Norton[22] as an information-based management tool which lays out four perspectives with goals and measures for each. A typical company's scorecard for financial, customer, internal business, and innovation and learning perspectives is illustrated in Box 2–5.

When it was originally introduced, the balanced business scorecard represented an advance in the field of performance measurement. Unfortunately, as they began to implement the balanced business scorecard, many companies complained that they ended up with a series of somewhat disconnected measures for individual areas within the company but felt constrained by a lack of ability to interrelate processes within the company to achieve the end goals. For example, to achieve customer satisfaction takes efforts *throughout* a company, ranging from research and development and new skills training in the development and production areas to better market analysis and improved customer service. A balanced business scorecard approach does not lend itself to a "horizontal" approach to understanding the requirements throughout the company for improving customer retention. More importantly, it does not lay out for companies a convenient framework to compare alternative strategic approaches (e.g., should a company seek out one type of customer rather than continue to serve its current array of customers?). It also fails to provide a framework

BOX 2-5

Elements of a Balanced Business Scorecard

Goals	Measures
The financial perspective	
survive	cash flow
succeed	quarterly sales growth and operating income by division
prosper	increased market share and return on equity
The customer perspective	
new products	percent of sales from new products
responsive supply	on-time delivery (defined by customer)
preferred supplier	share of key account's purchases ranking by key accounts
customer partnership	number of cooperative efforts
The internal business perspective	
technological capability	manufacturing geometry vs. competition
manufacturing	cycle time
excellence	unit cost
	yield
The innovation and learning perspective	
technology leadership	time to develop next generation of products
manufacturing learning	process time to maturity
time to market	new product introduction vs. competition

Source: Robert S. Kaplan and David P. Norton, "The Balanced Scorecard—Measures That Drive Performance," *Harvard Business Review*, January-February, 1992, p. 76.

for companies to understand how all their processes are synergistically related. The Balanced Scorecard's four boxes, while suggesting a series of useful ratios, do not provide the interlinkages and, therefore, remain functional silos in their own right. Moreover, they can actually defeat the purpose of devising comprehensive performance measures intended to break down functional silos within companies (e.g., to get everyone throughout the company to focus on improving customer retention).

John Cook, the managing director (in Australia, equivalent to CEO) for Kellogg's Australia, put in place a *quality-based management system* based on The Deming Centre International's Tactical Planning Matrix (see Figure 2–4). The system encompasses the entire activity of the company in a systemic way, beginning with the external needs being expressed to, and incorporated within, the strategic planning system. The system depends on establishing priorities to improve the company's internal capability system to transform inputs into appropriate outputs more effectively The focus is on developing the key components of the value-adding activity, focusing on the nonfinancial measures of performance, namely, the activities that are going to transform those inputs into the outputs. Dr. Francis, in addressing The Conference Board's International Working Group, explains the premise:

FIGURE 2–4

Tactical Planning Matrix

	Established direction	Ensure provider support	Meet the market	Plan and coordinate functions	Provide capacity	Excecute operations	Importance	Performance
Value		2	3	3	1	3	7	5
Quality product	1	3	2	2	2	3	4	6
Profit	1	2	3	3	1	3	4	4
Asset growth	3		3	2	3		2	5
New technology	2	1	2	1	3	1	7	2
Strong organization	2	2		3			5	2
Current capability	3	3	5	3	2	4		
Imputed importance	7	8	8	10	7	7		
Opportunity ratio	7	8	5	10	10	5		

Source: The Deming Centre International

How do you create value? What is the value-creating mechanism within the company? The argument here, upon which all of this is based, is unless we understand the mechanism by which those inputs are translated into the outputs, there is no way that we as managers or chief executives can manage for performance. Unless you know: (a) what the activities are; and (b) their impact on the outputs, you cannot manage for performance.

If you do know the relationships, then you can get some measure of relative importance of these activities. Then, if you map those onto the current capabilities of those activities, you can decide which of these activities should receive the highest priority. Internal investments then will be driven by the opportunity ratio.[23]

In the Kellogg's Australia example, this process was used to drive the company's strategies, and from these opportunity ratios were derived the three major strategies which were then used to drive the company's overall competitive strategy. The tactical planning matrix (TPM) includes estimates of the effects on output performance of an enhancement of internal functional capabilities. Developed by The Deming Centre International, the TPM utilizes systemic measures of estimating the reliability of corporate and operational functions. These provide new tools for executives and directors to run the company more like a Swiss watch, with its components running together and interacting to add value. The TPM provides information for the constructive oversight of the company by directors and executives—to establish a prioritized program of corporate enhancement. It can also be used as a medium or language of communication between boards of directors and management and between directors and shareholders.

The Tactical Planning Matrix is a model of an executive's decision-making process. It takes a company's output requirements, as driven by strategic imperatives, links them with the internal functions which produce them, and derives the tactical priorities for enhancing the value-creating capacity of the company. Within the TPM in Figure 2–4, the list of outputs is drawn up on the left side of the matrix. These include not only the shareholder outputs but also the customer outputs and any other outputs that are essential to the long-term survival of the company in a systemic way. They all must be produced by a company because, for example, a failure to produce a quality product will impact on profits and vice versa. The *relative importance* of these as defined by the chief executive is drawn up on the right side of the matrix, plus the performance of the company last year. These are in a scale of relative importance. Next, across the top is an exhaustive list of essential functions which ultimately are required to produce all of the outputs. It is essential to separate outputs into those that managers can control and those they cannot. The entries in the columns in the matrix are the degree of impact that these functions have on the outputs. With that measured, the procedure involves weighting these measurements in order to develop the *imputed importance of those functions,* a measure of how important each and every function is with respect to producing all the outputs for which managers are accountable. This is the process of translating inputs that can be controlled by individual managers into the outputs for one company as a whole, enabling an understanding of the relative importance of each of these functions.

The functions across the top of the matrix can be determined in two ways. The first would be to ask, what functions does the company currently execute? But the weakness with this "as is" model is that there may be some things the company should be doing that it hasn't even thought of doing. Thus, to make this a "to be" model or a "should be" model, Francis asks: What should we be doing? What functions should we have that we haven't got?

In addition, merely because some function is important in the matrix does not mean that is where investment should be made, since that function may currently be operating perfectly well. Consider how it is currently performing. What is its current capability? If it is an important function and also currently incapable, surely that is where managers should invest. On the other hand, if it is important and it is doing very well, managers should not invest there. The ratio of the one to the next gives you the bottom line, which is the *opportunity ratio*—where the leverage lies for enhancing the outputs, from the dollars invested to maximizing the output.

This is the "brain" of the management system. It quantitatively maps the organizational functional capabilities onto the performance of its outputs. The fact is that managers cannot control the outputs, at least not directly, because the outputs depend on the contribution of so many functions. Yet the survival of the business depends on those outputs, and managers are held accountable for them. What the manager can control is the functions and the resources applied to them, which then will have an impact on the outputs. So the managers do control the outputs, but only indirectly inasmuch as they pass through this matrix. They can only understand their control if they understand the impact of one on the other. Essentially the TPM framework deals with not only probabilities or reliability estimates, but also numbers auditable in some way by an independent third party.

DISCLOSING KEY PERFORMANCE DATA

Companies are being pressured to expand the amount and quality of performance data released to the public. In 1994, the California Public Employees' Retirement System (CalPERS) announced that it would begin factoring labor management relations and other aspects of human resource management and workplace practices into analyses of company performance in connection with the fund's investment and voting decisions. In addition, the Department of Labor, which monitors private pension funds, issued an Interpretive Bulletin in July 1994 urging fiduciaries to monitor more closely portfolio companies' investment in training and efforts to develop their workforces.

Yet many question how extensively this kind of intangible performance measurement information can and will be used to make investment decisions. A study conducted at the Ernst & Young Center for Business Innovation by Harvard Business School Professor Robert G. Eccles and his colleague Sarah C. Mavrinac explores how corporate managers, financial analysts, and portfolio managers hold strikingly different views on how much information is provided, needed, and used in evaluating corporations.[24] Michael R. Vitale from Ernst & Young discussed the findings of the study at a Conference Board International Working Group meeting:

- Corporate managers, financial analysts, and portfolio managers all agree that the capital markets focus excessively on quarterly earnings.
- 58 percent of corporate managers believe their share price is either slightly or significantly undervalued.
- More corporate managers in high-tech companies believe their stock is either slightly or significantly undervalued than managers in service or mature manufacturing industries.
- Corporate managers think they are providing a high degree of information to the investment community, but the investment community does not share this opinion.
- Analysts and portfolio managers say they want much more information about the strategic plans of companies and about certain nonfinancial measures of performance.
- Corporate managers rate the relative importance of measures of performance somewhat differently than do financial analysts and portfolio managers.

- Despite their claims to want more information, both corporations and analysts currently rate certain "intangibles" such as employee satisfaction, turnover, and training very low in importance.
- Litigation concerns rank highest among the influences on the timing, amount, and nature of corporate information disclosed.
- There is a substantial amount of fingerpointing between the markets and companies: Companies perceive that the markets are not listening very well, and the markets perceive that companies are not communicating very well.[25]

This study confirms that a substantial communications gap exists among surveyed corporations, analysts, and portfolio managers.

Studies conducted by Matthew Gaved at the London School of Economics and presented to The Conference Board show what emphasis institutional investors in the United Kingdom place on certain types of nonfinancial information compared to U.S. counterparts (see Table 2–3).

TABLE 2–3

Factors Used to Evaluate Companies: A Comparison of Information Needs of U.S. and U.K. Institutional Investors

Factors Used in Evaluation	Percent of Institutions in the United States Ranking as Very Important	Percent of Institutions in the United Kingdom Ranking as Very Important
Objectives versus results	84%	68%
Financial history	72	52
Contingent liabilities	68	68
Strategy	68	68
Challenges/risks/uncertainty	68	60
Bad news	68	52
Markets	56	72
Geographical segmentation	56	64
Shareholder equity changes	48	56
Capital expenditure	40	56
Research & development	32	64

Source: Matthew Gaved, "Shareholder Communications: Institutional Ownership & Influence in the United Kingdom," Presentation to The Conference Board's Working Group on Communicating Corporate Performance, New York City, April 24, 1996: citing 1995 survey in the United Kingdom undertaken by Shelley Taylor.

In the United Kingdom, shareholder ownership is considerably more concentrated than it is in the United States, with approximately 75 percent of shares of the largest FT-SE 100 companies in the hands of fund managers (including 28 percent held by pension funds, 22 percent held by insurance companies, 6.8 percent held by unit trusts, and 16.3 percent held by overseas institutional investors). This compares with the approximately 57 percent of the stock in U.S. *Business Week's* largest 1,000 corporations held by institutional investors. Moreover, funds tend to take much higher stakes in U.K. companies—more along the lines of the Warren Buffet–style, level 1 "relationship investor" described in Chapter 1. Gaved's data show that, in a sample of 75 out of the top 100 FT-SE companies:

- 18 companies had one shareholder holding 10 percent or more of the company's stock.
- 20 companies had several large financial shareholders holding from 3 to10 percent of the company's stock.
- 20 companies had a single financial shareholder holding from 3 to 10 percent of the company's stock.
- 17 companies had other major shareholders with at least 3 percent of the company's stock.[26]

This higher degree of shareholder concentration in the United Kingdom has traditionally been accompanied by closer ties between funds and corporations, with broker intermediaries tending to communicate with companies on more strategic, intangible issues. Thus, in the United Kingdom, which tends to have a more "relationship investing" atmosphere among institutions, less emphasis is placed on financial history and more on certain intangibles such as research and development.

The Conference Board working group members vigorously debated whether the financial community actually needs additional information about new performance measures linked to corporate strategic plans. Some believe communicating additional information is not necessary, since many active "fundamental" analysts track companies in-depth. Others argue that new measures will give these same fundamental analysts new ways to view performance which focus on the potential for improved valuation. While the Harvard Business School/Ernst & Young study shows analysts do want more nonfinancial information, it also shows that analysts appear to be uncertain as to how they would factor in certain types of nonfinancial performance information if it were provided. This appears to be a cause and effect, or "chicken and egg," problem that may be resolved if key perform-ance indicators—both financial and nonfinancial—are more explicitly and extensively developed within the business community.

Progress has been made in this regard by companies such as Skandia AFS, Whirlpool, and The Bank of Montreal, as well as by the Royal Society for the encouragement of Arts, Manufactures, and Commerce (RSA). Efforts have begun to yield key strategic measures that can be standardized and disclosed to outside companies. According to Leif Edvinsson, director of intellectual capital for Skandia AFS (Assurance and Financial Services), the company has embarked on a program to make the company's intellec-tual capital—its "hidden value"—more tangible. To Skandia, intellectual capital is the result of the linkage of *human capital* (training and the accumulation of knowledge, skills, and experience) with *organizational processes* in the company to translate that human capital into customer satisfaction, high-quality output, productivity, and, ultimately, improved financial performance. Moreover, Skandia is one of the first corporations[27] to develop an annual report on intellectual capital which gathers a consid-erable number of figures into areas such as "customer," "processes," and "renewal." Skandia began to report a number of indicators to the public in a supplement to its 1994 annual report entitled *Visualizing Intellectual Capital in Skandia:*

Customer focus:
- Market share.
- Customers lost.
- Satisfied customers index (scale 1–5).

Renewal and development focus:
- Competence development expense/employee.
- Satisfied employee index (scale 1–5).
- Marketing expense/managed assets.
- Marketing expense/customer.

Information Technology Focus Indicators:
- Information technology investments as a percent of total expenses.
- Information technology employees as a percent of all employees.

Innovation focus indicators.
- Business development expenses as a percent of total expenses.
- Production from new launches.

Price Waterhouse's Change Management Team has worked with diverse companies, such as General Motors in Detroit and Mine Safety Appliances in Pittsburgh, to develop a series of performance measurements that are consistent over time and can, in some cases, be disclosed to external constituents. These measures include:

- Average time to market for new products.
- Design for manufacturability (a series of factors that indicate how easy it is to make the new product).
- New product sales dollars as a percentage of total sales dollars.
- Number of engineering changes after production release.
- Number of part numbers (and percentage of parts standardized among products).
- Concept-to-customer time milestones met.
- R&D investment as a percentage of sales.
- Planned and actual return on new product investment.
- Target product cost achievement.[28]

A task force of the RSA's Tomorrow's Company Inquiry[29] has considered a "Prototype plc Annual Report" developed by RSA Fellow Alan Benjamin, which brings together some of the key performance measures of most concern for each type of stakeholder. Measures include:

- *For customers:* sales, market share, and percentage of retained customers.
- *For providers of capital:* dividends and the percentage of long-term shareholders.
- *For employees:* the value of the company's knowledge bank, training investment as a percentage of profits, and reduced noise levels.
- *For suppliers:* a "co-operative" budget and the volume of shared data.

At the Bank of Montreal, Executive Vice-President and Chief Financial Officer Robert Wells believes that "it is imperative to find the drivers that are critical to the success of your business, and to structure your performance measurement around these few items. We also believe that part of the success you gain from focusing on performance measurement comes from communicating these measures publicly to all stakeholders."[30] The Annual Report for the Bank of Montreal spells out a number of strategic goals, measurements, and accomplishments.

Efforts to develop new performance measurements appear to be farther along outside the United States primarily because shareholder litigation is less common and companies feel more confident in disclosing more information. That situation may change in the United States following the passage of legislation providing for securities litigation reform. The "Private Securities Litigation Reform Act of 1995" (HR 1058) was passed by both the Senate and House of Representatives, then vetoed by President Clinton. The veto was subsequently overridden by Congress and the bill enacted into law on December 22, 1995. The law affects procedures, standards, and recoveries in securities litigation cases where shareholders claim they lost money because management acted in some manner contrary to what it had disclosed to the public. Title I provides a safe harbor (e.g., companies cannot be sued) for certain statements companies choose to disclose, raises pleading standards for fraud actions (e.g., making it harder to bring a suit), and limits attorneys' fees in class actions (e.g., where a single shareholder brings an action on behalf of a class or group of shareholders). It is possible that the quality and quantity of information companies make available to the public will increase as a result of this legislation. However, corporate legal counsel are still cautious about the nature and amount of information management discloses to all or part of the investing public, lest such information eventually becomes the basis for a lawsuit.

Even prior to enactment of this law, some U.S. companies had voluntarily begun to increase their disclosure of intangibles. In 1991, Whirlpool Chairman and CEO David Whitwam authorized the company to begin presentations to analysts with details on such topics as product and service quality, brand loyalty, brand share, and trade-partner satisfaction, with the standard review of financial results following these presentations. Whirlpool executives grade their performance with both financial and nonfinancial metrics into a "report card" (see Box 2–6, "Whirlpool's Performance Report Card"). Such disclosure, however, is still relatively rare in the United States.

LINKING KEY MEASURES TO THE BOTTOM LINE

The *Fortune* data on cumulative shareholder returns for the 10 most admired companies cited in the beginning of this chapter indicate a general tendency for most admired companies to outperform the S&P 500 in 1995 and over the 10-year period, 1985–1995, and for the least admired companies to fare

BOX 2–6

Whirlpool's Performance Report Card

Whirlpool's performance measures are based on both financial and nonfinancial metrics.

- **Financial**
  - economic value added
  - return on equity
- **Customer satisfaction**
  - market share
  - customer satisfaction (by survey)
  - brand loyalty
  - satisfaction with service
  - trade-partner satisfaction
  - product availability
- **Total quality**
  - worldwide excellence (quality) score
  - defect levels
  - cycle time
  - service incidence rates
- **People commitment**
  - employee commitment survey
- **Growth and innovation**
  - percent new product sales

Source: Bill Birchard, "The Call for Full Disclosure," *CFO Magazine,* 10, no. 12, December 1994, pp. 31 and 33.

worse. These data, however, are not systematic, and none of The Conference Board's case study companies report having devised a method to quantify precisely the link between improving the bottom line and using key performance measurements in a systematic strategic process. This is not surprising since, if the process works, it results in systemic change throughout the organization; it would, therefore, be difficult to isolate quantitative effects in such a dynamic situation. Moreover, even if mathematical correlation were identifiable, that correlation would not necessarily prove causation (e.g., simply because two events happen at the same time, one does not necessarily cause the other).

Case study company managers and CEOs appear to recognize these data limitations. Rather than putting off their key performance measurement programs until they find quantifiable linkages, they have generally taken it for granted that instituting and adhering to key performance measurement systems will improve profitability. According to Mark Green of Pitney Bowes: "We believe that there is a strong relationship to financial performance by focusing on the nonfinancial." Green believes that financial measures, while important, tend not to be the leading indicators, whereas the nonfinancial measures tend to foretell financial results. Another case study presenter sums it up: "There has not been any kind of conclusive analysis that focuses on how quality, productivity, or the customer market directly ties into the bottom line. We've just assumed that these three—the client, the employee, and the bottom line—are so inextricably linked that we have to focus on all three in order to produce the results in the bottom line that our investors are looking for."

Secretary of Labor Robert B. Reich, speaking to the SEC, asserts that improved workplace practices hold the key to competitive performance:

> Corporate success is maximized only when every worker at every level is enlisted as a partner in the all-out effort to achieve top performance. Training and empowering employees enables them to deliver the high-quality, low-cost products and services demanded by today's global, technologically sophisticated markets.[31]

Innovative workplace practices produce performance gains that can, to a great extent, be measured. The types of measures that can be utilized include customer retention, market share, defect rates, on-time deliveries, speed of new products to market, value added per employee, labor turnover, absenteeism, accidents, average span of control, number of management levels, training expense as a percent of payroll or per employee, and process value analysis. The Department of Labor is acting as a clearinghouse for information linking workplace practices to improved performance; some of the more significant studies are summarized in Box 2–7, "Workplace Practices and Performance Improvement: The Department of Labor's Survey of Studies."

The Conference Board's study of key nonfinancial performance measurements has uncovered a mounting trend within U.S. and global businesses to develop and expand performance measures to run businesses and chart their future. Case study companies are instituting performance measurement techniques to track processes formerly thought to be intangible, such as improving the value of intellectual capital, customer satisfaction, and

BOX 2-7

Workplace Practices and Performance Improvement: The Department of Labor's Survey of Studies

- Firms that introduced formal training programs after 1983 experienced a 19 percent larger rise in productivity by 1986 on average than did firms that did not introduce such a program.

- The presence of problem-solving teams, gain sharing, training, and employment security in steel industry finishing lines resulted in significantly increased productivity. Ninety-eight percent of the runs were on schedule—compared with 88 percent in lines not using such innovative practices.

- Automobile plants with innovative work systems—such as extensive training, performance-based compensation, work teams, and reassignment of quality control responsibility to line workers—manufactured vehicles in an average of 22 hours with 0.5 defects per vehicle. In contrast, more traditional plants using similar technology took 30 hours with 0.8 defects per vehicle.

- A study analyzing a firm's valuation levels found that firms noted for their progressive use of employee development and process management practices had price-to-book valuation ratios significantly higher than their industry peers not investing in these workplace practices.

- A study reviewing share price returns to firms recognized for the "above-average implementation" of Total Quality Management (TQM) practices found these firms accruing excess returns of 15 percent over the five years after the start of the TQM program. A second study constructed a portfolio of firms noted for their use of TQM. This portfolio outperformed the Standard & Poor's 500 portfolio by some 1 to 2 percent per year over the 1989–1992 period.

- A survey of 700 firms from all major industries found that companies utilizing a greater number of innovative human resource practices had higher annual shareholder return from 1986–1991 and higher gross return on capital. For example, the top 25 percent of firms—those using the greatest number of "best practices"—had an 11 percent rate of return on capital, more than twice as high as the remaining companies.

Note: Studies are described in full in *Road to High-Performance Workplaces: A Guide to Better Jobs and Better Business Results 1994*, U.S. Department of Labor, Office of the American Workplace.

Source: Robert B. Reich, "Statement of the Secretary of Labor Before the Securities and Exchange Commission, Hearing on Safe Harbor Protection for Corporate Disclosure of High-Performance Work Practices," February 13, 1995, pp. 4–5.

workplace practices. Companies say that key performance measures, when linked to the company's overall strategic vision and goals, can improve profitability and be used to provide appropriate incentives to executives through their compensation packages.

While there is general acceptance that key measures of performance can be useful tools to manage companies, there is considerable controversy over the extent to which the details of performance measures can and should be communicated between managements, boards, and shareholders. There is, at present, significant debate surrounding the legality and advisability of disclosing certain types of intangible performance information. Yet there is a pressing need to explore ways corporations can communicate with their current and potential investors (as opposed to the traders in the markets) concerning their key performance measures, strategic intentions, and plans to add value to their enterprises in the future. This need is coming both from corporations, which want to tell a more complete story and be evaluated by their investors on a more comprehensive basis, and from certain institutional investors who, as will be discussed in the next chapter, are increasingly willing to take the time to evaluate companies on their overall performance.

ENDNOTES

1. Anne B. Fisher, "America's Most Admired Companies: Corporate Reputations," *Fortune,* March 6, 1996, pp. 90–98.
2. Competitiveness Policy Council, Subcouncil on Corporate Governance and Financial Markets, *The Will to Act,* Washington D.C., December 7, 1992, pp. 22–23.
3. Ibid., pp. 23–24.
4. Competitiveness Policy Council, Subcouncil on Capital Allocation, *Lifting All Boats: Increasing the Payoff From Private Investment in the U.S. Economy,* Washington D.C., September 1995, pp. ii–iii.
5. Carolyn Kay Brancato, *New Corporate Performance Measures,* Report 1118-95-RR, The Conference Board, New York, New York, 1995.
6. Ibid., p. 13.
7. John Geanuracos and Ian Meiklejohn, *Performance Measurement: The New Agenda; Using Non-Financial Indicators to Improve Profitability* (London: Business Intelligence, 1993), p. 6.
8. Ibid., p. 14.
9. Brancato, p. 14.

10. Geanuracos and Meiklejohn, p. 9.

11. Brancato, p. 36.

12. Ibid.

13. Ibid.

14. Ibid., p. 37.

15. Ibid.

16. Ibid., p. 38.

17. Ibid.

18. Ibid., p. 39.

19. Ibid., p. 40.

20. Ibid., p. 41.

21. Ibid.

22. See two articles by Robert S. Kaplan and David P. Norton, "The Balanced Scorecard—Measures That Drive Performance," *Harvard Business Review,* January–February 1992 and "Putting the Balanced Scorecard to Work," *Harvard Business Review,* September–October, 1993.

23. Brancato, p. 43.

24. See Robert G. Eccles and Sarah C. Mavrinac, *Improving the Corporate Disclosure Process,* Harvard Graduate School of Business Administration, Working Paper 94-061, 1994.

25. Brancato, p. 52.

26. Matthew Gaved, "Shareholder Communications: Institutional Ownership & Influence in the United Kingdom," Presentation to The Conference Board's Working Group on Communicating Corporate Performance, New York City, April 24, 1996.

27. Thomas A. Stewart, "Your Company's Most Valuable Asset: Intellectual Capital," *Fortune,* October 3, 1994, p. 69.

28. The Price Waterhouse Change Integration Team, *The Paradox Principles: How High-Performance Companies Manage Chaos, Complexity, and Contradiction to Achieve Superior Results* (Chicago: Irwin Professional Publishing, 1996), p. 250.

29. In January 1993, the RSA brought together senior executives from 25 leading U.K. companies to develop a shared vision of Tomorrow's Company. The inquiry's objective was a practical one: to stimulate competitive performance by encouraging business leaders and those who influence their decision making and to reexamine the sources of sustainable business success. See: Royal Society for the Encouragement of Arts, Manufactures & Commerce, *Tomorrow's Company: The Role of Business in a Changing World* (London: Royal Society for the Encouragement of

Arts Manufacturers & Commerce, Interim Report, February 1994; and Final Report, June 1995.)

30. Letter from R.B. Wells, Executive Vice President and Chief Financial Officer, Bank of Montreal, to the author, dated December 20, 1995.

31. Robert B. Reich, "Statement of the Secretary of Labor Before the Securities and Exchange Commission, Hearing on Safe Harbor Protection for Corporate Disclosure of High-Performance Work Practices," February 13, 1995, p. 3.

II

BEST PRACTICES IN CORPORATE GOVERNANCE

3

INSTITUTIONAL INVESTORS
BECOME ACTIVISTS

During the past decade, U.S. institutional investors such as pension funds and even mutual funds and bank trusts have come to realize the full force of the financial power they command. Many have clearly moved from the Berle and Means model of passive, dispersed, and faceless individual shareholders to institutions challenging managements on a variety of issues and in a variety of styles—some favoring negotiation, others preferring more direct confrontation. A number of umbrella groups also help mobilize U.S. institutional investor economic and political clout beyond what could be achieved by even a single large institution (see Box 3–1 for a description of some of the major U.S. shareholders groups). Moreover, institutional activism is rapidly spreading from the United States to Europe, Australia, and even Asia. This chapter traces the development of U.S. and global shareholder activism in the context of the continuing debate over how corporations create value for themselves and their shareholders; the next chapter discusses best practices in corporate governance and why they make good business sense.

BOX 3-1

The Major U.S. Shareholder Groups

CIC
: The Corporate Information Center was formed in late 1969 by the National Council of Churches to collect information on the social aspects of business activities for church groups.

CII
: The Council of Institutional Investors was formed in 1984 by the Treasurer of the State of California to protest the payment of greenmail by certain corporations. It is currently based in Washington D.C. and is comprised of more than 100 state and local public and labor pension funds as well as a small but growing number of corporate pension funds. This is probably the most aggressive shareholder advocacy group in the United States.

ICCR
: The Interfaith Center of Corporate Responsibility in New York focuses on social and ethical issues. It is an active advocacy group which continues to file shareholder resolutions on such issues as Northern Ireland, South Africa (remains on the list because of company reinvestment in the area), the CERES environmental principles, equal employment opportunity, tobacco spin-offs, and human rights in Burma.

IRRC
: The Investor Responsibility Research Center, Inc. formed in December 1972 to provide timely and impartial analysis concerning corporate social responsibility issues. The group is currently headquartered in Washington D.C. and now ana-

(continued)

STAGES OF SHAREHOLDER ACTIVISM

Institutional investor activism is now focused more intently on performance issues, having proceeded through a series of developmental stages (see Box 3–2): (1) pressing corporations to adopt shareholder resolutions on "social" issues; (2) opposing management when corporations institute certain antitakeover devices; (3) urging corporations to make structural changes in their boards of directors and voting procedures; (4) analyzing the performance of corporations and their boards of directors to identify underperforming companies to be targeted for shareholder action; and (5)

The Major U.S. Shareholder Groups—Concluded

	-lyzes both social and corporate governance issues. The group does not file shareholder resolutions, but provides proxy tracking and voting analysis services.
ISS	Institutional Shareholder Services, Inc. was established by the former Assistant Secretary of Labor for Pension and Welfare Benefits, Robert A.G. Monks, to advise institutional investors on how to carry out their fiduciary responsibility to vote their shares. It provides proxy voting services and re-search and consulting advice to institutions. It is based in Bethesda, Maryland just outside of Washington D.C.
IRAA	The Investors' Rights Association of America (IRAA) is the newly formed successor to the grass roots group founded by T. Boone Pickens called United Shareholders Association (USA), which closed its doors in 1994. The IRAA acts on behalf of the collective group of individual shareholders and aggressively sponsors shareholder governance proposals. It is based in Washington D.C.
Labor Groups	These include the Laborers' International Union of North America, The International Brotherhood of Teamsters, and the AFL-CIO, all of whom control substantial pension fund assets directly (which distinguishes them from the above "umbrella groups" which, while representing various institutional investors, do not control their assets).

focusing not only on financial but on nonfinancial measures of corporate performance (e.g., workplace practices, quality, innovativeness, customer satisfaction) to understand the ability of the corporation to perform not only over an historic period but to generate a stream of future benefits. Ironically, some of these nonfinancial measures now perceived to relate to the financial viability of the corporation (e.g., workplace practices) were precisely those with which the early "social responsibility" activists were concerned during the 1930s—only then these measures were not perceived to impact on financial issues and were, therefore, eschewed by the main-

BOX 3–2

Stages of U.S. Institutional Investor Activism

- *Social investing.* For decades, certain individual shareholders pressured corporations to adopt social policies concerning consumer protection, the environment, and withholding investments in countries perceived to be undemocratic such as the former South Africa. A few "gadfly" individuals in the United States made public statements at annual company meetings to attract media attention. These individuals were eventually joined by certain institutional investors, primarily pension fund managers for church groups. Progressively, these individuals and institutions learned that utilizing proxy voting tactics could be at least as effective as their media strategy, and might, in fact, provide more leverage over the company if enough votes could be amassed among the general shareholder population. A number of social issues continue to be raised today, especially by church groups and, until recently, many state legislatures banned public pension funds from investing in companies doing business in South Africa. On the whole, however, the largest public and private pension funds have tended to be more concerned with financially based issues.

- *Fighting antitakeover initiatives.* During the mid-1980s, institutions were faced with an array of what they perceived to be management entrenchment devices to reduce shareholder value and eliminate the market for corporate control. Devices included payment of "greenmail" by management (takeover devices are explained in the text of this chapter) or awarding "golden parachutes" to provide executives with large compensation packages if they lost their jobs following a merger. Managements also instituted a series of initiatives to prevent shareholders from receiving a premium offered by a bidder (via "poison pills" and other strategies). Institutions embraced the proxy voting mechanism (developed in the social investing phase) to oppose management attempts to block takeovers and to protect their right to decide whether to "tender" or surrender their shares to a bidding company for the premium generally offered.

- *Pressing for structural governance changes within the corporation.* In the late 1980s and early 1990s, U.S. institutions increasingly focused on the formal structure of the corporation and the role of its board of directors. These structural issues included: whether there should be a separate CEO and chairman; the number of "outside"

(continued)

U.S. Institutional Investor Activism—Concluded

directors who were independent of management; the composition of key board committees such as the audit, nominating, and compensation committees; proxy voting mechanics; and other issues institutions could affect or influence through proxy voting mechanisms. Institutional shareholders learned that voting their stock represented an economic value, not only in takeovers, but to influence the direction of the corporation. Federal and state regulatory oversight of certain institutional investors reinforced this belief by requiring fiduciaries to vote their stock as a matter of fiduciary responsibility. During this phase, institutions concentrated on the board as the means to improve the corporation and its accountability to them, and they chose certain corporate governance structures as the pivotal point of pressure most easily accessible to them through the now familiar proxy voting mechanism.

■ *Monitoring performance.* While important, many institutions now consider the structural governance initiatives to be important for engendering confidence in management, but recognize that they are essentially surrogate measures for corporate performance. By the mid-1990s, therefore, institutions had shifted their focus to performance-related issues including measuring and evaluating the performance of the board, the CEO, and the company. Executive compensation and the link, if any, between executive pay and corporate performance also concerns institutions as they scrutinize corporate performance more closely.

■ *Incorporating nonfinancial performance issues into indicators of corporate performance.* A small number of public pension funds have gone beyond targeting corporations for governance intercession by looking at their historic, cumulative shareholder returns. They are now pressing for meetings with senior management and, in some cases, boards of directors to discuss the strategic direction of the company. Certain types of nonfinancial measures of corporate performance, such as workplace practices, are being included in these discussions since these institutions increasingly believe that these measures are explicitly tied to prospective financial results and, therefore, provide an indication of the ability of the corporation to perform in the future.

Source: Carolyn Kay Brancato, *Getting Listed on Wall Street: The Irwin Guide to Financial Reporting Standards in the U.S.* (Chicago: Irwin Professional Publishing, 1996), pp. 163-164.

stream pension fund institutions and left to individual and church-related pension fund "social activists."

Most institutional investor activists now want corporate structures (e.g., composition of the board of directors, democratic voting procedures) to afford them a certain baseline degree of confidence that, as former CalPERS CEO Dale Hanson put it: "someone is minding the store." But the distinct shift in institutional investor focus towards corporate performance suggests a maturing relationship between investors and companies. It also supports distinctions made in Chapter 1 between shareholders as investors or traders who have varying expectations of the companies in which they invest. Some institutional investors are now attempting to define acceptable levels of performance which reflect an in-depth view of the intrinsic value of the companies whose stock they hold. A memorandum written by key staff at CalPERS, a leading institutional activist, traces the development towards performance related activism:

> Initially, "Corporate Governance" was viewed only in the limited historical context from which it was created—i.e., since it was the takeover disputes of the early- to mid-1980s that caused CalPERS to enter this arena, early efforts focused on takeover issues . . . During these early days, we did not look at whether the adoption of one of these antitakeover measures had any impact on the company's performance. At that time, it was enough that the *issue* existed and might, at some point in the future, be used to oppose a takeover that might be favored by shareholders. By 1987, we had learned that the effectiveness of our efforts in these areas . . . [was] being diminished because of procedural obstacles. We then broadened our focus to include confidential voting, and other ballot counting issues. We continued to be issue-oriented, however, rather than performance-oriented. . . . [emphasis original]
>
> We gradually became convinced that a focus on antitakeover and proxy issues—in a vacuum—was too narrow . . . we began to refocus on the bottom line—corporate economic performance.[1]

Monitoring corporate performance to create shareholder value, however, can mean different things to different shareholders. Some institutions, like CalPERS, are rejecting the level 4 shareholder focus of merely creating short-term profit, as described in the first chapter of this book. Their mid-1990s, broader view of performance looks at creating intrinsic value for investors, increasingly perceived to include both financial and nonfinancial matters which reflect the *viability* of the corporation—e.g., its ability to generate a stream of profit.

U.S. shareholder activism as practiced in the 1990s has its origins in the 1930s with individual shareholder concern over corporate accountability. As institutions became involved, activism took two directions: the social- and religious-based institutions concentrated on social issues; while the public pension funds were jarred into action based on financial issues stemming from the abuses of the early 1980s takeover period. This book is primarily concerned with financially motivated institutional investors (as opposed to social issue- or religious-based institutions).[2] Until now, these financially motivated institutions have directed their shareholder activism primarily against companies that either have acted egregiously to abridge the rights of shareholders or underperformed in terms of the overall market or individual industry averages, as measured by the classic measurement of shareholder value—cumulative shareholder returns measured by stock price appreciation plus dividend return.

But a select group of the leading institutional investors is now reaching towards a much more proactive stance with regard to valuing the companies in their portfolios. These institutions are increasingly concerned with gauging the *potential for future performance* of the company, its management, and its board of directors. This valuation perspective requires these institutions to become more aware of factors (both financial and nonfinancial, as described in Chapter 2) which contribute to the potential of the corporation to increase firm value and, therefore, shareholder value in the future. Oddly enough, many of these nonfinancial issues are reminiscent of some social concerns, such as workplace practices and environmental compliance, formerly associated only with the social- and religious-based institutional investors (see Box 3–3). These nonfinancial concerns are no longer viewed as "nice" for society's sake although they detract from the bottom line; they are increasingly perceived to add to the financial viability of the corporation. Decades after some of the more public shareholder struggles over, for example, consumer and environmental issues at General Motors, a number of pension funds have begun to believe that certain heretofore social issues will ultimately have an impact upon the quality of their investment. These classic issues have focused on South Africa (until recently); alcohol, tobacco, and gambling; military weapons and services; effects on the environment, including nuclear power; company relations with the community; company relations with employees; treatment of women and minorities; and product quality and attitude towards consumers. Some of these issues are increasingly

BOX 3–3

Church Efforts to Inject Ethical Standards Into the Corporate Fabric

In 1908 the Federal Council of Churches adopted the following Social Creed of the Churches.

The Federal Council of the Churches of Christ in America stands:

- For equal rights and complete justice for all men in all stations of life.
- For the abolition of child labor.
- For such regulation of the conditions of toil for women as shall safeguard the physical and moral health of the community.
- For the suppression of the "Sweating System."
- For the gradual and reasonable reduction of the hours of labor to the lowest practicable point, and for that degree of leisure for all, which is the condition of the highest human life.
- For a release from employment one day in seven.
- For the right of all men to the opportunity for self-maintenance, a right ever to be wisely and strongly safeguarded against encroachments of every kind.
- For the right of workers to some protection against the hardships often resulting from the swift crises of industrial change.
- For a living wage as a minimum in every industry, and for the highest wage that each industry can afford.
- For the protection of the worker from dangerous machinery, occupational disease, injuries, and mortality.
- For the principle of conciliation and arbitration in industrial dissensions.
- For the abatement of poverty.
- For the most equitable division of the products of industry that can ultimately be devised.

Source: Peter Kinder, Steven D. Lydenberg, and Amy L. Domini, *Investing for Good: Making Money While Being Socially Responsible* (New York: Harper-Collins, 1993), p. 14.

viewed as spilling over to affect the economics of the corporation; they then become the responsibility of the fiduciary to monitor. There is increasingly, therefore, a blending of some of the concerns of these two branches of the institutional investor activist movement to incorporate a more intrinsic view of what constitutes the value of the corporation.

In order to push for increases in intrinsic firm value, however, institutional investors will need better financial and nonfinancial information to use in their future oriented performance-based analysis. Moreover, rather than seeing this increased performance-based activism as a threat, corporations can become allied with those institutions which encourage it to make the strategic investments in both tangible and intangible areas that will enable the company to generate a stream of income in the future. Both corporations and institutions will benefit from this approach.

THE SOCIAL RESPONSIBILITY STAGE

U.S. shareholders have been actively pressuring managements to address social issues through the proxy voting process for more than 60 years. According to the Investor Responsibility Research Center (IRRC),[3] Lewis Gilbert, owner of 10 shares of Consolidated Gas Company of New York, attended his first annual meeting in 1932 and was appalled by the absence of communication between company management and shareholders. After being ignored by management at the meeting, he joined with his brother John to form the first group of shareholder activists. In 1995 the Gilberts were still listed by the IRRC as sponsoring shareholder resolutions at American Express, Ashland Oil, and the Bank of New York to revise procedures for electing directors at these companies. The Gilberts attempted, through their persistent questioning of management, to transform annual meetings from "perfunctory legal rituals" into forums for discussions between management and shareholders. They also demonstrated that minority shareholders could be more effective if they did not sell their shares when they disagreed with management; rather, they should serve as a pressure group for corporate reform of policies and actions. The Gilberts threw a rock into the water as they pressured managements to be accountable to shareholders—and that rock has generated ripples for decades.

The Gilberts, though arguing on behalf of individual shareholders, focused on many of the same issues which concern today's largest institutional investors. It was their intention to:

- Make management more accountable.
- Increase disclosure of financial data.
- Safeguard the power of shareholders to elect directors by:

1. Opposing staggered boards whereby fewer than all directors are elected at one time.

2. Supporting cumulative voting whereby shareholders could swing their total votes behind the number of directors they support, rather than having to vote for the full slate of candidates.

- Improve shareholder benefits by:

1. Installing preemptive rights which would allow current owners to take advantage of new stock issues.

2. Opposing stock option plans which unduly benefit management.

- Curb excessive executive compensation plans.

The Gilberts may have been considered annoying "gadflies" by the companies they targeted, but they sparked the imagination of others like Saul Alinsky. Alinsky was one of the early advocates of using the platform of the corporate annual meeting and the publicity stemming from direct confrontations with management to press for social change. In 1966, Alinsky lead a group called FIGHT to pressure Eastman Kodak to hire and train 600 blacks at the company's Rochester, New York facility. FIGHT urged shareholders to assign it their proxies, withhold their proxies, or vote directly against management. While FIGHT did not achieve sufficient proxies to defeat Kodak, the company did agree to improve its minority hiring.[4]

By the late 1960s, (see Box 3–4 for a chronology of activism from the 1930s to 1970) a number of anti–Vietnam War issues were directed at companies such as Honeywell and Dow Chemical, ushering in what should be regarded as the first truly organized and widespread stage of shareholder activism—the "social investing movement." Building on the Kodak strategy, activists sought to create an "event" and use the media surrounding the annual meeting to win support for a social cause. In the Honeywell and Dow cases, shareholders attempted to personalize the war by locating visible and tangible local corporate targets such as these companies producing weapons and napalm. The Honeywell 1970 annual meeting apparently fell short of the peaceful yet provocative meeting that both management and the activists reportedly expected.

On April 28, more than 1,000 demonstrators congregated outside Honeywell's headquarters. As shareholders were registering to enter the meeting, a group of protesters tried to storm the entrance. *Time* magazine reported the scene as follows: "When flying beer bottles shattered glass doors and windows, 60 city policemen wearing gas masks formed a skirmish line to clear the entrance. About 300 demonstrators, many of them stripped to the waist and daubed in red and white grease paint, managed to get inside." Against a background of shouting from proxy-wielding protesters, Chairman Binger quickly ran through the meeting's official business. He announced that management controlled enough proxies to elect its slate of directors and adjourned the meeting just 10 minutes after it had been called to order. . . .

In varying degrees the chaos at Honeywell's annual meeting was repeated throughout the 1970 proxy season. The protests against corporations reflected in part a volatile social climate characterized by public outcry against government, the war, and anything else associated with "the establishment." A longer-lasting theme of the attack on corporations in 1970 stemmed from rising public awareness of and increased concern about the impact of corporate practices on society.[5]

In 1970, the SEC disallowed a Dow shareholder resolution that requested the board to consider amending the company's certificate of incorporation so that the company would no longer be able to make napalm. At issue was the right of management to engage in business decisions without interference from shareholders even if those business decisions have a social impact.[6] The court, however, overruled the SEC, delivering a strong endorsement of shareholder review of corporate decisions with political implications. Of key relevance was the fact that Dow admitted that its napalm operations lost money, and that the decision the company made to continue to manufacture and market napalm was made not because of business considerations, but in spite of them.

> We think that there is a clear and compelling distinction between management's legitimate need for freedom to apply its expertise in matters of day-to-day business judgment, and management's patently illegitimate claim of power to treat modern corporations with their vast resources as personal satrapies implementing personal, political, or moral predilections. It could scarcely be argued that management is more qualified or more entitled to make these kinds of decisions than the shareholders who are the true beneficial owners of the corporation. . . .[7]

The court's action effectively launched the social investing movement by permitting social responsibility issues to be included among shareholder resolutions. The court (U.S. Court of Appeals for the District of Columbia) made its ruling in July 1970. Meanwhile, the General Motors shareholder activist case was in progress.

BOX 3–4

Chronology of Shareholder Activism: 1932-1970

1932   Lewis Gilbert, owner of 10 shares of **Consolidated Gas Co. of New York** attends his first meeting, vows to devote himself to the cause of the public shareholder, and with his brother John Gilbert forms first group of shareholder activists.

1940   The Gilberts challenge **American Tobacco Company's** executive compensation incentive bonus plan.

1942   Securities and Exchange Commission (SEC) adopts Rule 14a-8 requiring companies to include shareholder resolutions in their proxy statements. The resolutions must be of concern to all shareholders and relate to the ordinary conduct of business. Resolutions are to be disseminated in the proxy materials at the company's expense and discussed at annual meetings.

1946   SEC issues opinion allowing **Greyhound** to exclude shareholder resolution that it abolish segregated seating on buses on the grounds that Rule 14a-8 is not intended to permit proposals of "a general political, social or economic nature." In 1952 the SEC amends its rules to comply with the Greyhound opinion.

1966   **Eastman Kodak** is pressured by FIGHT to hire and train black workers. FIGHT urges proxy battle and assignment of proxies to the organization, but does not attain sufficient number. Kodak agrees to improvements in minority hiring. Saul Alinsky (the organizer of FIGHT) views proxy participation as the means of democratizing corporate America.

1969   Heir to the Pillsbury flour company fortune, Charles Pillsbury, leads proxy battle against **Honeywell** over the manufacture of antipersonnel

(continued)

At the time that Campaign GM was launched, the court had not yet overturned the SEC's ruling in the Dow case. Therefore, the SEC took a much narrower position favoring what management could exclude. Even so, the SEC permitted two out of nine resolutions to be included in the company's proxy materials. This confirmed the activists' stance that shareholders should not observe the "Wall Street Walk"—sell their shares if they are displeased with management—but rather should stand and fight. The

Chronology—Concluded

weapons. He buys one share then requests shareholder list from company so he can share his concerns about Honeywell's production of fragmentation bombs and other war material with other owners.

1970   Shareholder groups led by Dr. Quentin Young of the Medical Committee for Human Rights press **Dow Chemical** for proposal requesting its board to consider amending the company's certificate of incorporation to exclude the production of napalm. SEC rules against shareholders; court overturns SEC's decision and paves the way for social responsibility resolutions on the proxy. In 1976 SEC solidifies the court's position by refining Rule 14a-8 so that companies can exclude only proposals involving business matters that are mundane in nature and do not involve any substantial policy or other considerations.

1970   The Project on Corporate Responsibility, in conjunction with Ralph Nader's Campaign GM, targets **General Motors** as the symbol of corporate America to pressure them in a broad range of social policy areas including product safety and environmental pollution. The SEC permits two out of nine shareholder resolutions forwarded with social responsibility content to be included in the General Motors proxy materials. At the annual meeting on May 22, 1970 dissidents achieve less than 3 percent of the vote, but General Motors agrees to create a Public Policy Committee composed of five outside directors to monitor social performance.

Sources: Robert A.G. Monks and Nell Minow, *Power and Accountability* (New York: Harper-Collins, 1991) and Lauren Talner, *The Origins of Shareholder Activism* (Washington D.C., The Investor Responsibility Research Center, July 1983).

coupling of the GM and the Dow cases in early 1970 clearly solidified the social responsibility movement.

The GM case was in many ways a landmark case. Four public interest lawyers formed the Project on Corporate Responsibility as a means for corporate reform. They reasoned that the corporation, with its vast resources, is like a private government and, therefore, must be more responsive to society's needs in a range of areas such as product safety, employment discrimination, and environmental pollution. The corporation singled out was not chosen because of anything in particular it did or did not do, but because of what it was—a symbol of all of corporate America. The Project enlisted the support of consumer advocate Ralph Nader, and the strategy was originally to run Nader for the board of directors. Nader declined, although he did attract national attention to its cause by launching the Campaign to Make General Motors Responsible.

The Project's strategy then shifted to using the proxy process to press for three proposals: (1) amend GM's charter to limit the company's operations to those consistent with "public health, safety and welfare;" (2) establish a shareholder committee on corporate responsibility, proposed to be composed of 15 to 25 representatives of environmental, civil rights, labor, academic, and other groups to be chosen by a trio made up of a member of GM's board, a representative of the United Auto Workers and a Campaign GM spokesman. The committee would be charged with reporting to shareholders within a year on GM's efforts to reduce pollution, develop safer products, encourage opportunities for minorities, and facilitate low-cost mass transit systems; and (3) place public interest representatives on GM's board of directors by expanding the board by three such places. Six more proposals were shortly added seeking to commit GM to specific policies in the areas of auto safety, pollution control, mass transit, and minority hiring.

In late February 1970, GM informed the Project on Corporate Responsibility and the SEC that it planned to exclude from its 1970 proxy statement all nine proposals, citing Rule 14a-8 and the prerogatives of management to exclude proposals submitted primarily for the purpose of promoting general economic, political, racial, religious, social, or similar causes. GM held that it had jurisdiction in all the areas under the ordinary course of business rationale.[8] The decision the SEC was to make with regard to access to the proxy was crucial; if shareholders couldn't get on the proxy, dissidents would not be able to afford to mail information on their perspective to all the company's shareholders, and their proposals would have no chance of being discussed. Moreover, they would not even be guaranteed a place at the annual meeting to discuss their proposals.

The SEC, after weighing the arguments, decided to allow two of the nine proposals to be included in GM's proxy statement—the resolution to expand the board of directors to make room for public representatives and the resolution to establish a shareholder committee on corporate responsibility. At the May 22, 1970 annual meeting, neither resolution received the

3 percent of the shares voted that would have made them eligible for resubmission in 1971. Nevertheless, each side claimed victory, since the dissidents argued that they achieved public focus on their issues and management claimed that the small vote was a gratifying expression of confidence. In August 1970, the company did, however, create a Public Policy Committee composed of five outside directors to monitor social performance. According to the IRRC, a few months later, the company appointed its first black director and also formed a special committee of scientists to study the environmental effects of GM products. A "round two" of Campaign GM action was launched the following year, attempting to enlist the support of large institutional investors such as universities and foundations, but it was less successful since most of these institutions were not persuaded that their fiduciary responsibilities extended to curing the social ills which might be engendered by the corporations in which they invest. This form of activism would take a number of years to cultivate.

The SEC's decision in the General Motors case was followed up and extended by the court's decision in the Dow case, marking 1970 as the year in which shareholder responsibility issues came to the ballot. To this day, the SEC and the courts have continued to go back and forth on the issue of what properly constitutes a shareholder resolution and when shareholders can be denied a say in areas which are the province of management as an item of "ordinary" business. Shareholders have, for example, pressed tobacco companies to get out of the tobacco business and have argued for change in areas over which management would certainly have claimed to have the sole jurisdiction. To managements this is one of the most unsettling of the ripples in the water, since it is still not clear where managements' prerogatives end and shareholders' demands begin. The fundamental questions raised in these early activist cases, concerning the purpose of the corporation and on whose behalf the managers act, are still very much in the forefront of the shareholder activist movement.

1980s—THE TAKEOVER WARS

The early 1980s saw the birth of what is generally regarded as the modern institutional investor movement in the United States. During the takeover wars, the financial vehicles available to raiders caused the market for corporate control to focus largely on financial gain in the short term and not on the viability of companies to generate investment profits. Moreover, until that time, most institutional investors would never have considered voting against management. Reactions by target managements taken in response to raiders, however, led to a breach of investor confidence. Institutional investors began to perceive that managements were acting to entrench themselves and not necessarily in the best interest of shareholders. New to the issue of institutional investor activism, early public pension fund efforts were directed at making sure the managements accorded shareholders their rights; in so doing, institutional investors were swept along by the tender offer and premium process, which led to a corresponding breach of confidence by corporate managements (especially in profitable, cash-rich companies) who felt unrewarded by their efforts and sold out by their investors to the highest bidding raider. The most formidable task now before corporations and their institutional investors is to restore confidence by repairing both sets of failed expectations—a task made significantly more manageable with the move towards performance based activism.

The 1980s takeover wave began with "Saturday night special" raids on corporations. A bidder, or raider, would typically buy a block of stock, making a bid for 51 percent of shares outstanding, then having gained control would "mop up" the transaction for the remaining 49 percent of shares at a significantly lower "back end" price. Shareholders felt coerced by these "two-tier" bids into tendering their shares for fear they would be "frozen out" and left in the 49 percent of minority shareholders forced to accept the lower back end price. Once a raider surfaced, "arbitrageurs" would eagerly buy up the target company stock, splitting the difference between the announced tender offer bid and the current price. For example, if XYZ company was selling for $50 per share, and a raider announced a tender offer for 51 percent of outstanding shares for $100 per share, the arbitrageurs would enter the market and drive the price up to a risk calculated amount, around $65 per share, depending on the solidity of the deal and the "back end" tender offer price for the remaining 49 percent of shares. Shareholders were then faced with an assured profit of $15 per share if they sold immediately. Institutional investors became concerned that they might be in breach of their own fiduciary duties if they did not sell immediately or ultimately tender their shares to the raider. This frequently resulted in a "stampede" to either sell or tender.

Meanwhile, following the enactment of the Employment Retirement Income Security Act (ERISA) in 1974, investment money began to shift from large individual accounts in brokerage houses to institutional ownership especially through pension funds, as described in Chapter 1. Vast quantities of assets were being amassed in the accounts of institutional investors, which were tax exempt and immune from any tax consequences of trading stock.

Companies first put "into play" tended to be oil companies for which the book value generally was considerably higher than the current market share value. This made it worth more to buy oil company assets than to drill for new reserves, and further increased the attractiveness of the raider's two-tier technique, since the raider would be relatively certain he could sell off the company's assets for more than the purchase price, assuring a positive trading return.

As legendary takeover figures such as T. Boone Pickens, Carl Icahn, Sir James Goldsmith, and Saul Steinberg initiated bids on some of America's largest corporations, the corporate response to these raiders was to fend them off by instituting various antitakeover devices (see Box 3–5 for a description of major corporate defensive tactics). Unfortunately, many of these devices protected managements at the financial expense of the broad base of shareholders. Companies, in their efforts to avoid the raiders, triggered the wrath of the institutional investors and inadvertently nurtured the institutional investor movement as it is known today. CalPERS, one of the leaders in the U.S. institutional investor movement, became involved at this time.

> CalPERS' involvement in what has become known as "Corporate Governance" began in 1984. That was a relatively tumultuous period in the public markets, where hostile takeover bids were pitted against corporate entrenchment devices. The CalPERS Board became concerned that, while corporate dynasties were rising and falling, the economic impact of these high-stake disputes upon other investors was being ignored. . . .[9]

Greenmail

One of the earliest devices managements and boards used in the 1980s to fend off raiders was to pay *greenmail*. Greenmail is a form of financial blackmail that occurs when a company repurchases from a shareholder a block of stock at a premium over the current market price, for the purpose of preventing a takeover attempt. Noted financiers typically bought chunks of stock, threatened to initiate a takeover, and then waited to be bought out at a premium over market value. Major repurchase transactions exceeded $20 million during the burgeoning takeover period from 1979 to 1984. With hefty premiums over the market price in excess of 35 percent paid to Saul Steinberg, Rupert Murdoch, Sir James Goldsmith, and others, institutions

BOX 3–5

Corporate Defensive Provisions of Concern to Institutional Investors

TAKEOVER RELATED PROVISIONS

Antigreenmail Provisions

Greenmail refers to the practice of accumulating a block of stock in a company, then selling the stock back to the company in a private transaction at an above-market price. In exchange for the greenmail payment, the greenmail recipient often signs a standstill agreement, which limits his ability to seek control of the company for a certain period of time. In an effort to discourage greenmail, some companies have adopted charter and bylaw amendments that prohibit such above-market purchases unless the same offer is made to all shareholders or unless shareholders approve the transaction by a majority or supermajority vote. Technically, antigreenmail provisions are not takeover defenses; taken in tandem with other measures, however, some observers say the provisions deter the accumulation of large blocks of stock that often precede a takeover attempt.

Consider Nonfinancial Effects of Mergers

Some companies have adopted provisions that require or allow their boards of directors to evaluate the impact a proposed change in control could have on employees, host communities, suppliers, and other constituencies. Some state laws allow corporations' directors to consider such factors, whether or not the company has specifically adopted a charter or bylaw provision permitting it to do so.

Fair Price Provisions

Fair price provisions require a bidder to pay all shareholders a "fair price"— usually defined as the highest price the bidder paid for any of the shares it acquired in a target company during a specified period of time before the commencement of a tender offer. Most fair price provisions do not apply if a merger is approved by the target's board or if the bidder obtains a specified, supermajority level of approval for the merger from the target's shareholders.

Poison Pills

Shareholder rights plans are among the more complicated antitakeover devices. Although their terms and conditions vary considerably, the purpose

(continued)

Corporate Defensive Provisions—Continued

of a poison pill is to force all potential bidders to negotiate with a target company's board of directors. If the board approves the deal, it is often able to redeem the pill. If the board does not approve the bid and the potential acquirer proceeds anyway, the pill is "triggered," causing actions that would make the target financially unattractive or dilute the voting power of the potential acquirer.

Under a typical plan, shareholders are issued rights to purchase stock in their own company or in the acquiring company at a discount price (usually half) if a hostile bidder acquires a certain percentage (usually 10, 15, or 20 percent) of the outstanding shares. Unlike antitakeover charter and bylaw amendments, poison pills do not generally have to be submitted to shareholders for ratification. Requests to authorize large amounts of additional common or preferred stock, which do require shareholder approval, frequently are seen as standby measures for companies that have adopted, or may adopt, poison pills.

Supermajority Vote to Approve Merger

Supermajority provisions establish shareholder vote requirements that are higher than the minimum levels set by state law to approve a merger or other business combination. They typically require the approval of the holders of two-thirds, 75 or 80 percent, or more of the shares for actions that otherwise would require simple majority approval. Supermajority vote requirements are often combined with fair price provisions.

PROVISIONS RELATED TO COMPANY BOARDS OF DIRECTORS

Classified Board

A classified board is one in which directors are divided into separate classes, with the directors in each class elected to overlapping three-year terms. Staggering directors' terms makes it more difficult for dissidents to seize control of a target company immediately, even if they control the majority of a company's stock, since only one-third of the directors stand for election in any one year.

Cumulative Voting

Cumulative voting permits shareholders to apportion the total number of votes they are entitled to cast in the election of directors in any fashion they

(continued)

Corporate Defensive Provisions—Continued

desire. The total number is equal to the number of directors to be elected at the meeting multiplied by the number of shares voted. With cumulative voting, each shareholder may cast the total number of votes he or she is entitled to cast for one director or apportion them among the candidates desired.

The use of cumulative voting enables the holders of a minority of a company's stock to elect one or more directors even if they are unable to muster sufficient support on a straight voting basis; for example, the owners of 11 percent of the voting shares in a corporation that is electing 10 directors can be assured of electing one director if they vote all the shares cumulatively for one nominee. The greater the number of directors to be elected, the lower the level of support needed to elect directors cumulatively.

SHAREHOLDER VOTING ISSUES

Confidential Voting

Firms that use secret ballots designate either an independent third party or company employee sworn to secrecy to tabulate and review all proxy votes. In most instances, management agrees not to look at individual proxy cards. Most companies reserve the right to examine individual proxy cards in the event of a contested election. The intended purpose of secret ballots is to eliminate pressures and potential conflicts of interest faced by fiduciaries who vote shares on behalf of others.

Dual Class Stock

Some companies have two or more classes of common stock. The voting rights attached to each class of stock may (but do not always) vary from the one vote per share standard.

(continued)

questioned management motives for transferring this wealth to the raiders at their expense. The same financiers were routinely involved, and a group of five of them—the Bass Brothers, Sir James Goldsmith, Carl Icahn, Carl Lindner, Rupert Murdoch, and Saul Steinberg—received 26 percent of the value of all premiums paid over market value from 1979 through 1984, and 47 percent of the value of all premiums paid over market value in 1984.[10]

Corporate Defensive Provisions—Concluded

Under some voting schemes, one class of stock will be granted super voting rights—typically 5, 10, or more votes per share. In other instances, a class of shares may carry no voting rights. Some companies also provide one or more classes of stock with special rights, such as the ability to name a certain percentage of the directors. In other instances, such as at General Motors, stock is split into separate classes that reflect the company's various business operations.

Dual class capitalization plans are not antitakeover measures per se; they only help management (or another insider group) deter takeovers when they control the class of stock with higher or special voting rights.

Limited Shareholder Ability to Act by Written Consent or to Call a Special Meeting

Some companies have adopted charter or bylaw amendments that restrict or prohibit shareholders from taking action by written consent or calling a special meeting. Typically, the written consent limits will: (1) set a supermajority approval standard; (2) require unanimous consent; or (3) ban the practice outright.

Unequal Voting Rights

Unequal voting rights provisions limit the voting rights of certain types of holders or grant special rights to a particular class of shareholder. One variety, time-phased voting, gives shareholders who have owned their stock for a specified period of time, typically four years, a higher number of votes per share than more recent purchasers. Another unequal voting device, known as a substantial shareholder provision, reduces or caps the voting power of the holder once a certain ownership threshold, typically 10 or 20 percent, has been reached.

Source: Investor Responsibility Research Center, *Corporate Takeover Defenses,* 1993.

Managements defended their discriminatory payments of greenmail on grounds they were keeping their companies from falling into the hands of "fast buck" financiers who would strip the company of assets and reduce overall, long-term shareholder value. Some of the raiders justified their actions in populist terms, arguing that companies were worth more if they were broken up and that they were legitimate financiers intent on increasing value for all shareholders. Institutions were clearly caught in the middle of swarms of raiders making offers and counteroffers.

In one notable case, Saul Steinberg's Reliance Group Holdings Inc. purchased 4.2 million shares, or 12 percent, of Walt Disney Productions. Reliance launched a tender offer for control of Disney, but it withdrew its offer when Walt Disney bought it out at a profit to Reliance of $60 million. Immediately after the repurchase agreement was announced, the stock plummeted and, shortly thereafter, numerous shareholder suits were filed. Pursuant to these suits, the California Superior Court in July 1984 found in favor of the plaintiffs and issued a preliminary injunction against the Steinberg group, restricting the group's ability to transfer, invest, or dispose of the profits from the Disney repurchase. In May 1985, the California Court of Appeals affirmed the lower court's ruling, indicating that it was not persuaded by the directors' argument that the repurchases they undertook in response to the Steinberg group's accumulation of shares were to protect Disney shareholders. Rather, the court found that these actions were difficult to understand except as defense strategies against a hostile takeover in which the company was trying to make itself appear less attractive. The opinion also referred to the greenmailers' profits as "ill-gotten gain," especially in light of the fact that Disney was borrowing the $325 million repurchase price and additionally burdening the company with an increased debt load which could adversely affected Disney's credit rating.[11]

Trader versus Investor Value

The greenmail cases of the early 1980s marked the beginning of the need to differentiate trader from investor value. Although the Disney case was rather straightforward, another particularly byzantine case serves as an example of how the concept of shareholder value versus investor value developed in the context of these takeover transactions. T. Boone Pickens, Jr., CEO of Mesa Petroleum, often stated that he was not a greenmailer, only a force for increasing shareholder value. One transaction involved Phillips Petroleum and began December 4, 1984 when Mesa Petroleum Co. announced that, along with various partners, it had acquired 8.8 million shares, or 5.7 percent, of Phillips' outstanding stock and that it planned to make a tender offer for at least 15 million shares, or about 10 percent of the company's stock, for $60 per share. This tender offer price compared favorably with the approximately $35 per share during the summer of 1984 and a trading range of $40 to $43.75 per share during the month of November 1984. After a series of legal maneuverings involving the Oklahoma and Delaware courts, Phillips and Mesa reached an agreement on December 23, 1984 which would have ended Mesa's hostile takeover threat. The terms of the agreement provided Mesa with its expenses (up to $25 million) plus a buyback of its Phillips shares at $53 in cash for a reported profit of $89 million. Phillips agreed to a restructuring and recapitalization plan pursuant to which: (1) 38 percent of Phillips common stock would be swapped and converted to debt securities; (2) Phillips would buy back $1 billion of its stock in open market transactions to improve earnings per share; and (3) a sizable number of shares would be sold to an employee incentive stock ownership plan.

Company officials valued the transaction for the remaining shareholders at $60 per share, but the share price immediately dropped from approximately $55 per share to $45.25 per share upon announcement. Shortly thereafter, during January and early February 1985, as the recapitalization plan was being considered by shareholders, Irwin Jacobs and Carl Icahn announced their own purchases of Phillips stock. The former announced his intention to vote against the recapitalization, while the latter, with 8.5 percent of the stock, announced his intention to launch a tender offer for about half of the outstanding shares at $55 per share unless the company itself would propose a leveraged buyout in which all shareholders would receive $55 per share in cash. Subsequent moves by Icahn and the company resulted in a new, sweetened recapitalization plan, which involved a swap of 50 percent of the outstanding shares for a $4.5 billion package of debt securities the company valued at $62 per share. The "when distributed" Phillips common stock, which was to be the remaining common stock outstanding after the distribution of the new debt package, traded at $37 per share immediately after the swap. This meant an approximate average per share of $49.50 for all shareholders except Pickens' group, which had earlier been bought out at $53 per share.

Pickens maintained that he never accepted greenmail and that, indeed, his actions had led to an initial deal which benefited shareholders. Furthermore, by identifying an "undervalued company" that was subsequently "put into play" by Icahn and others, he argued that the shareholders benefited even more from his populist attack. Others contend that the differential and the terms applicable to his buyout compared to what the other shareholders received made him a greenmailer. Moreover, while the traders/shareholders reaped profit from the fact that Phillips was put in play, investors interested in the company's viability to generate a stream of profits were not so advantaged. This is a clear case when traders can be distinguished from investors.

By the mid-1980s, two forces acted to curb greenmail abuses. The first was the court ruling in the Walt Disney case; the second was a change in the tax laws excluding "excess greenmail payments" from the normal business expense deductibility provisions of the Internal Revenue Service (IRS) code. Until the court ruled with respect to the Walt Disney case, boards of directors were generally given almost unreviewable discretion to repurchase shares under the "Business Judgment Rule." This rule reflects various court rulings that have held that the directors of a corporation, who owe a responsibility to the corporation, can be found to have acted with prudent business judgment, even if their decisions turned out to be wrong, as long as they have followed procedures and have acted in the best interests of the corporation. Under this theory, it is difficult to sue the directors unless a plaintiff can prove fraud or theft of corporate assets.

Before the Disney case, companies argued that there were a number of general business reasons for undertaking stock repurchases even from dissident shareholders—and they won. To the extent that the holder of a block of stock is truly dissident and at odds on significant policy matters with management and at least a majority of the board, case law under the Business Judgment Rule generally recognized that eliminating such dissidence was a proper corporate goal. Moreover, as two legal commentators of the era put it: "There is something to be said in favor of an issuer avoiding a situation in which one or several large stockholders, acting in his or their own interest, can select the bidder and the acquisition price and set in train a series of events that may result in the acquisition of the issuer at the wrong time, by the wrong acquirer and at the wrong price."[12] In the leading case on the subject, ". . . the Delaware Supreme Court stated that if the 'sole or primary motive' for the share repurchase was to perpetuate the board in power, then the repurchase was improper. If, however, the repurchase occurred because there was a policy difference between the raider and current management, then using corporate funds to terminate the interest of the raider was legitimate and protected under the Business Judgment Rule."[13] Thus, until the landmark ruling in the Walt Disney case, courts generally gave target companies' directors almost complete discretion.

The Council of Institutional Investors

Following the Disney case, institutional investors, especially those heading public pension funds, began to sue to block greenmail payments. In addition, in 1984, under the leadership of California State Treasurer Jesse Unruth, they formed the Council of Institutional Investors (CII) to serve as a forum for corporate governance issues. The Council had its first working meeting in February 1985, when public pension fund members met to question the payment of greenmail in the Walt Disney and Phillips Petroleum cases. Some of these institutional investors began to use the proxy process to press for antigreenmail corporate charter amendments. These were designed to eliminate greenmail by providing that, unless approved by a vote of a majority of the shares owned by the nonparticipating shareholders, a corporation cannot purchase any of its shares at a premium over the market price from a shareholder who has held a certain percentage or more of stock for less than a certain number of years. These antigreenmail charter proposals could be approved either by shareholder vote or by the vote of the board of directors. In 1984 two companies adopted them, and by mid-1985 shareholders in approximately 60 companies had voted in favor of these amendments, while boards of directors for another three companies had approved them. The Investor Responsibility Research Center (IRRC) reports that antigreenmail charter proposals generally received higher levels of positive votes by shareholders than other antitakeover proposals during this period. The IRRC reports that, although the amendments may prevent the increase in stock price that usually accompanies share accumulations by corporate raiders, shareholders apparently believe that the benefits of the proposals outweigh the costs.[14] By the mid-1980s, the practice of greenmail became less widespread, both because of antigreenmail resolutions and because of changes in the tax code which taxed excess greenmail profits. In the 1,500 companies tracked by the IRRC, the number of companies with antigreenmail defenses in place rose only to 90 in 1995, a much smaller number than for other defensive measures (see Table 3–1).

Despite the Congressional furor over takeover abuses, virtually no federal legislation was enacted to curb takeovers during the 1980s except to effect changes in the tax code to remove tax deductibility for excess greenmail and golden parachute executive employment payments. The whole takeover debate is probably most remembered not for its legislative history, but because it served as an incubator for institutional shareholder concern over whether management was acting to entrench itself or in the best interest of its shareholders.

Junk Bonds

The initial takeover wave gave way to more frenzied activities by the mid-1980s as junk bonds (so named because they were used to finance high-risk and therefore high-yield projects) began to be used to finance takeovers. The new financial vehicles used in mergers further underscored

TABLE 3-1

Summary of Corporate Governance Provisions for 1,500 Companies Tracked by the Investor Responsibility Research Center

Provision	1990	1993	1995
Advance notice requirement	N/A	N/A	657
Antigreenmail	84	93	90
Blank check preferred stock	N/A	N/A	1275
Classified board	850	862	895
Confidential voting	48	139	176
Consider nonfinancial effects of merger	96	111	108
Cumulative voting	263	233	216
Dual class stock	112	122	124
Eliminate cumulative voting	131	150	156
Fair price	475	492	487
Golden parachutes	N/A	N/A	799
Limit right to call special meeting	355	424	466
Limit action by written consent	352	416	467
Poison pill	759	795	799
Supermajority vote to approve merger	252	269	267
Unequal voting rights	34	31	30

Source: Ann Yerger, "Changes in Takeover Tactics Outline in Profile," *Corporate Governance Bulletin,* Investor Responsibility Research Center, July–September 1995, XII, no. 3, p. 22.

the difference between generating investor and trading value. Prior to this time, the traditional method of financing takeovers had been to rely on bank capital and/or swaps and trades of stock to complete transactions. Ironically, high-yield junk bonds had traditionally been used to raise investment capital in two principal instances: (1) to enable companies with poor credit ratings to finance expansion (these were called "fallen angels" or companies emerging from bankruptcies, which included the major U.S. railroads); or (2) to enable investment banking firms such as Drexel Burnham Lambert to provide capital for emerging companies which were promising but lacked sufficient track records to attract bank financing. During the mid- to late 1980s, a new use was found for high-yield bonds: to provide raiders with the capital they needed to launch takeover battles. Frequently the takeover bid was not secured by anything other than the assets of the target company. High-yield junk bonds were floated in the marketplace and very short term "bridge" loans were actually made by investment banking houses eager to complete the transactions (a rare "merchant banking" type of activity more prevalent in the United Kingdom than in this country until that time). These loans tended to be made in conjunction with a multitier debt structure, reflecting an inverted pyramid likely to topple if interest rates rose and the increasingly excessively highly leveraged transactions were subjected to profit constraints. The multiplicity of deals was limited only by the imagination of the investment bankers, and eventually even the major companies began to raid each other, feeding in a frenzy of notable transactions referred to as "Pac Man" deals (each side eats the other), with white knight saviors (that is, a company willing to buy another company to keep it away from a raider). Corporations armed themselves with a series of shark-repellent, poison pill, and other tactics to thwart potential raiders. They also became increasingly critical of the public pension funds for selling them out. Moreover, they increased the pressure on private pension funds not to participate in the takeover rage. Each side entrenched itself strongly and firmly.

In their book, *Power and Accountability,* Robert Monks and Nell Minow report that, on December 12, 1986 Theodore F. Brophy, chairman of the board of GTE, wrote to other chief executive officers about his concern over the unfriendly merger and acquisition activity and what he considered to be the increasingly unhealthy, short-term, speculative nature of the nation's financial markets. Recognizing the powerful impact of voting a pension plan's proxies on merger and acquisition activity, the Chief Executive Officer of GTE implored other CEOs to ensure that their plans were monitored and voted in accordance with instructions to money managers and not to vote in favor of certain merger proposals without the sponsor's specific approval.

Considerable controversy surrounded the voting practices of pension plan sponsors and their delegated fiduciaries, such as money managers. Money managers, for example, reported being afraid to vote against corporations in areas of mergers and acquisitions for fear these corporations would withdraw from them their plan sponsorship monies. This gave rise to a movement by shareholders to institute confidential voting in the proxy process,[15] which was soundly opposed by managements. By 1995, the IRRC reported that only 176 of the companies in its universe of 1,500 had agreed to institute confidential voting mechanisms, either under pressure from shareholders or voluntarily (see Table 3–1).

In the past, institutions had routinely voted with managements under the "Wall Street Walk" theory—if shareholders do not like management, they sell the stock. Now, with their increasing holdings, some of which were in indexed portfolios, institutions felt somewhat conflicted about the raiders' tactics on the one hand and on the other their fiduciary responsibilities when faced with the extremely high premiums over current market value that accompanied many of these deals. The companies also felt sold out by the institutional investors, since many of them could not resist the temptation to take the premiums and transfer the stock to arbitrageurs—essentially taking the money and running. Regulatory authorities with oversight attempted to clarify the responsibilities of the pension funds. Weighing into the debate as well was the Internal Revenue Service, which was linked to the Department of Labor's ERISA regulatory scheme by virtue of the IRS requirement to certify that plans are not-for-profit and thereby tax exempt. In 1989 the IRS and the Department of Labor issued a joint letter indicating that it was their opinion that, should a fiduciary wish to decline a tender offer, it could do so and not violate its fiduciary responsibilities, so long as that offer was considered to have the potential to benefit the investor in the long term.[16]

FIDUCIARY RESPONSIBILITY AND CORPORATE PERFORMANCE

Many institutional investors, most notably the private pension funds, operate under regulations established under the Employment Retirement Income Security Act (ERISA) of 1974. Regulatory oversight in this area has also moved from a focus on takeover issues to procedural issues (requiring fiduciaries to vote their stock) to performance related issues (pushing fiduciaries to become involved in evaluation performance of the companies in their portfolios).

Robert Monks, former administrator of the Department of Labor's Pension and Welfare Benefits Administration, says no one anticipated the impact from establishing ERISA would be so dramatic on the course of investments in the United States. According to Monks: "I once asked the chief sponsor of ERISA, the late Senator Jacob Javits, whether he had any idea that the money gathered under this statute would reach such proportions, and he said, 'I have never been accused of modesty, but I will tell you in all sincerity that it never occurred to me.'"[17] Monks and Minow describe the idea behind ERISA as simple: Congress wanted to make it worthwhile for private companies to create pension plans for their employees, and then it wanted to protect the money after the plans had been created. The statute was designed to resolve conflicts of interest and liability that had left the private pension system uncertain and, in some cases, chaotic. One massive, federal law would pre-empt all state law in this area. ERISA pension funds are modeled on trust law, whereby a fiduciary must act for the "exclusive benefit" of pension plan participants. This is an attempt to prevent pension plan sponsors from investing undue amounts in risky, illiquid or self-dealing transactions. Initially ERISA applied only to private corporate pension plans, but, through a series of state laws, most public pension funds are by reference and regulation covered by the same ERISA principles.

Former SEC Commissioner Bevis Longstreth describes what constitutes a prudent person's behavior with respect to investing ERISA funds.

> The duties of an ERISA fiduciary relating strictly to prudence are twofold. First, he must act in all matters regarding the pension plan, not simply its investments, "with the care, skill, prudence, and diligence under the circumstances then prevailing that any prudent man acting in any like capacity and familiar with such matters would use in the conduct of an enterprise of a like character and with like aims." Diversification, which trust law treats as one facet of the general duty of prudent investment, appears in ERISA as a separate statutory duty. The fiduciary must "diversif[y] the investments of the plan so as to minimize the risk of large losses, unless under the circumstances it is clearly prudent not to do so."[18]

The duties belonging to a fiduciary are also defined by the statute to apply to a pension fund's investment managers as well as its trustees. According to Longstreth, ERISA also posits a formidable scheme of sanctions for breach of fiduciary duty. A fiduciary who makes an imprudent investment or violates the duty to diversify plan assets is personally liable for any losses and is subject to suit in federal court by the Secretary of Labor, a plan participant or beneficiary, or another fiduciary. The regulations interpreting ERISA's prudent person standard reflect a "safe harbor" process, whereby the statutory duty to act as a prudent man will be satisfied with respect to a particular investment if the fiduciary has thoroughly considered the following: the investment's place in the whole portfolio; the risk of loss and the opportunity for gain; and the diversification, liquidity, cash flow, and overall return requirements of the pension plan. With takeovers and their potential for realizing significant short-term profits through exercising the tender-offer stipulations, "prudent" institutional investors were faced with a dilemma: Should they sell and take the premium, or should they hold for the long term and back management as they had traditionally done?

In the mid- to late 1980s, many of the largest public pension funds had become active in the antitakeover arena, but private corporate pension funds were, understandably, reluctant to pressure other corporations to remove their protective devices. Money managers and bank custodians, even if assured anonymity in the few cases of confidential voting which existed, were also reluctant to exercise their voting power in contests for corporate control to vote against their current or potential clients. Thus, proxy voting, never vigorous to begin with, became something that private pension funds and delegated fiduciaries such as money managers and banks wanted to avoid.

The Avon Letter Requires Proxy Voting

In 1988, however, the Department of Labor (DOL) pension administrator Robert Monks began to force fiduciaries, such as the reluctant private corporate pension fund managers, to vote their proxies. Monks wrote a letter of instruction (such letters issued by the DOL are similar to opinions set forth by a judge in a court of law) addressed to Helmuth Fandel, the chairman of the retirement board of Avon Products Inc. and dated February 23, 1988 (the "Avon letter"). The letter clearly set forth Monks' opinion that ownership powers, including proxy voting, have an economic value; are an asset of a pension plan; and are therefore subject to the same fiduciary standards as other plan assets. In the Avon letter, the Department of Labor asserted that the fiduciary act of managing plan assets that are shares of corporate stock includes voting proxies pertaining to those shares. The responsibility for voting proxies therefore lies exclusively with the plan trustee unless the trustee delegates this authority to a named fiduciary, which might be, for example, an investment manager. This investment manager would not be relieved of the fiduciary responsibility to vote proxies merely because he or she was following directions of some other person regarding the voting of these proxies, or, in turn, had delegated this responsibility to yet another person. Compliance with this provision requires proper documentation of the activities that are subject to monitoring, including maintaining accurate records of proxy voting.

The Avon letter was followed by a series of increasingly focused statements and rulings by the Department of Labor that—along with the rising activism of public pension funds—provided considerable momentum to the corporate governance movement. The Department of Labor was taking a position it clearly vowed to monitor: that the right to vote must be exercised with the same fiduciary standards as money is invested—with care, skill, prudence, and diligence. According to Monks and Minow, the 1989 Department of Labor's "Proxy Project Report" underscored the department's commitment to this issue:

> A fiduciary who fails to vote, or casts a vote without considering the impact of the question, or votes blindly with management would appear to violate his duty to manage planned assets solely in the interests of the participants and beneficiaries of the plan. We will be vigilant in assuring that pension fund fiduciaries handle proxy voting as they handle any other corporate asset—namely not for the benefit of themselves or third parties, but for the benefit of participants and beneficiaries.[19]

Even after the departure of Monks from the DOL, the department has persistently, and under various Republican and Democratic administrations alike, put pressure on fiduciaries to become more active in corporate governance. In a letter from Monks' successor at the DOL, dated January 23, 1990 and, ironically, addressed to Robert Monks himself (who had left the Department of Labor to found Institutional Shareholder Services, Inc. (ISS)), the Department of Labor further extended the pension funds' voting responsibility. In this letter, the DOL established the directive that a fiduciary has the obligation to monitor the voting activities of the investment managers it hires and that the named fiduciary, which might be, for example, an investment manager, must act solely in the interest of the *participants and the beneficiaries* and without regard to his or her relationship to the *plan sponsor*. This ruling was intended to keep the pressure up to vote proxies by ensuring that not only prime fiduciaries but also investment managers to whom these prime fiduciaries have delegated voting authority will, in turn, vote their shares with regard to shareholder interest.

The Department of Labor Recommends Monitoring Governance and Performance

DOL Interpretive Bulletin 94-2, issued on July 28, 1994, codifies all the Department of Labor's statements, letters, and prior rulings with regard to the duty of employee benefit plan fiduciaries to vote proxies. The DOL Bulletin reiterates the department's earlier position that voting proxies is a fiduciary act of plan asset management. Recognizing that pension plan investments wield considerable influence, Secretary of Labor Robert B. Reich issued the 1994 bulletin to urge pension plan officials to actively monitor the management of companies in which they invest. Reich is quoted in the press release accompanying the Interpretive Bulletin: "Responsible shareholder activism by pension plan managers can improve the long-term company performance, increasing the return to plan participants and strengthening the competitive advantage of American business." The Interpretive Bulletin states that pension plan managers may actively monitor and communicate with corporate management, independently or together with other shareholders, as a means to improve corporate performance and investment return. The DOL reaffirms its longstanding position that plan officials are responsible for voting proxies, unless that responsibility has been delegated to an investment manager. In that case, plan officials should monitor the manager's activities, a principle that was established with the letter to ISS discussed above. The Bulletin clarifies that these principles also apply to proxies on foreign investments. Plan officials, however, can properly decline to vote foreign investment proxies where they judge the cost would outweigh any benefits. The DOL's Interpretive Bulletin puts fiduciaries under considerable pressure, unless they can justify their lack of action on the basis of excessive cost, to become actively involved in a broad range of corporate governance issues if there is reason to believe that such monitoring or communication is likely to enhance the value of the fiduciary's investment. The DOL cites areas for activism, including voting for board of director candidates who are independent, evaluating executive compensation, evaluating a corporation's investment in its workforce, and monitoring financial and nonfinancial measures of corporate performance:

> An investment policy that contemplates activities intended to monitor or influence the management of corporations in which the plan owns stock is consistent with a fiduciary's obligations under ERISA, where the responsible fiduciary concludes that there is a reasonable expectation that such monitoring or communication with management, by the plan alone or together with other shareholders, is likely to enhance the value of the plan's investment in a corporation, after taking into account the costs involved. Such a reasonable expectation may exist in various circumstances, for example, where plan investments in corporate stock are held as long-term investments or where a plan may not be able to easily dispose [of] such an investment.
>
> Active monitoring and communication activities are generally concerned with such issues as the independence and expertise of candidates for the corporation's board of directors and assuring that the board has sufficient information to carry out its responsibility to monitor management. Other issues may include such matters as consideration of the appropriateness of executive compensation, the corporation's policy regarding mergers and acquisitions, the extent of debt financing and capitalization, the nature of long-term business plans, the corporation's investment in training to develop

its workforce, other workplace practices, and financial and nonfinancial measures of corporate performance. Active monitoring and communication may be carried out through a variety of methods including by means of correspondence and meeting with corporate management as well as by exercising the legal rights of a shareholder.[20]

POISON PILLS: FROM PROCEDURE TO PERFORMANCE

The poison pill warrants a special place in the history of institutional investor activism since it marks the issue that provided the transition between institutional investor concern over governance structural issues and corporate performance issues. Poison pills derive their name from their onerous provisions; they generally take the form of rights or warrants issues to shareholders that are worthless unless they are triggered by a hostile acquisition attempt. For example, if a raider crosses a 20 percent stock purchase threshold without obtaining the approval of the company's board, other shareholders get a two-for-one split, but the raider does not; therefore, he suffers an immediate dilution. Courts have generally upheld the board's decision to institute a pill under the business judgment rule,[21] although shareholders have argued that a unilateral decision to put a pill in place abrogates their rights. While instituting a poison pill has been a dominant antitakeover defense, ironically, debate over whether to put a pill in place has been the catalyst for some key institutional investors like CalPERS to alter their activist approach to become more performance oriented. The evolution is explained in a CalPERS' memorandum on its Corporate Governance Program:

> [We] changed our approach to Corporate Governance. We gradually became convinced that a focus on antitakeover and proxy issues—in a vacuum—was too narrow. We learned that the presence of an antitakeover device at a company does not absolutely make that company "bad," any more than its absence can absolutely make the company "good." We found that, if a company is being managed so as to place shareholder interests above all others, then it will take advantage of such a device only if necessary to benefit its shareholders. With this additional insight, we began to refocus on the bottom line—corporate economic performance.[22]

During the 1980s, poison pills became a "lightning rod" for shareholder activism and, for many years, were categorically opposed by all institutional investors. Embittered battles developed when corporations instituted poison pills, the courts overturned the first type of pill, and new evolutions in pill defenses were then instituted and upheld. Yet the pill has generated more than acrimony, since debate over its enactment has precipitated debate over long-term shareholder value and whether a profitable and viable company should be protected from raiders who are interested only in breaking it up for short-term gain. The pill can now be used as a vehicle to focus on investor value in the best interests of the company and the institutional shareholders with long-term investment objectives. Some of the recent stances institutional investors have taken to side with management (against raiders and other dissidents, such as union pension funds) over the issue of the pill may surprise and confuse corporate governance observers. But, by virtue of the fact that all institutional investors do not unilaterally wish to expose management to raiders for short-term trading profit, it has become clear that some of these institutions have moved from a strict focus on procedure to a more complex analytical focus on the elements of good corporate performance.

At an October 5, 1994 Corporate Governance Conference at the J.L. Kellogg Graduate School of Management in Chicago, takeover defense lawyer Martin Lipton noted that many of the pills instituted during the 1980s takeover period would soon celebrate their tenth anniversary. Companies would soon have to choose whether to renew the pills or to allow them to expire. While enactment of a poison pill is still the sole responsibility of the board, many shareholder groups have declared their interest in the issue. Sarah Teslik, executive director of CII, has written to companies in advance of the 1996 proxy season asking for comment on their plans for the pills. Teslik notes that "our interests and our holding periods are long-term. We are thus particularly concerned about company actions that affect our ability to preserve meaningful, ongoing shareholder accountability."[23]

The Lipton Legacy of Poison Pills

Developed by attorney Martin Lipton, who prefers to call poison pills stock purchase rights plans, the first poison pill in its current form was utilized in July 1984 in the Household International Finance case to protect the company against a two-tier takeover bid. According to Lipton, more than 1,700 companies have adopted the pill since 1984; approximately 1,400 companies still have them in effect today. During 1995, poison pills were in effect in 799 companies out of the IRRC's 1,500-company database (see Table 3–1).

The vast majority of poison pills have been adopted since the November 1985 decision of the Delaware Supreme Court upheld a company's right to adopt a poison pill without shareholder approval in *Moran v. Household International*. Poison pills have undergone significant metamorphoses in response to various court challenges over the years. The plan currently advocated by Lipton provides more protection for the company than the original "flip-over rights plan" because it includes a narrower "flip-in" feature.

> The plan involves a dividend distribution to common shareholders of rights which, in the event of a squeeze-out, become rights to purchase the acquiring company's stock at a 50 percent discount (the "flip-over feature") and, in the event of an acquisition of 20 percent or more of the company's stock, become rights to purchase the company's common stock at a 50 percent discount (the "flip-in feature"). Following a 20 percent acquisition (but provided there has been no 50 percent acquisition), the board of directors is also given the ability to exchange one share of the company's common stock for each valid right. The plan enables the board of directors to reduce the 20 percent threshold to not less than 10 percent in order to deal with specific situations.[24]

Institutional Shareholders Services, Inc. (ISS) notes that poison pills raise questions of shareholder democracy, since they amount to major *de facto* shifts of voting rights away from shareholders to management on matters pertaining to the sale of the corporation. ISS contends that plans give target boards of directors absolute veto power over any proposed business combination, no matter how beneficial it might be for the shareholders. All the board need do is refuse to redeem the pill, and no bidder would dare trigger its poison. Yet, because they are implemented as warrants or rights offerings, the plans can be put in place without shareholder approval.[25]

Lipton and other proponents of poison pills argue that rights plans are reasonable defensive mechanisms against abusive takeover techniques and that their adoption is governed by the Business Judgment Rule, an argument that has been upheld by the courts not only in the *Household* case but also in the *Time-Warner* case. In the latter case, the Delaware Supreme Court endorsed the Time-Warner merger by adopting the reasoning that a board may manage a company to achieve the long-term goals the board sets. The court emphasized that the target board has no duty to sell the company when it is not for sale; that a merger of equals that does not involve a sale of control is not a sale of the company; and that a company may proceed with such a merger under the protection of the Business Judgment Rule in the face of a premium bid for the company.[26]

According to Lipton, the *Paramount* decision expressly stated that it did not apply to a situation where a company is following its own strategic plan and has not initiated a takeover situation. *Paramount* did not invalidate the pill. To the contrary, it cited approvingly the *Household* decision. The Lipton currently proposed rights plan is seen by some corporations as a critical element in enabling a board of directors to remain independent and pursue its long-term business strategy. Lipton notes that the *Time* case, while not directly addressing the issue of rights plans, expressly rejected two Delaware chancery court decisions which require the redemption of rights plans at the "in stage" of takeover battles where the target has proffered a restructuring alternative. The Delaware Supreme Court decision clearly established the right of a board of directors in the exercise of its reasonable business judgment to "just say no" to a takeover bid and continue to follow the company's long-term business plan. The *Paramount* case constitutes a strong endorsement of the *Time* case and of the deference that is due to business judgment decisions by directors in pursuing strategic stock mergers and other long-term business strategies outside the context of the change of control.[27]

Shareholder Consent for Time-Warner's Poison Pill

Institutional investors have a long history of having attempted to use the proxy voting process to require a company's board of directors to rescind a poison pill it has enacted as a defense. However, in a landmark case involving Time-Warner, institutional investors gave support to a board-instituted pill because they did not believe the potential raider, Seagram, was likely to add as much shareholder value as would be achieved if Time-Warner were left alone.

The *Time-Warner* case represents an important shift institutional investors have made from concentrating solely on procedure to evaluating performance, since it indicates a willingness of institutional investors to work with the company to structure an appropriate response to a raider. In May 1993, the Bronfman family announced through its Seagram's subsidiary that it had acquired a 5 percent stake in Time-Warner, making a 13(d) filing for investment purposes only. The standard 13(d) language is, however, subject to change and, according to Philip Lochner, senior vice president and general counsel of Time-Warner, many observers felt that conflicting signals were generated by the Seagram purchase. The CEO of Seagram, Ed Bronfman, Jr., seemed to have a personal desire to get back into the movie business, although Lochner noted that it was difficult to see a strategic fit between the movie business and Seagram's liquor business.

The poison pill issue at Time-Warner came to head when the Bronfman family bought a 15 percent stake in January 1994. Institutional investors were concerned that if Seagram were to enjoy a control premium and make a bid that would be favorable for the majority of shareholders to the detriment of the minority of shareholders, they might not share in the control premium.

New Compromises on Poison Pills

Some elements of the institutional investor community have become guardedly supportive of poison pills although they attach certain stipulations to their enactment: (1) shareholders should approve their adoption by the board of directions; (2) they should be limited in the time they are in effect and should contain "sunset" provisions for their phase-out unless specifically voted back; (3) they would be redeemed only if there were an all-cash share offer.

In 1989, Robert C. Pozen, general counsel and managing director of Fidelity Investments, proposed limiting the time that the poison pill is in effect, depending on the composition of the management team and the nature of its strategic plan. This limited term pill would be eliminated automatically unless a new poison pill were approved by the then-current shareholders.[28] Pozen notes an early and at that time rare example of a time limited pill adopted by Pennzoil in 1988 for five years in order to give current management enough time to put the proceeds from a litigation settlement from Texaco to work in a prudent manner. Pozen also cites an example whereby the Pittsburgh-based National Intergroup Inc., a diversified holding company, worked with the State of Wisconsin Investment Board (SWIB), which owned about 7 percent of the company's voting stock, to devise a time limited poison pill. This pill automatically expires after three years unless continued by a vote of the shareholders. The pills would be "chewable" if they were subject to approval by shareholders and were time limited.

SWIB (an active investor) has continued to be one of the most vigilant institutional investors with regard to the poison pill. In 1993, SWIB and other institutional investors worked with Allergan management to forge a compromise on the elements of a pill which would achieve a successful shareholder approval (see Box 3–6 for the elements of this poison pill.)

After an initial 10-year cycle, corporations throughout the United States will be dealing with readoption of their poison pills. The pressures

BOX 3-6

The Allergan Model Poison Pill

TRIGGER

The poison pill is triggered when a group or individual has accumulated 15 percent or more of the outstanding shares of the company's common stock.

MECHANISM

Each common share carries with it a right to purchase one-half share of common stock for $XX. The rights cannot be sold separately from the common stock, do not receive dividends, or have voting rights. The rights are redeemable at $0.01 per share until the pill is triggered. In the event that the company is acquired in a hostile takeover, each holder of a right will be entitled to receive at the then-current exercise price a number of shares of the surviving company having a market value of two times the exercise price of one right.

PILL REDEMPTION

The pill can be redeemed in two ways. First, it may be redeemed by a majority vote of the board of directors. Second, under the amended plan, if a party makes an offer for all of the company's shares (subject to certain conditions) and the company has not redeemed the pill or presented a "financially superior" transaction within 60 days of the offer, the pill will be placed to a shareholder vote. A majority vote is required to retain the pill. To trigger a vote: 1) the offer must be for all outstanding shares at the same price; 2) any cash portion of the offer must be fully financed; 3) any noncash portion of the offer must be made in the form of securities listed on the NYSE; and 4) the offer price may not be subject to due diligence.

Source: "Preemptive Action: Companies Tailor Proposals to Suit Shareholders," *The 1995 Proxy Season: Settling For More* (Bethesda Maryland: Institutional Shareholder Services, CDA Investment Technologies, Inc., 1995), p. 55.

are great, considering renewed mergers and acquisition activity during 1995. The readoption of the poison pill puts to the forefront the role that shareholders have in deciding whether a company should be sold. Institutional investors clearly do not want a return to the "Saturday-night-special" raiders of the 1980s, who attacked profitable companies and offered less than fair terms to shareholders. On the other hand, a cash tender offer to all, or an 80 percent cash and 20 percent stock offer, might not be considered an abusive takeover proposal and might be in the best interest of the shareholders. Pozen says that Fidelity has voted for pills in certain circumstances, and this vote does not pose a fiduciary problem to the mutual fund.

Rather than oppose all pills on all grounds, certain shareholders have begun to look at pills on a case-by-case basis, weighing the confidence they have in the management of the company compared to the benefit of a raider concluding a takeover transaction. The battle lines are still drawn, however, as Martin Lipton continues to maintain that a "chewable" pill is not an effective pill. The debate continues to focus on who has the ultimate power to decide to sell the company, management or shareholders. But even more important than the specifics of the debate over renewal of poison pills is the fact that the issue underscores a subtle split in the investor activism movement as new types of activists challenge managements in styles and with motivations which may not be shared by the major, "mainstream" public pension fund activists who have, until the past two years, dominated the shareholder scene. The new activists, described in the next section, may actually act as a catalyst for managements to discuss in-depth performance issues with the more mainstream pension funds—such discussions, if undertaken wisely, may help corporations with a baseline of good corporate governance withstand new types of activist pressures.

NEW ACTIVISTS: GROUPS OF INDIVIDUALS AND LABOR

As the discussion about poison pills indicates, various classes of shareholders are now becoming more clearly defined as either traders or investors. Furthermore, companies can now seek out institutions that behave more like investors and may, under certain circumstances, find significant allies among them against either the tactics of groups like the IRAA or the motivations of labor-related pension funds.

The Investors' Rights Association (IRAA) is the newest of the shareholder activist groups and the successor to the former United Shareholders' Association (USA) as representative of individual shareholders. More "mainstream" activists, such as CalPERS, issue target lists of underperforming companies and favor direct negotiation with managements and, if necessary, boards of directors. Filing shareholder resolutions is only a last resort. Other mainstream activists, such as TIAA-CREF, do not even disclose their target companies, preferring quiet, behind-the-scenes diplomacy. By comparison, IRAA's President Tom Flanagan believes in blanketing corporations with proposals and maximizing media attention prior to initiating negotiations.

> In contrast to some of the larger, more established activist funds, IRAA has taken a different approach to targeting companies for action. Flanagan indicated that the large institutions have more leverage and can "deal with management on the telephone, while the little guys can't get through." Therefore, the smaller investors resort to submitting shareholder proposals in order to make their voices heard. While some of the major pension funds believe shareholder proposals should be used as a last resort, IRAA contends that such proposals are the first resort.[29]

Privately, however, some veterans of the activist movement question whether these tactics are counterproductive, and many companies, given their choice, seem more inclined to negotiate with veterans with whom they feel they can establish better rapport.

Another new group of activists on the shareholder rights scene are leaders of the "Taft-Hartley" union pension funds. The U.S. Department of Labor reports that there are in excess of 3,100 Taft-Hartley pension funds, so named because the Taft-Hartley Labor Act of 1947 allowed for union-managed pension funds to be established through collective bargaining with multiple employers. (This means that the carpenter's union controls a fund for all their workers, but the pension money is contributed by the companies that actually employ the carpenters.) According to journalist Paul Sweeney, writing in The Conference Board's magazine for corporate executives, *Across the Board:*

> Total assets of these funds amounted to $215 billion, according to the three-year-old Labor Department figures—which means they are likely to total $250 billion to $300 billion now. It also means that labor-union shareholders cannot be taken lightly.
>
> Consider the Teamsters. All told, Teamster-affiliated pension funds total about $48 billion, says [Teamsters' national coordinator for corporate affairs Bart] Naylor, about one-third of which is invested in equities that include a cross-section of major U.S. companies. Because their portfolio holdings are not aggressively traded, the Teamsters increasingly rely on a corporate-governance strategy to add investment value to its equity holdings.[30]

These funds have only recently become active in corporate governance and are, by virtue of their tactics, now highly visible. While public employee funds have shifted their approach from sponsoring shareholder proposals to more behind-the-scenes diplomacy, the number of shareholder proposals filed by Taft-Hartley funds has skyrocketed. Moreover, it appears that these funds have achieved a certain degree of success. In 1994, 15 labor-affiliated groups sponsored 80 corporate governance proposals and won more majority votes than all other institutional investors combined.[31]

During the 1995 proxy voting season, labor sponsored 48 out of a total of 123 shareholder proposals (see Table 3–2), while public pension funds sponsored only 15 proposals (CalPERS sponsored only 2 and the New York City Employees Retirement System sponsored only 9).

During the 1995 proxy season, more than 17 proposals on the subject of poison pills were introduced—all by groups with ties to labor unions—to either redeem a poison pill in place or to require a shareholder vote for one. Ten proposals actually came to a vote (the remainder were negotiated to a satisfactory conclusion or withdrawn). Proposals at SuperValu and Ryder Systems passed with more than 65 percent of the shareholder vote; a third proposal asking that the board withdraw the pill at Central Maine Power received 50.4 percent of the shareholder vote, which was followed by board action to rescind the pill.[32] The success of these resolutions is unprecedented and the power of the unions was clearly being felt by these corporations. (See Figures 3–1 and 3–2 for a breakdown of the proposals and their sponsors during the 1994 and 1995 proxy seasons.)

Taft-Hartley funds are gearing up for an active 1996 proxy season. Funds affiliated with the International Brotherhood of Teamsters will pursue the following governance improvements, which governance coordinator Bart Naylor considers necessary to achieve greater corporate accountability.[33]

Targeted Company	Action Sought
• Timer Warner, Inc.	Splitting positions of Chairman and CEO
• ITT Corp.	Splitting positions of Chairman and CEO
• Consolidated Freightways, Inc.	Adopt cumulative voting; declassify board
• Waste Management International PLC	Declassify board
• Philip Morris Cos. Inc.	Redemption of poison pill
• Ryder Systems, Inc.	Redemption of poison pill
• Toys R Us Inc.	Institute confidential voting
• Yellow Corp.	Institute confidential voting
• Minnesota Mining/Manufacturing	Transfer state of incorporation

Some corporations contend that anti–poison pill and other resolutions from these labor groups may be "facade" shareholder governance actions

TABLE 3-2

Shareholder Sponsors of Corporate Governance Proposals: 1994–1995

	1994	1995
Labor unions		
Amalg. Bank of New York's Labor Oriented LongView Collective Inv. Fund	3	7
Amalg. Clothing and Textile Workers Union	3	3
Communications Workers of America	1	1
International Union of Operating Engineers	2	6
Laborers' International Union of N.A.	2	13
Oil, Chem. & Atomic Workers Int'l Union	3	1
Teamsters	11	4
United Brotherhood of Carpenters and Joiners of America	3	8
United Paperworkers International Union	0	1
Subtotal Labor Unions	32	48
Public pensions		
California Public Employees' Retirement	1	2
NY City Employees Retirement System	10	9
NY City Fire Department Pension Fund	2	0
NY City Police Pension Fund	3	2
NY City Teachers' Retirement System	7	1
State of Wisconsin Investment Board	0	1
Subtotal Public Pensions	23	15
Religious organizations		
Christian Brothers Investment Services	0	1
Interfaith Center on Corporate Responsibility	10	13
General Board of Pensions of the United Methodist Church	0	1
Subtotal Religious	10	15
Other shareholder groups		
College Retirement Equities Fund	0	3
Investors Rights Association of America	N/A	42
U.S. Trust	1	0
Subtotal Other	1	45
Total	66	123

Source: Georgeson & Company, Inc., *Corporate Governance: 1995 Annual Meeting Season Wrap-Up*, 1995, p. 6.

FIGURE 3-1

Corporate Governance Proposals: 1995

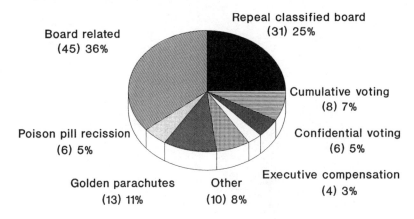

Repeal classified board
(31) 25%

Board related
(45) 36%

Cumulative voting
(8) 7%

Poison pill recission
(6) 5%

Confidential voting
(6) 5%

Golden parachutes   Other   Executive compensation
(13) 11%   (10) 8%   (4) 3%

Source: Georgeson & Company, Inc., *Corporate Governance: 1996 Annual Meeting Season Wrap-Up*, p. 5.

directed at pressuring management in labor management disputes rather than pressing for better corporate governance and shareholder protections. In his review of labor-proxy voting practices, Sweeney observes:

> The idea that the Teamsters or carpenters should have a say in the way any publicly owned companies are managed is manifestly foreign to the average senior executive . . .
>
> Part of the reason for management suspicion, if not outright truculence, is the abiding belief that unions are less-than-sincere proponents of a corporate-governance agenda. That is especially true at companies like Caterpiller Inc., which has been embroiled in a vitriolic labor dispute with the United Auto Workers, and trucking companies that have been the target of labor action by the Teamsters.
>
> "Many companies view union use of the proxy vote as simply an extension of the collective-bargaining process," says James Heard, president of Institutional Shareholder Services. . . .[34]

Some companies have fought back against putting labor related proposals to a vote by requesting the SEC issue "no action" letters through its administrative process. Under section 14(a)8 of the Securities Act, companies can ask the SEC to disallow a shareholder proposal on several grounds:

124

FIGURE 3–2

Sponsors of Corporate Governance Proposals: 1994–1995

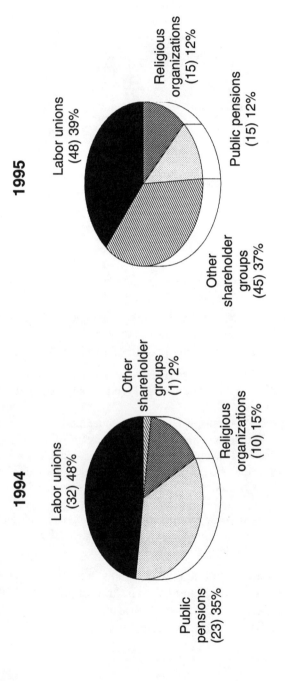

1994

Labor unions
(32) 48%

Other shareholder groups
(1) 2%

Religious organizations
(10) 15%

Public pensions
(23) 35%

1995

Labor unions
(48) 39%

Religious organizations
(15) 12%

Public pensions
(15) 12%

Other shareholder groups
(45) 37%

Source: Georgeson & Company, Inc., *Corporate Governance: 1995 Annual Meeting Season Wrap-Up*, p. 5.

(1) it is designed to redress a personal claim or grievance; (2) it is designed to benefit the proponent; or (3) it is not in the interests of the other securities holders at large.[35] Indeed, the SEC issued approximately four *no action* letters for 25 proposals submitted during the 1995 proxy season by the Laborers Union. The SEC also sent the Teamsters a *no action* letter for its proposal to tie the compensation of top executives at Consolidated Freightways to the pay of its members.

Obviously, the position of a labor union that owns significant stock in a corporation can create a number of questions about potential conflicts of interest, since that fund's beneficiaries include not only current employees but retired employees as well. In any event, many corporations have quietly begun behind the scenes to negotiate with some of the more "mainstream" public pension funds on certain matters which they believe to be motivated by a narrow labor contingent at the expense of the general shareholder base. For example, Consolidated Freightways consulted with a major shareholder, the State of Wisconsin Board, over the Teamsters' proposal to put a poison pill up for shareholder vote. But labor has learned to use corporate governance issues well and has clearly picked a number of universally desirable issues—such as declassifying a staggered board to insure that all directors are up for election at the same time and instituting confidential proxy voting—issues which, regardless of their underlying motivation, clearly meet the voting guidelines of "mainstream" activist funds. The lesson corporations can learn from this trend is to make sure that their underlying governance procedures meet the general shareholder consensus of good corporate governance. These companies will be in a better position to deal with those institutions interested in performance-oriented issues of intrinsic shareholder value and long-term corporate performance.

INSTITUTIONAL ACTIVISM AND STRATEGIC MEASURES OF CORPORATE PERFORMANCE

On March 1, 1990 the largest U.S. institutional investor, Teachers Insurance and Annuity Association-College Retirement Equities Fund (TIAA-CREF), which would ordinarily be thought of as concerned primarily with financial and investment concerns, instituted a Social Choice Fund to which beneficiaries can specifically channel their investments. In 1993, TIAA-CREF issued the following statement regarding social responsibility:

> TIAA-CREF believes building long-term shareholder value is consistent with directors giving careful consideration to social responsibility issues and

the common good of the community. The board should develop policies and practices to address the following issues:

- The environmental impact of the corporation's operations and products.
- Equal employment opportunities for all segments of our population.
- Open channels of communications permitting employees, customers, suppliers, and the community to freely express their concerns.
- Effective employee training and development.
- Evaluation of corporate actions that can negatively affect the common good of the community and its residents.
- Prohibition of deliberate and knowing exploitation of any of the nonshareholder constituencies.[36]

On June 15, 1994 CalPERS announced that it had "adopted a study which links workplace performance with improved corporate performance and will utilize the findings as a factor in its annual corporate governance review."[37] The study, conducted by the Gordon Group, examines a series of workplace policies that affect worker productivity, including increased rights and responsibilities for employees, training programs, and employee feedback. According to Charles Valdes, chairman of the CalPERS Investment Committee, the study provides information which supports the intuitive conclusion that good workplace practices result in a stronger, more productive company. Precisely how these workplace practices will be factored into the investment decisions of companies was not discussed, although Dr. William D. Crist, president of the CalPERS Board of Administration, indicated that CalPERS is "confident that considering workplace practices as a variable in our analysis of company performance will enhance our corporate governance program."[38]

Several important factors differentiate the TIAA-CREF and CalPERS "social responsibility" statements and perspectives of the early 1990s from those of the early 1970s. The first is that they are being made by the very largest institutional investors, with in excess of $225 billion at their disposal. These are not the emotional rantings of church groups or "gadfly" individuals, but pension funds which have traditionally and until very recently taken their charge as one solely focused on earning financial returns to pay beneficiary pensions. The second is the determination of these institutional shareholders to link the social issues with the well-being of the corporation and, in so doing, justify their concern over these issues on grounds which are consistent with their fiduciary duty of care owed to their beneficiaries. They are saying, in effect, that to make money and satisfy shareholders' concern for increasing returns, corporations must fashion certain social programs in areas such as employee and consumer satisfaction. Instead of approaching the issue as was done decades ago, by attacking companies such as General Motors on vague and general grounds that they are quasi-governmental bodies with a duty to society at large, these pension funds are now taking the approach that intrinsic shareholder value of the companies in which they invest is inextricably linked to certain of these heretofore social issues, now determined by comprehensive financial and nonfinancial corporate performance measurements.

INSTITUTIONAL INVESTORS EXPORT THEIR ACTIVISM

U.S. equity markets represent approximately a third of world capitalization and 37 percent of the value of all shares traded in global markets. U.S. institutional investors have increased their presence in foreign equity markets, not only in terms of their equity positions, but also with regard to the level and intensity of their participation in international corporate governance. The principal U.S. institutions making foreign equity investments (pension funds and mutual funds) increased their equity holdings from $97.5 billion in 1990 to $281.7 billion in 1994. This represents an aggregate increase in pension fund assets devoted to foreign equities from 3.1 percent in 1990 to 5.5 percent in 1994, and an increase in mutual fund assets from 1.7 percent to 3.9 percent.

Moreover, international investment (and corporate governance clout) is highly concentrated in a small number of the 25 largest public and private pension funds which represent the major investors in international equities. As of September 30, 1994 the largest 25 public and private pension funds held a total of $85.3 billion in international stocks, which accounted for 29.6 percent of all foreign equity investments made by all U.S. investors. Their investments in international equities began to escalate from a mere $17.7 billion in 1989 to $61.9 billion in 1993 then to $85.3 billion in 1994. For the top 25, this represents an increase in the percentage of their portfolios devoted to international equities from 3.8 percent in 1989 to 7.7 percent in 1993 and a further jump to 10.5 percent in 1994. (see Figure 3–3).

There can be no doubt that some of the sweeping corporate governance reforms discussed in the next chapter are derived from the willingness of U.S. institutional investors to act in the international proxy voting arena. In

1991, U.S. investors reported voting only 24 percent of their global proxies; however, by 1995, the percentage had climbed to 72 percent. Initially it appeared that U.S. investors were using U.S. proxy voting guidelines to apply to their foreign investments. According to the Investor Responsibility Research Center, more than 50 percent of those reporting in 1993 used U.S. guidelines (while only 40 percent used separate global guidelines); by 1995 U.S. investors had clearly become more sensitive to the differences associated with the governance structures of their global portfolio companies. The balance has now tipped in favor of implementing separate global guidelines (60 percent reported using them compared to 40 percent who applied their U.S. guidelines globally).

Finally, the ability and willingness of U.S. institutions to become active with regard to their global holdings is reinforced by two developments: (1) the Department of Labor has pressed pension funds under its jurisdiction to broaden the notion of what is required of them, as a matter of their fiduciary responsibility, to include voting their global proxies; and (2) non-U.S. institutions, including fund managers in places such as the United Kingdom, have become willing to coordinate with U.S. institutions in such notable proxy battles as the Hanson PLC case—the first international proxy contest.

> ... before June 1993, Lord James Hanson, chairman of the giant British industrial conglomerate Hanson plc, had probably never heard of the Houston Firefighters Relief and Retirement Fund. But he was certainly aware of the fund after June 1993, for in that month, officials of the fund joined with pension fund directors from the United Mine Workers of America and the State of Wisconsin Investment Board, and with leading investors from the United Kingdom, to defeat an attempt Hanson was making to limit shareholders' rights. The landmark case marked the first trans-Atlantic proxy battle waged at a British company, and shareholders emerged victorious. They forced Hanson to retract proposals that would have restricted shareholders' ability to nominate directors, to propose amendments to corporate resolutions, and even to speak at future general meetings. Days before the June 25 general meeting, Lord Hanson withdrew the proposals, saying that the company had apparently given the mistaken impression it was seeking "draconian" power over shareholders to restrict their rights.
>
> A year later, Maurice Saatchi, chairman of the British Saatchi & Saatchi Co., got his wake-up call from institutional investors. A shareholder group that included two major U.S. institutions, the State of Wisconsin Investment Board and the General Electric Company's pension trust, forced Saatchi's dismissal in 1994 by protesting an excessive stock option package and the

FIGURE 3-3

International Equities as a Percentage of Assets of the Largest 25 U.S. Pension Funds: 1989 and 1994

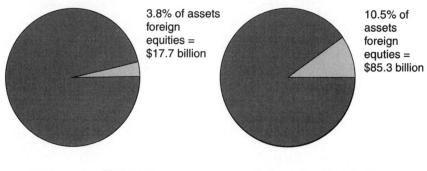

3.8% of assets foreign equities = $17.7 billion

10.5% of assets foreign equties = $85.3 billion

1989 assets—$465.5 billion   1994 assets—$812.6 billion

company's dismal performance since his installation as chairman. U.S. institutional investors have begun to make demands in Mexico, France, and even places where shareholders' rights are notoriously circumscribed—Germany and Japan.[39]

The increasing presence of U.S. institutional investors on the world equity market is likely to act as a continual catalyst for worldwide debate over corporate governance, the subject of the next chapter.

ENDNOTES

1. James E. Burton, Richard H. Koppes, Sheryl K. Pressler, and Kayla J. Gillan, Internal Memorandum to Members of the Investment Committee of the California Public Employees' Retirement System (CalPERS), August 14, 1995, pp. 1–2.

2. A 1993 Conference Board survey of U.S. corporations finds investors' interest in social issues well behind company performance issues. Performance issues were of concern to institutional investors at 68 percent of U.S. companies, while social issues were of concern at 21 percent of companies. See Ronald E. Berenbeim, "Company Relations With Institutional Investors," The Conference Board, Report No. 1070-94-RR, 1994, p. 15.

3. Lauren Talner, *The Origins of Shareholder Activism* (Washington DC: The Investor Responsibility Research Center, July 1983), p. 2.

4. Robert A.G. Monks and Nell Minow, *Power and Accountability* (New York: Harper-Collins, 1991), p. 231.

5. Talner, p. 11.

6. Talner, p. 23.

7. Monks and Minow, pp. 231-232. (Citing the decision in the case *Medical Committee for Human Rights* v. *SEC, 432 F.2d 659,678.*)

8. Talner, pp. 14–15.

9. Burton, Koppes, Pressler, and Gillan, p. 1

10. For data on this subject see Carolyn Kay Brancato, "Greenmail and the Market for Corporate Control: Impact on Shareholders, Issues of Fairness and Recent Developments," Congressional Research Service, Report No. 85-181E, August 27, 1985.

11. For further discussion of the Walt Disney and Phillips Petroleum cases see Ibid.

12. Charles M. Nathan and Marilyn Sobel, "Corporate Stock Repurchases in the Context of Unsolicited Takeover Bids," *Business Lawyer,* July 1980, p.1,551.

13. Roger Dennis, "Two-Tiered Tender Offers and Greenmail: Is New Legislation Needed?," *Georgia Law Review,* 19, no. 281, 1985, p. 306.

14. "1985 Proxy Season Laden With Shark Repellents," *Corporate Governance Bulletin,* Investor Responsibility Research Center, II, no. 3 (June 1985), p. 52.

15. See James E. Heard and Howard D. Sherman, *Conflicts of Interest in the Proxy Voting System* (Washington DC: Investor Responsibility Research Center, 1987).

16. See U.S. Department of Labor and U.S. Treasury Department, Joint Press Release and Joint Statement on Role of ERISA Plans in Takeovers, January 31, 1989.

17. Monks and Minow, p. 187.

18. Bevis Longstreth, *Modern Investment Management and the Prudent Man Rule* (New York: Oxford University Press, 1986), pp. 32–33.

19. U.S. Department of Labor, "1989 Proxy Project Report," as cited in Monks and Minow, p. 194.

20. U.S. Department of Labor, Interpretive Bulletin 94-2, Pension and Welfare Benefits Administration, Part 2509, Interpretive Bulletins Relating to the Employment Retirement Income Security Act of 1974, pp. 26–28.

21. Institutional Shareholder Services (ISS) reports that, in considering the validity of poison pills, courts traditionally focus on two primary features:

whether the board has acted in good faith and on an informed basis and whether the board is obligated to redeem the pill when confronted with a takeover bid. ISS quotes legal expert, David Martin, Jr., who notes that Delaware courts require boards to show two points with regard to a board's good-faith efforts: "(i) that they had reasonable grounds for believing that a danger to the corporate enterprise, which includes protecting stockholders from harm, existed, and (ii) that the defensive mechanism adopted was reasonable in relation to the threat posed." In the case of a hostile takeover bid, the courts will examine a company's existing antitakeover measures and the terms of the hostile offer to determine whether a company should redeem the rights. Joseph Sargent, "Investors Eye Expiration Dates for First Wave of Poison Pills," *ISSUE ALERT,* Institutional Shareholder Services, Inc., Bethesda Maryland, December 1995, X, no. 11, p. 5.

22. Burton, Koppes, Pressler, and Gillen, p. 2.
23. Sargent, p. 1.
24. Wachtell, Lipton, Rosen, and Katz, "Common Share Purchase Rights Plan," Client Memorandum, September 1994, pp 2–3.
25. Institutional Shareholder Services, Inc., *The ISS Corporate Ownership Manual* (Bethesda, Maryland: Institutional Shareholder Services, Inc., January 1990), 1Ed., Ch. 4, pp. 4–22.
26. Wachtell, Lipton, p. 1.
27. Ibid.
28. Robert C. Pozen, "A Prescription: Give Poison Pills Expiration Dates," *The Wall Street Journal,* November 1, 1989, p. C1.
29. Peter R. Gleason, "Activists Ready Campaigns for 1996 Proxy Season," *ISSUE ALERT,* Institutional Shareholder Services, January 1996, XI, no. 1, p. 5.
30. Paul Sweeney, "Clash by Proxy," *Across the Board,* May 1996, p. 22.
31. Susan Kellock and Craig Rosenbert, "The Role of Taft-Hartley Funds in the Corporate Governance Debate," *Corporate Governance Advisor,* May/June 1995, 3, no. 3, p. 13.
32. Peg O'Hara and Patrick McGurn, "Shareholder Interests Shift Somewhat in 1995 Proxy Season," *Corporate Governance Bulletin,* Investor Responsibility Research Center, July-September 1995, XII, no. 3, p. 19.
33. Bart Naylor, "International Brotherhood of Teamsters Prepares for Proxy Season," *ISSUE ALERT,* Institutional Shareholder Services, January 1996, XI, no. 1, p. 3.
34. Sweeney, p. 23.
35. Ibid.

36. TIAA-CREF Policy Statement
37. News Release, California Public Employees' Retirement System, June 15, 1994, p. 1.
38. Ibid., p. 2.
39. Carolyn K. Brancato, *Getting Listed on Wall Street: The Irwin Guide to Financial Reporting Standards in the U.S.* (Burr Ridge, IL: Irwin Professional Publishing, 1996), pp. xii-xiii.

4

GOOD CORPORATE GOVERNANCE IS GOOD BUSINESS

In the United States, improvements in corporate governance are taking place not only as a result of institutional investor activism; they have also become important agendas for public corporations ranging from the giant General Motors[1] to the more closely held Campbell Soup Company, which has championed the concept that "good governance is good business."[2] U.S. boards of directors have been grappling with key issues such as the scope of their responsibilities; the composition of the board; the number and nature of board committees; procedures for providing information between boards, managements, and shareholders; methods to evaluate CEOs and board members, either individually or collectively; and procedures to assure accountability to shareholders, such as proxy voting arrangements. (They are also charged with approving the corporation's compensation plans for its executives and themselves, which will be discussed in Chapter 6 under the general topic of aligning the interests of the corporation with that of its shareholders.) This chapter discusses "best practices" evolving in U.S. corporate governance, as well as international trends which are, in many cases, tracking these U.S. developments.

THE CORPORATE BOARD'S SCOPE OF RESPONSIBILITIES

Robert Monks and Nell Minow provide interesting historical background on how terminology for "the board" and "the chairman" came to be used:

> U.S. boards carried on a tradition that began with the earliest form of corporate organization, the joint stock companies. In the British colonies, as in Great Britain itself, the group of people who oversaw the company would meet regularly. Fine furniture was expensive in those days, and few people in trade had chairs or tables to contain the group. So the men sat on stools, around a long board laid across two sawhorses. The group was named "the board," after the makeshift table they worked at. And the leader of the group, who did not have to sit on a stool, by reason of his prestigious perch, was named the "chair-man."[3]

Noted attorney Ira M. Millstein traces the development of the modern corporate board from the Berle and Means corporate model to one which must respond to the collective ownership of institutional investors:

> Managers at one point—the hey-day of managerial capitalism—came to view themselves as the corporation itself. Boards and shareholders existed more in theory than in fact. Ownership was a concept, not a reality.
>
> Now, ownership has changed, becoming more concentrated in the hands of institutions. True, it is still fragmented because individual institutions, through theories of diversification, own the securities of hundreds if not thousands of corporations. But different from the past, through collective ownership institutions appear powerful, have found a shareholder voice, and that shareholder voice is being heard. And that is the difference—the voice and, to an extent if [institutional investors will] use it, more concentrated capital and the ability to purchase larger stakes in individual enterprises to enhance the voice.[4]

In the United States, boards derive their power from state laws, which charge them to direct the business and affairs of the corporation on behalf of the shareholders. The board is ultimately responsible for determining what is in the best interests of the corporation, with a duty implicit in the so-called "Business Judgment Rule," which requires a range of duties of loyalty and the responsible conduct of the business.[5] But beyond the basics that directors should not engage in self-dealing at the expense of the corporation, there is vigorous debate about which constituents or *stakeholders* should be taken into account when directors discharge their duties of loyalty—loyalty to whom? This question becomes all the more important in light of the emerging consensus that the corporation will enhance its value if it considers nontangibles, such as employee and customer satisfaction.

Millstein argues that, notwithstanding the range of its duties and the pressures exerted upon it to please a variety of constituents, the foremost responsibility of the board is to steer toward the "polestar" of attaining corporate profit and shareholder gain. This view conforms to that held by corporate executives and directors as well as major U.S. institutional investors. It was articulated in 1991 in a seminal document, *A New Compact for Owners and Directors,* which was crafted by a group of eminent corporate attorneys and representatives of major public pension funds— with notably diverse perspectives. While recognizing that different owners have different goals and investment expectations, the *Compact* provides that:

> Shareholders should recognize and respect that the only goal common to all shareholders is the ongoing prosperity of the company. . . . Shareholders should not pressure companies to be managed to favor their own goals at the expense of the goals of others. Directors and managers should manage a company to be a profitable and viable enterprise over the long term. Business decisions generally should not be focused on achieving returns to the shareholder in the short term at the expense of the long-term growth and success of the company. Shareholders should not act in ways that frustrate or detract from the ongoing prosperity of the company.[6]

The National Association of Corporate Directors (NACD) also makes clear that boards of directors bear primary responsibility to the corporation's owners—its shareholders—and should be committed to maximizing shareholder wealth in the long run.[7] TIAA-CREF, a major institutional investor, echos this sentiment in its Policy Statement on Corporate Governance: "It is recognized that the primary responsibility of the board of directors is to foster the long-term success of the corporation consistent with its fiduciary responsibility to the shareholders."[8] But the definition of what it takes to achieve long-term success has been changing to accommodate a somewhat broader spectrum of concerns for directors.

Millstein notes that, during the 1980s, a number of "corporate constituency statutes" were enacted by state legislatures at the behest of managements. These permitted boards to assume that corporate profit and shareholder gain were only one objective; jobs, community welfare, and other values of stakeholders were put on an equal plane and employees, suppliers, and customers were given a right to sue for alleged economic harm. But there has always been a certain sense of cynicism that these statutes were enacted more to protect managements against raiders than to genuinely take into account the interests of employees, customers, and suppliers. Moreover, Millstein argues that accountability to everyone means being accountable to no one, and that the board should direct its efforts to improving corporate profitability and shareholder value.

These values are affirmed by a 1995 NACD survey on the viewpoints of corporate CEOs in nine countries (see Figure 4–1). When asked to describe the most significant corporate governance issues they face, more than 50 percent of the CEOs said that corporate performance was their number one priority (more than 80 percent said it was among their top three priorities), followed by nearly 20 percent who rated strategic planning as their number one priority (just over 70 percent said it rated among their top three priorities). Paying attention to *stakeholder* relations was low on their lists—viewed as their top priority by less than 2 percent of CEOs (just under 20 percent rated it among their top three priorities).[9]

Despite the controversy over how much boards should concern themselves with satisfying stakeholders versus shareholders, Millstein does concede that the modern corporation clearly creates interdependencies with a variety of groups (employees, customers, suppliers, and members of communities in which the corporation operates), which must be balanced by boards and managers: "It can be a difficult balancing act—better yet, a difficult integration act—for managers, but there can be no long-term profitability and shareholder gain without an attempt to integrate fair treatment of all those who depend on the corporation."[10] The NACD concurs:

> Experienced directors recognize and accept the fact that the reality of the issues they deal with turns out to be far more complicated than "total and sole responsibility to our shareholders." The value of shareholder returns depends, in no small measure, on several important corporate stakeholders, including employees, customers, suppliers, and local communities. An effective board must, therefore, be aware of the legitimate claims stakeholders may have on the corporation, and be prepared to see to it that such claims are equitably honored.[11]

The principal voice in the United Kingdom also appears to take the view that the directors' duty of loyalty is to the shareholders alone. This perspective is implicit in the report of The Committee on The Financial Aspects of Corporate Governance,[12] referred to as "The Cadbury Report" after its esteemed Chairman, Sir Adrian Cadbury. *The Cadbury Report,* released on December 1, 1992 endorses the concept that the shareholders are the owners of the company and the directors report to them on their stewardship (and only directly to them—not through other entities, such as

FIGURE 4-1

CEO Priorities: Corporate Governance Issues

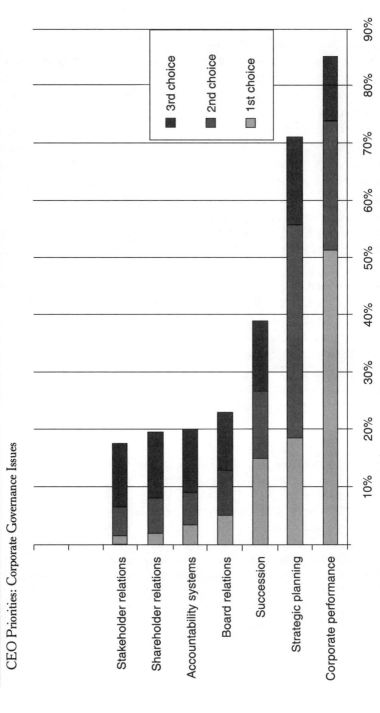

Source: National Association of Corporate Directors and Deloitte & Touche, CEO Viewpoint Survey, Deloitte & Touche Review, May 1, 1995, p. 1.

shareholder committees). In rejecting the concept of shareholder committees, *The Cadbury Report* notes that it does not see evidence explaining how it would be possible to form shareholder committees "in such a way that they would be both truly representative of all the company's shareholders and able to keep in regular touch with their changing constituencies. Unless these tests of legitimacy are met, the Committee is unable to see how shareholder committees can become the accepted link between a board and its shareholders."[13]

In the United Kingdom, however, there is growing debate regarding the proper responsibility of the corporation to society. Mark Goyder, Programme Director for a major study on *Tomorrow's Company* being conducted by The Royal Society for the encouragement of Arts, Manufactures & Commerce, contends that the corporation must pursue an "inclusive" approach and incorporate more explicitly the needs of major *stakeholder* constituents such as employees, customers, and suppliers. The *Tomorrow's Company* study, discussed in Chapter 2, is comprised of a group of approximately 25 of the largest U.K. corporations, including IBM of U.K. This is clearly the most expansive view in Europe. On the other side of the English Channel, however, perhaps the narrowest European view of a board's duties vis á vis its shareholders or stakeholders can be found in France. A major corporate governance report, *The Vienot Report,* was issued on July 10, 1995 by a group of major French businessmen, chaired by M. Marc Vienot, Chairman and CEO of Société Generale.[14] In *The Vienot Report,* the overriding duty of directors is to promote the company's prosperity:

> In Anglo-American countries, the emphasis [with regard to the duties of the board of directors] is on enhancing share value, whereas in continental Europe, and particularly in France, it tends to be on the company's interest. . . .
>
> The interest of the company may be understood as the overriding claim of the company considered as a separate economic agent, pursuing its own objectives which are distinct from those of shareholders, employees, creditors including the internal revenue authorities, suppliers and customers. It nonetheless represents the common interest of all of these persons, which is for the company to remain in business and prosper.
>
> The Committee thus believes that directors should at all time (sic) be concerned solely to promote the interests of the company.[15]

Finally, to round out the spectrum of opinion on the place of shareholders within the corporation, Japanese companies have traditionally been

run with the express purpose of protecting the enterprise, its employees, and
its suppliers, frequently members of the same trading group.

> There seems to be no doubt that Japanese companies put the "family" first
> (or immediately after customers). They argue that an employee who devotes
> his life to a business has morally a bigger stake in it than a shareholder. . . .
>
> What has made Japan different is not so much attitudes within the
> company—though these count—but the fact that outside the company the
> interested parties, banks and shareholders, share the company's view that the
> shareholders' interest does not have to be satisfied by a growing dividend
> stream. . . .[16]

The notion that shareholder return would be paramount has, until
recently, been a foreign concept in Japan. However, this is changing rapidly
with increasing pressures coming from a removal of government supports
for cross-shareholdings and of banking system supports for corporate debt
financing. Former advisor to the Governors of The Bank of England,
Jonathan Charkham notes: "The Japanese feeling about the company as a
family—in which shareholders are 'poor relations'—may in future be
somewhat modified if shareholders assert themselves."[17]

Thus, globalization trends are forcing Japanese companies to join their
European counterparts and enter international securities markets to obtain
capital. With this comes the need for companies to adjust their governance
structures to meet the expectations of a dominant U.S. institutional investor
presence. The Centre for European Policy Studies (CEPS) reported in 1995
that corporate governance issues will become of increasing concern to
European corporations because of the international diversification and
increasing cross-border activity of institutional investors. Specifically,
American and British pension funds represent about 72 percent of total
pension fund assets in the Western world; these can be instrumental in
changing corporate governance standards. Moreover, CEPS notes that the
trend in which institutional investors have increased their shareholdings of
listed companies over time in several European countries is likely to
continue, above all in continental Europe, due to developments in retirement
financing and health care:

> European countries currently rely to a large extent on publicly operated
> pay-as-you-go financed pension schemes, in which contributions from the
> active working population pay for the pensions of the retired. Growing
> pensioner-to-worker ratios and the restraints on public spending will make
> these schemes more and more untenable, and a larger share of pension
> contributions will have to be financed by privately managed funded labour-

market and/or individual pension schemes. Similar changes might also occur in the sector of health care, where parts of the tasks that are now carried out by the public sector will be divested and handed over to the private sector.

These developments will lead to an increase in the demand for equity and dis-intermediated finance by institutional investors, acting as the depositors of pension funds. They will push companies to adjust their financing methods and may well result in a reduction of the debt-to-equity ratios of European industry. The role of purely commercial banks (as opposed to investment or universal banks) might diminish in favour of securities markets.[18]

The role of institutional investors in this new capital market structure becomes paramount, as they supplant the traditional role banks have played as providers of debt. As former SEC Chairman Richard Breeden points out:

> Even in Germany and Japan (though for very different reasons), the traditional system of relationships is changing between a universal bank in Germany, and the companies in which it holds equity stakes, and the "main bank" in Japan and its relationship to a group of companies within a keiretsu. The German banks have been fairly quiet about it, but nonetheless the steps of Deutsche Bank and others to reduce the size of their industrial equity holdings suggests the beginning of a profound change in the capital market systems of Germany.[19]

This change is clearly signaled by a momentous event. In early October 1993, Daimler-Benz AG became the first German company to become publicly traded in the United States. The traditionally strong linkages between German companies and German banks, coupled with historically high savings rates in Germany compared with those in the United States, generally meant that most German companies had access to abundant quantities of capital within Germany. That may explain why there are only about 600 publicly traded companies in Germany. Daimler-Benz's bold departure from tradition presented a threat and a challenge to European banks. David Fairlamb described their predicament in a 1994 article in *Institutional Investor:*

> Like the biblical apple proffered to Eve, U.S. capital markets are as dangerous as they are enticing - so European bankers have learned. . . . Spurred on by the globalization of capital markets, the Europeans are now busily rethinking and reorganizing their U.S. operations . . . Unlike Eve, the Europeans have little choice. Their biggest corporate customers need access to the U.S. markets. The European banks also need to fight a rear-guard action against U.S. banks that are making inroads into Europe. "To be in investment banking but not to be in the U.S. means that the U.S. houses will have the upper hand

[globally],'' points out Giorgio Questa, chairman of IMI Capital Markets and vice chairman of Mabon Securities, a subsidiary of Italy's partly privatized merchant bank Istituto Mobiliare Italiano.[20]

European banks are clearly responding by shifting into new investment strategies, as can be seen by the unprecedented alliance between Deutsche Bank, on behalf of its European clients, and U.S. investment banking firms for the underwriting of the Daimler-Benz American Depositary Receipt (ADR) listing in the United States. This arrangement between German banks and Wall Street has heralded a new age in the globalization of U.S. securities markets.[21]

The European exposure to global institutional investors is also heightened by the wave of privatizations of state assets, especially in the banking, telecommunications, and energy industries. Major formerly state-owned companies are now up for sale to the public in Belgium, France, Germany, Italy, the Netherlands, Spain, and the United Kingdom. These trends will increase the importance of stock markets and augment their capitalization. CEPS notes the prime example of this is in Italy, where the stock market capitalization as a percent of gross domestic product is the lowest in the European Union (EU) and where the share of government ownership of listed companies amounted to 40 percent in 1991. While these newly privatized firms will clearly need expanded private sector equity financing, CEPS warns that a countervailing trend to keep privatized corporations nationally "anchored" (in order to retain a strong shareholding in the hands of nationals and to control national assets) may prevent corporate governance from becoming harmonized and transparent in the context of global standards:

> In several European member states, privatisations are placed with local companies and investors. In France, a core shareholding of the privatised companies is in general placed with French institutional investors and corporations ("les noyaux durs"). Local individual residents came in second place, but not much was left for foreign investors. The same strategy is followed in other European countries, such as Spain and Belgium. Clearly, however, such policies are irreconcilable with membership of an integrated European market.[22]

Finally, in other parts of the world, withdrawal of traditional sources of government funding will continue to put pressure on capital markets as newly privatized companies in the former Soviet Union and Eastern Bloc countries attempt to enter global securities markets. A former SEC Commissioner, Professor Roberta Karmel, notes:

It seems government funding is not in the cards anywhere in the world in the near future. The financial collapse of former Communist and Socialist countries and the huge budget deficits all over the Western world make it very difficult, if not impossible, for economic enterprises to continue to be financed through government grants almost everywhere. This has led to privatizations in developed Western countries and in emerging countries. These privatizations have been the driving force behind much of the internationalization of the securities markets, and in particular behind the decisions of various foreign issuers to enter the U.S. markets.[23]

The economic influence of U.S.-style institutional investor activists on global securities markets is immense and will certainly provide an attractive alternative as local equity markets struggle to provide sufficiently accessible capital. Moreover, as these institutional investors press for shareholder returns which reflect sustained corporate growth (which in turn recognizes that employees, customers, and suppliers are important to achieve these), there should be a gradual convergence of views on the role of the board in internationally equity financed corporations. This move toward the middle might occur from: (1) one end of the spectrum in Japan, which says that the company is less important than its constituents; and (2) the other end of the spectrum in France, which says that the company is all important notwithstanding its shareholder or other constituent base. In this middle ground, directors will not have to choose one constituency over another; shareholder value may be technically and legally paramount, but the basic definition of shareholder value will be broadened to explicitly assume that the health of the shareholders depends on achieving enhanced and sustained value for other constituents of the corporation. This will result in a convergence of opinion that all constituents are important since they are synergistically tied to the new concepts of corporate performance and the creation of shareholder value described in this book.

Finally, with regard to the role of the board in monitoring (and having an impact upon) the performance of the company, Millstein believes the linkage should be intuitive:

> I'm always surprised when people debate this linkage, for to me it is intuitive. No one questions that the CEO's actions matter to corporate performance. And since the board is charged with (1) hiring the best CEO it can find; (2) helping the CEO set goals and priorities for the long-term viability of the corporation; (3) monitoring his or her accomplishments against those goals; and (4) if necessary, replacing him or her in a timely manner, the board is linked to corporate performance.[24]

THE ROLE OF THE BOARD IN DETERMINING STRATEGY

A credible board—Millstein calls it a *certifying* board—can be management's greatest ally because "It can 'certify' to shareholders in times of trouble that management is regularly evaluated and is doing what the board expects, according to a strategic plan agreed to in advance by the board and management."[25] The role of the board in devising strategy for the corporation is generally left to individual corporations, although a 1993 Conference Board survey[26] finds that strategy formulation is the corporate activity that the board most influences. (This survey finds that boards also influence human resources and financial management and, to a lesser extent, operations control, risk management, and external relations.)

A more recent 1996 Conference Board study reports that, according to a survey and interviews conducted with CEOs, directors, and senior executives in 10 countries during 1995, boards are playing an increasing role in approving (not merely rubber stamping) corporate strategic plans.[27] Both board members and managements are, however, extremely sensitive to how they balance formulating strategy without micromanaging the company or second-guessing the CEO.

As with the state *constituents* statutes devised during the takeover years of the 1980s, the role of the board in strategic planning became associated with management entrenchment devices, which have also sidetracked and confused some important developments. In 1990, Time Inc. successfully fended off a hostile tender offer from Paramount Communications, on the grounds that it had a strategic plan which, if permitted to be enacted by incumbent management, would yield higher shareholder values than the raider's bid would afford shareholders. According to attorney Jon Masters, the court "applied the business judgment rule to uphold the strategic plan approved by Time's directors and explained that the precepts underlying the business judgment rule militate against a court's engaging in the process of attempting to appraise and evaluate the relative merits of a long-term versus a short-term investment goal for shareholders. ... Directors are not obliged to abandon a deliberately conceived corporate plan for a short-term shareholder profit unless there is clearly no basis to sustain the corporate strategy."[28]

The *Paramount-Time* decision, while it called attention to the needs of boards to become more sharply focused on strategy, had some negative effects. A number of boards developed rather cursory strategic plans so they could avail themselves of the so-called *Marty Lipton defense*—named after the prominent defense attorney who represented Time. Some companies, therefore, have found the need to overcome a pro forma strategic planning process to institute something of more lasting benefit to the corporation.

A number of major players in the current corporate governance debate have endorsed the board's growing role in strategic deliberation. The Subcouncil on Corporate Governance and Financial Markets of the U.S. Competitiveness Policy Council recommended in 1992 that boards establish appropriate procedures at the full board level to oversee the formulation and realization of the long-term strategic, financial, and organizational goals of the corporation.[29] With greater concern for failing U.K. businesses, *The Cadbury Report* approaches the strategic assessment question in a much more specific way by asking that directors state in their report that the business is a "going concern" with supporting assumptions or qualifications as necessary.[30] *The Toronto Stock Exchange Report* has one of the broadest recommendations for the board: "as part of the overall stewardship responsibility [it] should assume responsibility for . . . adoption of a strategic planning process."[31] In France, the board has responsibility for adoption, but the impetus for the strategic plan comes from the chairman. *The Vienot Report* states that a "clear strategy is not only a necessary condition for good management, it is also a fundamental component of the information to be supplied to shareholder and the market. The Committee believes that, while it is the Chairman's role to draw up and propose a strategy, this must be adopted by the board. By virtue of the same principle, it must consider and decide on all strategically important decisions . . ."[32]

But the most specific recommendation of all comes from the United States and CalPERS, which believes that boards should adopt a formal method for strategic oversight, such as a strategic or business audit.[33]

Indeed, The Conference Board's 1995 survey on the role of the board in strategic assessment finds that 60 percent of U.S. and European senior executives and directors say their boards have increased their deliberations of strategic issues during the previous three years; 51 percent say their board has a "greater" role in strategy formulation; and nearly half describe their board's current role as "actively engaged in the choice of strategic options."[34] The report observes three factors (see Box 4–1) that explain the trend toward more active director involvement in strategy formulation: (1) the need to compete for capital in world markets; (2) a developing consensus that strategic deliberation is a board responsibility; and (3) employee stock ownership and privatization.

BOX 4–1

Reasons for Greater Involvement by Boards in Strategic Deliberation

COMPETING FOR CAPITAL IN WORLD MARKETS

Growing numbers of U.S., Canadian, and European companies can no longer finance expansion solely with retained earnings or, in the case of former state-owned enterprises, with government subsidies. CEOs and directors say that more board meeting time is now devoted to discussion and monitoring of strategic plans that will attract investors and develop priorities for allocating limited capital and human resources.

Companies now confront pressure on a global scale from institutional investors that control increasing percentages of shares and seek a high rate of return. U.S. capital, in particular, is highly mobile. In September 1995, The Brancato Report on Institutional Investment estimated that U.S. investors owned $377 billion in foreign equities (7 to 8 percent of their total equity holdings). Since 1990, the 25 U.S. pension funds with the largest foreign holdings have increased the percentage of foreign assets in their portfolios nearly threefold (3.8 to 10.5 percent) and the dollar value of foreign equity assets held nearly fivefold ($17.7 to $85.5 billion).

DEVELOPING CONSENSUS THAT STRATEGIC DELIBERATION IS A BOARD RESPONSIBILITY

The 1992 release of *The Cadbury Report* in the United Kingdom was [one of] the first in a series of corporate governance commission reports and legislative initiatives in the United States, Canada, France, Spain, and South Africa to cite the more prominent examples . . . Regardless of the composition of the committee, there was widespread agreement on the need for greater director involvement in strategic assessment.

Most North American and European CEOs interviewed agreed with these recommendations for greater director participation in strategy discussions. The CEOs believe that thorough board discussion of the environmental factors that shape business prospects can add value to the company's review of its strategic options. Explaining the Campbell Soup Company's Principles on Corporate Governance, Campbell Corporate Secretary John J. Furey goes a step further and argues that director strategic assessment is a critical element in the board's ability to evaluate CEO and company performance.

(continued)

Reasons—Concluded

EMPLOYEE STOCK OWNERSHIP AND PRIVATIZATION

Employee stock ownership and the worldwide trend to privatization of industry has also resulted in the need for a board response to the shareholder assertion of an ownership role. Chairmen of recently privatized Swedish, Canadian, and U.K. companies say that directors of newly privatized companies typically spend more time than their predecessors in strategic deliberation because the board and not a finance ministry now charts the course for the company.

Source: Ronald E. Berenbeim, "The Corporate Board: A Growing Role in Strategic Assessment," The Conference Board, Report 1152-96-RR., Executive Summary, pp. 5–6.

FINANCIAL ACCOUNTABILITY: THE ROLE OF AUDITING

Virtually all the board's as well as the entire corporation's financial credibility to its shareholders (or other appropriate constituents) depends on the accuracy and independence of corporate financial reports. In a number of European countries, as well as Japan, boards are still struggling with certain basics which have long been taken for granted in the United States:

- Boards should employ outside, independent auditors.
- Outside, independent directors are to oversee and monitor their activities.

By contrast, in the United Kingdom major efforts have had to be directed at overcoming the onus of recent corporate scandals and failures (such as the failure of BCCI and the collapse of Robert Maxwell's media and communications empire and the subsequent discovery of the alleged transfer of $700 million from Maxwell's employees' pension fund to finance Maxwell's operations). These two incidents, which occurred in 1991 and 1992, reshaped the focus (and heightened the profile) of *The Cadbury Report*. This report refers to "the understandable public criticism of the audit process when companies collapse without apparent warning"[35] and states: "Had a Code such as ours been in existence in the past, we believe that a number of the recent examples of unexpected company failures and cases of fraud would have received attention earlier."[36] This report focused on the need for boards to be free to drive their companies forward, but recognized that boards must exercise that freedom within a framework of effective accountability. Thus, its recommendations, embodied in a "Code of Best Practice," deal primarily with the control and reporting functions of boards and the role of auditors.

Based on the *Cadbury* recommendations, The London Stock Exchange has adopted a listing requirement for companies with filing dates of June 30, 1993 or later, mandating disclosure of the extent to which a company complies with the Cadbury Code; failing compliance, a company must explain why, although there is no penalty for failing to adopt the code. Compliance therefore falls primarily under the guise of "moral suasion," not enactment of statutory codes, although *The Cadbury Report* contemplates that the Stock Exchange may include, in "appropriate cases, the publication of a formal statement of censure."

The Toronto Stock Exchange Committee on Corporate Governance in Canada issued its December 1994 governance guidelines not in response to the scandals of the United Kingdom, or to the takeover raiders' actions in the United States, but because of a concern over the performance of Canadian corporations emerging from the "stresses of the 1990–1991 recession." In the preface, Chairman Peter Dey notes that investors and other parties interested in the welfare of corporations that failed or have been significantly restructured have frequently been dissatisfied with the performance of their boards of directors and managements. They have asked the question featured in the title of the report: "Where Were the Directors?"[37] The *Toronto Stock Exchange Report* promulgates a list of governance guidelines for which it recommends that Toronto Stock Exchange companies be required to disclose whether they adhere to them or not—much like the London Stock Exchange adopted *The Cadbury Report* disclosure guidelines.

In contrast to these relatively recent and more modest disclosure approaches, it has been the practice in the United States to more aggressively assure shareholders of the veracity of the board's stewardship of their assets; the New York Stock Exchange has, since 1978, required all listed companies to have audit committees composed solely of independent directors. A Conference Board comparison of corporate boards in 546 U.S. companies contrasts how practices have changed over the past two decades. The survey finds that, in 1993, almost every company surveyed had an audit committee, whereas, in 1972, only 45 percent reported such a committee. The report noted, however, that this important, independent board committee faces major new challenges, including complex financial controls over far-flung operations, the increase in lawsuits alleging improper disclosure, and increasingly high-tech auditing procedures that are replacing paper-trail systems in some industries.[38]

Catching up to U.S. practice with regard to audit committees, *Cadbury* recommends that all companies establish audit committees. However, it does not go as far as to require that such committees be made of entirely of independent directors; *Cadbury* recommends that there should be a minimum of three members, with membership confined to the nonexecutive directors of the company, a majority of whom should be independent. The report further notes: "While experience of audit committees in this country is shorter, it is encouraging, and around two-thirds of the top 250 U.K. listed companies now have them in place."[39]

Lagging both the United States and the United Kingdom in this area of accountability, French recommendations in the 1995 *Vienot Report* are to have each board appoint an advisory committee principally charged with ensuring the appropriateness and consistency of accounting policies and verifying that internal procedures for collecting and checking information are such that they guarantee its accuracy. As to the composition of this advisory audit committee, it should include at least three directors, to the exclusion of executive directors and employees, and at least *one* independent director[40]—less than the more stringent requirements for independence of directors on audit committees in both the United Kingdom and the United States.

In Japan there are external auditors who are qualified accountants as well as internal auditors; however, the problem of financial accountability appears to rest more with the difficulty of finding "independent directors" outside the close knit structure of cross-shareholding trading groups referred to as *keiretsu*. In a Tokyo debate between a group of Japanese businessman and a delegation of U.S. corporate governance experts sponsored by the Pacific Institute in October 1993 (in which the author took part), one Japanese businessman, when asked about having independent directors to oversee the auditing process, responded: "Where am I going to get an outside, independent director—they do not exist in Japan—everyone is in a *keiretsu* trading group and no one would think of going outside the group." According to Jonathan Charkham, the role of the statutory auditor *(kansayaku)* should not be confused with either external or internal auditors. (Statutory auditors may well represent "a mere formality without substance" since their function is not to replace more generally accepted types of auditors but to provide retired employees or directors with a nominal form of shareholder oversight, ostensibly to ensure that business is conducted in accordance with applicable laws; they may, however, lack the clout to question superiors with the necessary acumen.[41])

The CEPS report underscores the need for improving the quality of the audit function within the EU, especially in the context of discussions about uniform standards in an integrated market for business and investors.

> So far, only the minimum qualifications for persons carrying out statutory audits have been harmonized through EU legislation in the 8th company law directive. ... A final issue of concern is the independence of auditors. Auditors are generally appointed by the AGM [CEO] and must give an independent opinion to the shareholders on the stewardship of the directors as reflected in the annual accounts. Shareholders rarely make an informed decision and appoint the auditors recommended to them by the directors. Auditors' independence might, however, be compromised by the other non-audit tasks performed for their client, or through other auditing tasks carried out for subsidiaries. . . .
>
> The independence of auditors should not be overemphasized, since what counts finally is the professional judgment of the auditor.[42]

An even greater difficulty European and Japanese companies have in adhering to the high standards of Anglo-American auditing practices stems from far more than their reluctance or inability to employ outside directors to oversee independent auditors—it is frequently a matter of deep-seated variances in basic accounting rules. The main accounting issue involves the need to reconcile home country accounting standards with U.S. Generally Accepted Accounting Principles (U.S. GAAP). Indeed, the issue of how to treat reserves was a key obstacle for the 1993 Daimler-Benz ADR New York Stock Exchange listing issue. During the listing process, variations in German and U.S. accounting standards were extensively reviewed. Under German accounting policies, companies are afforded considerable discretion in either reporting income through to the bottom line or placing earnings into reserves. In the United States, reserves under U.S. GAAP can be diverted from income only to provide for an adverse event that must be probable and estimable in amount; German companies may record reserves without such a stringent restriction, and they can later release them to improve sagging earnings. Former SEC Chairman Richard Breeden notes that, at one time, roughly 40 percent of the entire balance sheet of Daimler-Benz was represented by the single line item, "provisions." The so-called "hidden reserves" so notoriously associated with

German companies turned out, unexpectedly, to be reconciled with accounting methods which produced lower rather than higher reported earnings. (Most investors had assumed that the reserves would have produced a surplus for earnings, not a deficit.)

Breeden, who oversaw the Daimler-Benz listing in U.S. securities markets describes the effects of varying accounting methods:

> Though its sales had plummeted in the face of a steep downturn in Germany's economy, for the first half of 1993 Daimler-Benz reported a profit under German GAAP of almost DM200 million, a terrific result given the state of the German economy. However, this reported DM200 million profit came after an undisclosed release of more than DM1.5 billion in provisions into income. Under German GAAP, the story for investors would have ended at the DM200 million profit, though its board members and its largest shareholder, the Deutsche Bank, would have known about the results before adding back the provisions from prior years.
>
> For the same period under U.S. GAAP, the company reported a loss of just under DM1 billion. That fact is clearly shown in a two-page reconciliation to U.S. GAAP, where the addition of reserves earned in prior periods is simply backed out of the current year's results, along with other changes. Thus, all the investors in Daimler-Benz ... are now able to evaluate the company's current performance without the considerable layer of camouflage that other German companies are allowed to use to smooth out their reported earnings.[43]

In both Germany and Japan, as well as in certain other countries such as France, companies have traditionally kept high levels of reserves for a variety of reasons, including preparing for special contingencies and as a method of passing on shareholder equity untaxed to future generations in family owned businesses. Global shareholders may object to these reserves—assuming they are even disclosed—as lowering allocations to them through lower dividend payout. In addition, treatment of items such as goodwill on the balance sheet can give rise to controversial accounting discrepancies.

SEC rules for listing securities in U.S. securities markets require extensive disclosure and reconciliation of accounting differences, including estimates of how the issuer's bottom line would have been revised if full conformance with U.S. GAAP had been established. Companies may face substantial costs in reworking their accounting systems, although some new companies may determine that, as long as they are establishing accounting systems, it might be in their best interests to conform to U.S. standards for listing, since investors in the U.S. markets have come to trust and rely on the panoply of disclosure and accounting regularly provided them by companies utilizing U.S. capital markets.

On the other hand, there is considerable resistance to widespread adoption of U.S. GAAP. CEPS notes that, while international markets are tending towards U.S. accounting rules and, indeed, most European stock exchanges already accept financial statements prepared under U.S. GAAP for quotation, forced adherence to U.S. accounting standards is politically unacceptable to the European Union: "These rules have been developed in the U.S. and are adapted to its circumstances, over which Europe has no influence whatsoever."[44]

The SEC, however, has taken some steps towards recognizing that there is an advantage to international harmonization of accounting rules. On April 19, 1994 the SEC adopted a series of initiatives designed to simplify the registration and reporting process for foreign companies accessing the U.S. capital markets. The rules demonstrate the SEC's commitment to enhancing the competitiveness of the U.S. capital markets while at the same time honoring its regulatory mandate to protect U.S. investors and markets. Then SEC Commissioner J. Carter Beese Jr. summarized the initiatives: "What we are doing today is lowering impediments, not lowering thresholds."

The new rules: (1) relax certain of the financial statement burdens on foreign issuers[45] seeking access to the U.S. capital markets through public offerings or seeking listings on U.S. stock exchanges or NASDAQ; and (2) ease the eligibility requirements for these potential foreign issuers as well.[46] The SEC estimates that the number of currently reporting foreign issuers that will satisfy the new eligibility criteria will increase by approximately one-third. In addition, the SEC also extended certain aspects of its registration process to foreign companies. This action will enable eligible foreign companies to use one registration statement to register debt, equity, and other securities, without specifying in advance the amount of each class of securities to be offered. Consequently, foreign corporate treasurers will enjoy the same degree of financing flexibility as U.S. companies in meeting the short-term and long-term capital needs of their businesses.[47]

Observers credit various efforts by the International Accounting Standards Committee (IASC) and other organizations to pave the way for reconciliation of accounting differences among countries. The SEC's April 1994 ruling recognizing as authoritative the International Accounting Standard (IAS) pertaining to cash flow is regarded as an important event:

"Acceptance of International Standards is going to be the route both to international harmonization and mutual recognition."[48]

Indeed, CEPS endorses the possibility of the EU conforming with the standards developed by IASC. The International Organization of Securities' Supervisors (IOSCO) has commissioned the IASC to develop international standards (IASs) which would enable large corporations to use one set of consolidated financial statements to obtain a listing of their shares on any exchange. Discussions, though proceeding with difficulty, are still underway, with the main barrier being balancing the SEC's desire to retain U.S. accounting rules with the need for international harmonization.

COMPOSITION OF THE BOARD OF DIRECTORS

U.S. activist shareholders have, as a first line of attack, long been interested in various structural issues relating to the composition of the board, assuming that correcting any problems with structure would translate into better oversight and, ultimately, better corporate performance. Issues of most concern are: (1) whether the chairman should be separated from the CEO to make sure that a company's board is afforded the opportunity for appropriate oversight over management; and (2) the degree to which directors are "independent" of the corporation and can, therefore, be expected to act in the best interests of the corporation rather than their own.

Separating the Chairman from the CEO

According to The Conference Board, in the United States, the positions of chairman and CEO have long been combined in more than 75 percent of companies,[49] although the practice of separating the offices is almost universal in countries such as the United Kingdom and Australia. A 1995 survey conducted by the firm Korn/Ferry International found that 23 percent of the more than 1,000 companies surveyed have separated the positions, 10 percent were considering doing so, but 67 percent had not and were not intending to split the positions. Of those companies considering splitting the roles, a larger percent (13 percent) in retail and service companies were considering such a split, while a much smaller percent (6 percent) of directors in the largest $5 billion-and-over companies were considering this action.[50]

As the corporate governance debate has evolved through the various stages described in Chapter 3, shareholders have increasingly focused on *performance* rather than merely on *structure*. This has led to a somewhat more flexible general approach to the generic question of separating the roles of chairman and CEO on the part of some institutions. Some funds, such as TIAA-CREF and The State of Wisconsin Investment Board, have not therefore categorically insisted on such separations of power. Where performance is lagging, however, activists such as CalPERS will focus their shareholder voting and proxy efforts at their "Focus Ten" poorest performing companies to require that the positions be split "so that the Board is truly empowered to hold the CEO accountable."[51]

Within the past few years, a number of corporations as well as quasi-governmental institutions and advisory panels in the United States, the United Kingdom, Canada, and France, have issued corporate governance recommendations or guidelines focusing on the issue of separating the chairman and CEO positions and, if the positions are combined, on the possibility of boards electing a "lead director." One of the earliest of these groups, The Subcouncil on Corporate Governance and Financial Markets of the U.S. Competitiveness Policy Council, issued its report *The Will to Act* in December 1992. The Subcouncil found that boards of directors have become better organized and appear to be quicker to intervene in cases of poor corporate performance. It found that independent directors now dominate the membership of U.S. boards and key board committees. Audit committees of major companies are composed entirely of independent directors, and this is now the norm with compensation and nominating committees as well. CEO evaluation and selection is also performed by the independent directors. Finally, increasingly frequent announcements of restructurings, reorganizations, and replaced CEOs are encouraging signs that boards are asserting their independence and acting more decisively to deal with the issue of subpar performance. While noting that these are significant changes, and that wholesale change is clearly not merited, the Subcouncil found that improvements in the corporate governance process are still essential and accepted certain of the recommendations of two of its members—Martin Lipton and Jay Lorsche—who raised the issue of appointing a "lead director" to assist boards in their task of monitoring and evaluating corporate performance. The Subcouncil, therefore, recommended "a process for selecting, where appropriate and necessary, a director(s) with special leadership responsibilities."[52] It is not surprising that the General Motors Board of Directors' Guidelines (first issued in April 1994, then revised in July 1995) provide for complete flexibility in the separation of the roles, but it is interesting that they too endorse the selection of a "lead director" in the event that the chairman is an employee of the company:

The Board has adopted a policy that it have a Director selected by the outside Directors who will assume the responsibility of chairing the regularly scheduled meetings of outside Directors or other responsibilities which the outside Directors as a whole might designate from time to time. Currently, this role is filled by the non-executive Chairman of the Board. Should the Company be organized in such a way that the Chairman is an employee of the company, another Director would be selected for this responsibility.[53]

Both *The Will to Act* in the United States and *The Cadbury Report* in the United Kingdom were issued in December 1992. Unlike in the United States, but consistent with the common approach in the United Kingdom to separate the positions, *Cadbury* recommended separation of the posts and, in cases where the posts are combined, a "strong and independent element" most probably a "lead director:"

Given the importance and particular nature of the chairman's role, it should in principle be separate from that of the chief executive. If the two roles are combined in one person, it represents a considerable concentration of power. We recommend, therefore, that there should be a clearly accepted division of responsibilities at the head of a company, which will ensure a balance of power and authority, such that no one individual has unfettered powers of decision. When the chairman is also the chief executive, it is essential that there should be a strong and independent element on the board.[54]

In Canada, the December 1994 Toronto Stock Exchange Report is somewhat more moderate than *The Cadbury Report* in that it finds an "appropriate structure would be to (i) appoint a chair of the board who is not a member of management with responsibility to ensure the board discharges its responsibilities or (ii) adopt alternate means such as assigning this responsibility to a committee of the board or to a director, sometimes referred to as the "lead director."[55]

It is not surprising that the strength of the recommendation to separate the functions is strongest in the United Kingdom and Canada where the practice is more the norm than in the United States or in France, where the roles are most frequently combined. The *Vienot Report* notes that separating the positions was the rule in France prior to the Second World War and that "it was precisely because this led to difficulties that the present arrangement was adopted." The report notes that separation may well have its advantages where directors who are also exercising a management role represent a significant or even preponderant proportion of board membership. This is not the case in France, since not only does the law impose a ceiling on the number of *directeurs generaux* (executive directors) who are also board members, but this limit is rarely reached in practice. Moreover, flexibility should be the norm, since the chairman and the board together "assume responsibility for the success or failure of management as well as for the efficiency or shortcomings of supervision, and they must jointly adopt measures to satisfy shareholders on these points."[56]

The Independence of Directors

The whole thrust of recent governance developments in the United States, the United Kingdom, and Canada (and to a lesser extent in Continental Europe, but hardly at all in Japan) is to assure that there is a mechanism for *independent* oversight of management on behalf of shareholders by a "stewardship" group, such as the company's board of directors.

The practice of having a majority of directors be independent is well established in the United States. According to 1993 Conference Board survey in the United States:

- Sixty percent of corporations responding to the survey now have no directors who represent a major customer or a major supplier or who are related to, or have a significant business connection with, a member of the company's management.
- Outsiders comprise a majority of the board membership in 94 percent of the manufacturing and financial firms surveyed, and 93 percent of the membership in nonfinancial service companies.
- More than 60 percent of all companies have no more than two members of management on their board.

Table 4–1 shows the breakdown in the United States of the average number of directors in various industries, as well as the composition of inside versus outside directors. In 1995, U.S. boards continued to average 12 directors, the same total as in 1994 and in 1990. Box 4–2 summarizes independence of the board as viewed from various perspectives.

EVALUATING THE PERFORMANCE OF THE CEO AND THE BOARD

In 1991, *A New Compact for Owners and Directors,* drafted by a diverse group of corporate attorneys and institutional investors, recommended[57] performance evaluations for both CEO and the board itself:

For directors:

1. The board of directors should evaluate the performance of the chief executive officer regularly against established goals and strategies.

TABLE 4-1

Composition of U.S. Boards of Directors: 1995

Type and Size of Company	Average Number of Inside Directors	Average Number of Outside Directors	Average Number of Directors
Industrials			
$600 mil-$999 mil	3	7	10
$1 bil-$2.999 bil	3	8	11
$3 bil-$4.999 bil	2	9	11
$5 billion and over	3	10	13
Banks	3	14	17
Other financial institutions	3	9	12
Insurance companies	3	10	13
Retailers	3	8	11
Service companies	3	8	11
Average	3	9	12

Source: Korn/Ferry International, "22nd Annual Board of Directors Study," May 1995, p. 10.

2. This evaluation should be performed by "outside" directors.

3. All outside directors should meet alone, at least once a year, coordinated by a leader.

4. Directors should establish appropriate qualifications for board members and communicate those qualifications clearly to shareholders.

5. Outside directors should screen and recommend candidates based on qualifications established by the board.

For shareholders:

1. Institutional shareholders of public companies should see themselves as owners, not just investors.

2. Shareholders should not be involved in the conduct of the company's day-to-day operations.

3. Shareholders should evaluate the performance of directors regularly.

BOX 4–2

International Comparative Standards for Determining the Effectiveness of Boards of Directors

DEFINING INDEPENDENT DIRECTORS

National Association of Corporate Directors—A director is independent if he or she: (1) has never been an employee of the corporation or any of its subsidiaries; (2) is not a relative of any employee of the company; (3) provides no services to the company; (4) is not employed by any firm providing major services to the company; or (5) receives no compensation from the company, other than director fees.

General Motors Guidelines—Company has guidelines describing independent directors. It believes that all its directors meet these guidelines. Any question about independence is reviewed annually by the Committee on Director Affairs.

A former CEO can serve on the board, but will be considered an inside director for purposes of corporate governance.

Campbell Soup Company—All directors are independent except for one current Campbell executive. No former Campbell executives serve on its Board.

The Cadbury Report—A majority of nonexecutives on a board should be independent of the company. This means that, apart from their directors' fees and shareholdings, they should be independent of management and freed from any business or other relationship which could materially interfere with exercise of their independent judgment. It is for the board to decide in particular cases whether this definition is met. Information about the relevant interests of directors should be disclosed in the Directors' Report.

The Toronto Stock Exchange Report—The board of every corporation should be constituted with a majority of individuals who qualify as unrelated directors—free from any interest and any business or other relationship which could, or could reasonably be perceived to, materially interfere with the director's ability to act with a view to the best interests of the corporation.

The Vienot Report—Debate on the need for independent directors is largely irrelevant in France, given that French law limits the number of directors holding a contract of employment with a company to a third of board members and limits the number of executive directors on a board to five.

The appropriate balance between independent directors, shareholder directors, and executive directors varies from one company to another, although in general the last should in any case not be too numerous.

(continued)

International Comparative Standards—Continued

The Vienot Committee concludes that the boards of all listed companies should have at least two independent members, although it is up to each board to determine the most appropriate balance in its membership.

CROSS-SHAREHOLDERS AND INTERLOCKING BOARDS

Campbell Soup Company—There are no interlocking directorships, which would occur if a Campbell officer served on the Board of Company A while an officer of Company A served on the Campbell board, or when a Board member is a major supplier or customer of the company.

The Vienot Report—Favorable revisions in the French capital structure should raise companies' equity capital and diminish the prevalence of cross-shareholders—whose elimination as quickly as possible would appear highly desirable. Cross-shareholdings frequently, but not inevitably, result in reciprocal board membership. Companies should take care to avoid including an excessive number of such reciprocal directorships.

KEY COMMITTEE REQUIREMENTS

The New York Stock Exchange—Requires listed companies to have an audit committee composed entirely of independent board members.

The U.S. Securities and Exchange Commission—Requires the compensation committee of the board to be comprised entirely of independent directors.

General Motors Guidelines—There should be a majority of independent directors on the GM board. The board is willing to have members of Management, in addition to the CEO, as directors.

On all matters of corporate governance, the board assumes decisions will be made by the outside directors.

Campbell Soup Company—The audit, compensation, and organization and governance (nominating) committees consist entirely of independent directors.

(continued)

4. In evaluating the performance of directors, shareholders should be informed.

5. Shareholders should recognize and respect that the only goal common to all shareholders is the ongoing prosperity of the company.

International Comparative Standards—Concluded

CalPERS—All key committees such as the audit, compensation, and nominations committees should be comprised entirely of independent directors.

The Cadbury Report—Recommends that all listed companies establish an audit committee, with formal guidelines. There should be a minimum of three members confined to the nonexecutive directors of the company. Recommends boards appoint remuneration committees, consisting wholly or mainly of nonexecutive directors and chaired by a nonexecutive director. Membership in the committee should be disclosed in the Directors' Report. Nominating committees to review board appointments should have a majority of nonexecutive directors and be chaired by either the chairman or a nonexecutive director.

The Toronto Stock Exchange Report—Recommends that the audit committee of every corporation be composed only of outside directors. Every corporation should appoint a nominating committee of outside directors (a majority of whom are unrelated directors).

Committees of the board should generally be composed of outside directors, a majority of whom are unrelated directors.

The Vienot Report—The Committee advises boards against appointing directors to their remuneration or audit committees when these directors are reciprocal and represent another company where its own representatives are members of the equivalent committees.

The committee recommends that each board appoint an advisory audit committee to assess the reliability of procedures and examine major transactions which may have given rise to conflicts of interest. This committee should be able to meet, without the presence of corporate officers or executive directors. The audit committee should include at least three directors, to the exclusion of executive directors and employees and including at least one independent director.

Subsequent U.S. and international organizations and commissions discussed in this chapter have recommended specific procedures to improve board processes including:

- Size of the board.
- Number of committees.

- Assignment and rotation of committee members.
- Style of committee meetings (frequency, length, agenda).
- Board meeting structure (agenda, information flows, presentations, attendance of nondirectors, executive sessions of outside directors, and board access to senior management).
- Board membership criteria (selection and orientation of new candidates, term limits, retirement age).

The NACD's *Blue Ribbon Commission Report on Performance Evaluation of Chief Executive Officers, Boards, and Directors* discusses CEO performance evaluation, director selection, board evaluation, and director compensation (which will be discussed in Chapter 6 in this book). The NACD takes a different approach from some of the major commissions in that it avoids making extensive procedural recommendations in favor of a more generic approach to CEO and board evaluation on the theory that, if these evaluations are done properly, specifics like term and age limits as well as number and configuration of committees will take care of themselves. This viewpoint represents a major shift towards a performance oriented (rather than merely a structurally and procedurally oriented) view of the governance structure of the company.

CEO Performance Evaluation

The Korn/Ferry 1995 survey of directors finds that boards in U.S. companies are formally reviewing the performance of their CEOs to a much greater degree than critics of most corporate governance yet realize:

- 75 percent of companies report that their boards set clear objectives for evaluating the CEO.
- 67 percent say they have a formal process for evaluating the CEO annually.
- 20 percent report feedback to the CEO was given by the compensation committee or its chairman (65 percent), so it may be assumed that these evaluations are often part of the annual compensation review.
- 15 percent of these CEO evaluations involve the full board.
- 8 percent of these CEO evaluations involve the nominating committee or a special review committee.[58]

Korn/Ferry also reports that, among the companies that have a formal feedback session with the CEO, 77 percent say it is oral only while 23 percent say it is written as well as oral.[59]

The NACD provides guidelines for board evaluation of the CEO to be conducted in three stages: (1) defining the job, its roles, duties, and key responsibilities; (2) setting forth mutually agreeable performance objectives, measures, and standards; and (3) establishing an evaluation process. Performance objectives might include the following qualitative and quantitative performance factors which may be weighted differently in different situations: ability to meet corporate performance objectives including financial and operating performance goals in the short- and long-term; ability to meet strategic planning targets; providing integrity, vision, and leadership; and achieving succession planning with viable candidates acceptable to the board.[60] Suggested procedures in the evaluation process are described in Box 4–3.

A Conference Board 1993 survey reports that CEO evaluation has clearly been occurring (with or without formal procedures) as reflected by the fact that 9 percent of companies say the board as asked the CEO to resign or retire early.[61] A brief summary of some of these CEO firings is contained in Box 4–4.

Corporate Board Performance Evaluation

In its 1992 report *The Will to Act*, The Subcouncil on Corporate Governance and Financial Markets of the U.S. Competitiveness Policy Council recommended: "Boards should establish criteria and procedures for evaluating their own processes and performance, as well as the performance of the CEO. These criteria should be based on a clear understanding of the board's accountability to shareholders and, as appropriate, to various other constituents of the corporation."[62] At the time it was proposed, the recommendation was rather unusual, since only a small number of companies, notably Dayton Hudson, were known to perform board evaluations. By 1995, the process had become more widespread, with 26 percent of the 1995 Korn/Ferry survey companies responding that they evaluated the board's performance on a regular basis; this, however, left 74 percent of companies with no director evaluation process.

Institutional investors have stepped up their focus on the board, not only from a structural point of view (number of independent directors, committee structure, etc.) but from a performance point of view. As part of CalPERS' formal corporate governance program, it urges: "Periodic self-evaluation by the Board of its own procedures, practices and performance."[63]

There are several sensitive issues regarding board evaluation: (1) should it be done collectively or individually; (2) should it be performed

BOX 4–3

Key Elements in The National Association of Corporate Directors' CEO Evaluation Process

- The board appoints a designated independent director or directors to serve as leaders of the CEO evaluation process. In many cases, the designated director will be the nonexecutive chairman, or the chairman or a member of the governance committee, the compensation committee or a similar committee of independent directors.

- The CEO evaluates how he or she has performed in the current year (and perhaps in past years as well) against stated goals, including goals related to the annual plan and any longer-term strategic plan in effect for each of the years analyzed. This evaluation in most cases takes place annually and covers each performance objective and the major duties and responsibilities outlined in the CEO's job description.

- Following the CEO's self-assessment, the outside directors meet independently to discuss it.

- Outside directors then conduct their own evaluations, conveying them to the designated director for consolidation. Alternatively, a committee of directors may prepare a single, joint evaluation.

- The outside directors review and approve the consolidated evaluation.

- The designated director or directors meet privately with the CEO to discuss the consolidated evaluation.

- The CEO then meets with the outside directors to react to the evaluation and discuss appropriate next steps.

- Some companies use an experienced third-party facilitator to initiate the CEO evaluation process.

Source: National Association of Corporate Directors, "Report of the NACD Blue Ribbon Commission on Performance Evaluation of Chief Executive Officers, Boards, and Directors," Washington DC, 1994, p. 4.

orally or in writing; and (3) can any self-evaluation process be considered impartial if it is conducted by the very people who are being evaluated? A major Conference Board study[64] explores in detail these issues and notes that, for most companies, if the process has integrity, it will be viewed favorably.

At Campbell Soup Company, the board has established a Governance Committee which is charged with, among other things, determining the role and effectiveness of the Board and each committee in the company's governance process.

General Motors has embraced the notion of assessing the board's performance in its corporate governance guidelines, although it is clear that the assessment is to be done collectively—not individually.

> The Committee on Director Affairs is responsible to report annually to the Board an assessment of the Board's performance. This will be discussed with the full Board. This should be done following the end of each fiscal year and at the same time as the report on Board membership criteria.
>
> The assessment should be of the Board's contribution as a whole and specifically review areas in which the Board and/or the Management believes a better contribution could be made. Its purpose is to increase the effectiveness of the Board, not to target individual Board members.[65]

The NACD's Blue Ribbon Commission suggests three interrelated and highly synergistic criteria for board evaluation: (1) the CEO's performance; (2) company performance; and (3) board performance. Noting that the board functions as a group, the NACD nevertheless recommends that the evaluation process include some evaluation of individual performance. This evaluation:

> above and beyond the obvious concerns of attendance, preparation, and participation, is at least partially dependent on the objectives the board has set for itself. While the method used should be left to each individual company, clearly directors must be involved in this process of setting evaluation criteria. . . . This evaluation must be undertaken with great sensitivity, of course, focusing not on general personal attributes but rather on specific issues of performance, behavior, and contribution. For example, it is not very helpful to hear that a director is "ineffective." It is more helpful to learn that a director is unprepared at committee meetings and often leaves them early.
>
> Individual directors who do not appear to meet the performance criteria set by the board as a whole should be so informed and given ample opportunity and assistance to improve. Results from evaluation over time can be used to select the best candidates for renomination.[66]

The NACD also recommends that the director evaluation process begin with a meeting of the full board, perhaps followed by a meeting of the outside directors in executive session to discuss the structure and agenda of the board's self-evaluation. One director—or a small committee—could be assigned the principal responsibility. Each company should establish its

BOX 4–4

Boards Act to Evaluate (and Dismiss) CEOs

By the early 1990s, numbers of our largest corporations were obviously faltering. According to *Fortune,* IBM, GM, and Sears, which ranked numbers 1, 4, and 6, respectively, in a 1972 list of the world's 20 largest companies by stock market valuation, were no longer represented in the top 20 in 1992 and had lost a total of $32.4 billion in 1992, more than four times what the Gulf War cost the U.S. taxpayers. A dominant managerial system acting without true accountability is perceived by some to be partially to blame. . .

Today, boards—in general—are moving toward embracing their duty to act as guardians of the corporation and its shareholders, and not solely as passive supporters of management. In the past year [1992–1993], since the time when General Motors' high-quality board restructured itself and corporate management, events have moved at lightning speed—for the world of corporate governance.

In a two-week period in January [1993], boards of three other major U.S. corporations took significant action in their oversight role—acting to find and install corporate managers . . . who would become change agents . . .who could restore the global competitiveness our corporations require if they are to survive.. . . In those two weeks . . . Westinghouse's board modernized its bylaws in a variety of ways to empower itself to act and expose itself to easier removal if it didn't act. It then accepted the CEO's resignation and installed one of its own as nonexecutive chairman, while starting a search for [a more permanent] leader. At that corporate icon, IBM, the board first resisted stockholder pressure to remove a chairman/CEO who seemed unable suffi-

(continued)

own schedule for the frequency of review. Rather than adopt a list of principles—such as how many directors should be on a board and how many committees, and term and age limits—the NACD chose to shape the process of board evaluation by asking that boards address the key questions contained in Box 4–5.

SHAREHOLDER-BOARD RELATIONS

Probably no issue arouses more heated debate in the field of corporate governance than the issue of how much contact should exist, and for what purposes, between shareholders, managements, and boards of directors.

Boards Act—Concluded

ciently to change an age-old culture. Eventually, however, the board acted and installed one of its own as the leader in a search for the visionary change agent who would harness IBM's might and get it going again.

The most dramatic events happened at American Express. There, a very public discussion ensued about what the board should do with a chairman/CEO of whom the shareholders no longer approved, because corporate performance was not what they deemed appropriate. At first, it appeared that the chairman/CEO would remain in some important capacities. But then, according to press reports, a group of shareholders objected to a management structure that didn't clearly define who was to be the visionary change agent. This time, it wasn't the big public pension funds that stepped in and complained; rather it was such unlikely shareholder activists as J.P. Morgan Investment Management, Alliance Capital Management, Putnam Management, and other institutions who together represent about 20 percent of American Express' common stock. Allegedly, following a breakfast where their complaints were registered, the CEO/chairman resigned, a member of the board assumed the nonexecutive chairmanship of the board, and the board installed a new CEO.

Back at General Motors, the remolding of the board by the board continued. Former chairman and CEO Roger Smith resigned from the board, and three new directors were named . . .

Sources: Ira M. Millstein, "The State of Corporate Governance," presentation to The National Association of Corporate Directors, November 1, 1993, Washington DC , pp. 8–17; and Ira M. Millstein, "The Evolution of the Certifying Board," *The Business Lawyer*, 48, No. 4, August 1993, pp. 1,489–1,490.

The NACD report is actually quite revolutionary in its recommendation that, in some cases, especially in the case of underperforming companies, the board may want to enlist "the help of outside consultants, facilitators, industry analysts, or *knowledgeable shareholders*" (emphasis added).

A board may benefit from meeting with significant shareholders to discuss company performance or the board's role in monitoring that performance. In particular, shareholders may wish to discuss issues such as board structure, board composition, the nomination process (including possible candidates), and even the board evaluation process. Boards should establish a process for making the best use of shareholder perspectives. The board may wish to include in the proxy statement or annual report a description of the process

BOX 4–5

The Board Evaluation Process: Questions to Assist the Board in Assessing Its Role, Structure and Procedures

Director orientation and development. Is there agreement on director responsibilities? Are policies clearly articulated that define board eligibility criteria? Are new directors provided with adequate information about the company and the board? How does the board respond to directors who do not get satisfactory evaluations? Does it give useful, constructive comments? Does the evaluation process result in improved board performance?

Size and composition. Is the size of the board satisfactory? Do individual directors and does the board as a whole have the right mix of skills, experience, and other characteristics to be effective? Is the proportion of insider to outsider directors appropriate?

Information. Is the quality, quantity, and timing of information given to directors adequate? Are scheduled board meetings sufficiently frequent to allow directors to discuss the company's performance and the major issues that could affect its future? Is enough time devoted to reviewing strategic issues?

Teamwork. How well do members of the board work with each other? With the CEO? Do directors and the CEO work to create an open culture that encourages frank discussion? Do CEOs and directors recognize that evaluation is a two-way street?

Leadership. How effective is the board's leadership, both at the board and the committee level? How effective is each committee?

Individual contributions. Does the board have a process for evaluating each director's performance, behavior, and contribution to make sure he or she can perform satisfactorily? Is this process carried out on a regular basis? Are individual directors informed about the results of their performance reviews?

Effective board performance evaluation. Does this process result in improved performance for the board, its leadership, and its individual directors? Does it help boards overcome their weaknesses and build on their strengths?

Source: National Association of Corporate Directors, "Report of the NACD Blue Ribbon Commission on Performance Evaluation of Chief Executive Officers, Boards, and Directors," Washington DC, 1994, pp. 16–17.

and the name and address of a director designated to receive shareholder comments.[67]

In fact, since certain shareholders appear to be contacting not only managements but boards as well, structuring effective communications, including personal meetings with institutional investors, can rapidly become a critical issue to a company. The first step in a constructive communications process is for companies to understand with whom they are dealing.[68] Institutional investors generally have two types of people involved in communications with companies: personnel concerned with evaluating investments, and personnel concerned with evaluating corporate governance. On the investment decision-making side, many institutional investors who are actively managing their own portfolios function like Wall Street security analysts ("fundamental" analysts—so named because they are engaged in "basic" or "fundamental" research). These institutional investment personnel generally want to meet with the company's chief financial officer (as analysts do) and be involved in conference calls when senior management announces earnings results or significant events.

On the other hand, corporate governance personnel, frequently senior staff from the office of the pension fund's general counsel, are the primary people concerned with corporate governance issues. While they receive input from the investment personnel, they are the ones from the pension fund likely to write letters to and possibly request face-to-face meetings with not only senior management, but also the CEO, and perhaps outside or independent members of the board of directors as well.

Setting up face-to-face meetings among institutional investors and corporate management and/or board members raises a number of questions for both companies and shareholders. Speaking at the Kellogg Corporate Governance Conference on October 5, 1994 Michael A. Miles, former CEO of Philip Morris Companies, discussed the need for companies to develop specific policies to organize these special, high-level governance-related meetings with institutions. According to Miles, companies must address questions such as which shareholders the company should meet with and how it can avoid the charge of discrimination against small shareholders if it chooses to meet only with its largest institutional investors. Both corporations and institutions want to be careful to avoid transmitting "inside information"—the company because it needs to avoid improper disclosure and the institution because it does not want to be precluded from trading the company's stock.

Another important issue is at whose instigation the meeting should take place. Ceridian, for example, which was formed after a restructuring of Control Data, initiated what was reported to be a productive meeting with shareholders because it believed that institutional investors were not fully aware of some of the changes that were taking place following the restructuring. (The newly restructured company—from the prior Control Data— had lost over 90 percent of its shareholder value of the decade of the 1980s and accumulated a net operating loss carryforward of over a billion dollars.) Two months after the launch of Ceridian, a meeting was organized in 1992. The agenda was structured, and the parties—senior management, the company's board of directors, and a "dozen or so" representatives of institutions along with one person from an organization representing individual shareholders—met around a table in an collegial atmosphere. According to the company's Chairman and CEO Lawrence Perlman: "The purpose was to outline the strategy for this new company and to signal the priority we would give to building shareholder value, to listening to shareholders, and managing and governing the company in the interests of shareholders. . . ."[69]

In 1994, on the other hand, Philip Morris shareholders requested a meeting first with management and then with the company's outside directors, which did not go well. According to observers, after the company announced it was splitting off its tobacco units senior governance officials at six pension funds asked for a meeting with management, but their request was denied. Then the company announced there would be no split. The same six funds asked for another meeting—this time not only with management but with directors, including the independent directors. The long-awaited meeting took place on September 21, 1994 in Manhattan. Apparently the meeting was not structured as the institutions had expected, with independent directors (there was reportedly only one present). Moreover, expecting to be treated as "owners" and not "security analysts" the institutions were not pleased at what one referred to as "the teacher/student" setup in the room, obviously designed for analysts' presentations. About half of the pension fund representatives walked out of the meeting in protest, as did Sarah Teslik, Executive Director of the Council of Institutional Investors and the principal organizer of the meeting.

Many corporate executives experience a great deal of frustration in dealing with institutions. They have been used to meetings with securities analysts, which have, for decades, been the best vehicle for communicating with the investment community. However, according to a report by The Conference Board, a research organization which analyzes global business trends, some companies are adapting to a new communications environment and are beginning to understand the nuances of dealing with the various parts of the institutional investor community; they are very careful not to treat as analysts the senior corporate governance staff who think of themselves as owners of the companies in which they invest. In the report, a U.K. head of corporate development explains the difference in approach between dealing with institutional investors and dealing with the brokerage "sell-side" analysts:

> In short order we found that instead of dealing with a few industry analysts we had a much larger audience of current and potential shareholders with different informational requirements. The people from the brokerage houses were interested in share price volatility. The institutional analysts wanted to know about the prospective earning power of the industry, the assets of the business, and the quality of management and they would ask "Relative to the industry and the market is your share price underrated or overrated?" You cannot rely on intermediaries in responding to these kinds of inquiries because the relevant information includes discussions about the company's strategy and business plans.[70]

In considering the attendance list for company meetings with institutional shareholders, Miles recommends that corporate top management attend the meeting, regardless of whether the shareholders have requested the meeting involve the outside directors. This is primarily because top management may be able to answer questions that independent directors alone may not be able to. Shareholders, on the other hand, may not want top management to be present throughout the meeting; they may believe that the problem with the company stems from management and may wish to talk freely with the company's board of directors which, under state corporate law in the United States, appoints management. Most observers from the corporate and institutional investor communities agree, however, that the meetings should have a goal to achieve a reasonable outcome.

According to Korn/Ferry's 1995 board survey, 21 percent of companies report that institutional investors have formally contacted the board to discuss issues relating to corporate performance or governance. While only 6 percent of companies contacted said that institutional contacts made board deliberations less congenial, a number of positive impacts were reported from these institutional investor contacts: 19 percent said that the institutions increased the level of contribution by directors; 33 percent said that directors were more sensitive in evaluating CEO performance; and 36 percent said that directors were more sensitive in evaluating board performance.[71]

If the process of greater interaction is to work, it must have the kind of support it appears to receive from Ceridian's Chairman and CEO, Lawrence Perlman:

> Shareholder views on strategy and performance must be taken into account ... Many CEOs rightly complain about the short-term interests of institutional shareholders. Some people have even suggested minimum holding periods for voting rights. But the system doesn't distinguish between the two-month holder and the two-decade holder, so my advice to my fellow CEOs is get over it. Build and manage for the long-term creation of shareholder value, but remember that a successful long term is made up of a series of successful short terms.[72]

While it is certainty true that the "system" as a whole does not distinguish between short- and long-term holders, that fact may be less damaging for individual companies that are skilled not only in generating value but in communicating that fact to a stable, institutional shareholder base. The next chapter is intended to explore the types of marketing approaches managements can take to appeal to those shareholders for whom companies can build and manage long-term wealth.

ENDNOTES

1. "GM Board Guidelines on Significant Corporate Governance Issues," white paper which accompanied presentation, "Industry Leadership and the Responsibility of the Board of Directors," remarks by John G. Smale, Chairman, General Motors Corporation, at the Council of Institutional Investors, Washington D.C., April 15, 1994. These guidelines were subsequently updated on July 25, 1995. [Hereinafter cited as *GM Guidelines.*]
2. Campbell Soup Company, "Principles on Corporate Governance," attachment to *Notice of Annual Meeting of Shareholders,* October 6, 1995.
3. Robert A.G. Monks and Nell Minow, *Corporate Governance* (Cambridge, MA: Blackwell Business Publishers, 1995), p. 180.
4. Ira M. Millstein, "Distinguishing 'Ownership' and 'Control' in the 1990s," presentation at Institutional Shareholder Services Conference, Washington D.C., February 25, 1994, p. 8.
5. Ira M. Millstein, "The Professional Board," *The Business Lawyer,* 50, No. 4, August 1995, pp. 1,427–1,443.
6. The Working Group on Corporate Governance, "A New Compact for Owners and Directors," *Harvard Business Review,* July–August 1991, p. 141.

 7. National Association of Corporate Directors, "Report of the NACD Blue Ribbon Commission on Performance Evaluation of Chief Executive Officers, Boards, and Directors," Washington D.C., 1994, p. viii. [Hereinafter cited as *NACD CEO/Director Performance Report.*]

 8. TIAA-CREF, "Policy Statement on Corporate Governance," phamphlet, 1993, p. 2.

 9. Deloitte & Touche LLP, "CEO Viewpoints on Corporate Governance Issues," *Deloitte & Touche Review,* May 1, 1995, p. 1.

10. Millstein, "Distinguishing 'ownership' and 'control' in the 1990s," p. 5.

11. *NACD CEO/Director Performance Report,* p. viii.

12. The Committee on the Financial Aspects of Corporate Governance, *The Financial Aspects of Corporate Governance* (London: The Committee on the Financial Aspects of Corporate Governance and Gee and Co. Ltd., December 1, 1992). [Hereinafter cited as *The Cadbury Report.*]

13. *The Cadbury Report,* p. 48.

14. Conseil National du Patronat Francais and Association Francaise des Entreprises Privees, *The Boards of Directors of Listed Companies in France,* July 10, 1995.(translated edition) [Hereinafter cited as *The Vienot Report.*]

15. *The Vienot Report,* p. 5.

16. Jonathan P. Charkham, *Keeping Good Company: A Study of Corporate Governance in Five Countries* (Oxford: Clarendon Press, 1994), p. 116.

17. Ibid.

18. Centre for European Policy Studies (CEPS) Working Party, "Corporate Governance in Europe," CEPS Working Party Report No. 12, pp. 29–30. [Hereinafter cited as *CEPS.*]

19. Richard C. Breeden, "Foreign Companies and U.S. Securities Markets in a Time of Economic Transformation," *Fordham International Law Review* 17 (1994), pp. 79–80.

20. David Fairlamb, "The American Imperative," *Institutional Investor,* July 1994, p. 186.

21. For a more extensive discussion see Carolyn Kay Brancato, *Getting Listed on Wall Street: The Irwin Guide to Financial Reporting Standards in the U.S.* (Burr Ridge, IL: Irwin Professional Publishing, 1996).

22. *CEPS,* p. 37.

23. Roberta S. Karmel, "Living with U.S. Regulations: Complying with the Rules and Avoiding Litigation," *Fordham International Law Journal* 17 (1994), pp. 153–154.

24. Millstein, "Distinguishing 'ownership' and 'control' in the 1990s," p. 17.

25. Ibid., p. 19. See also Ira M. Millstein, "The Evolution of the Certifying Board," *The Business Lawyer*, 48, No. 4, August 1993, pp. 1,485–1,497.

26. See Jeremy Bacon, "Corporate Boards and Corporate Governance," The Conference Board, Report No. 1036, 1993.

27. See Ronald E. Berenbeim, "The Corporate Board: A Growing Role in Strategic Assessment," The Conference Board, Report 1152-96-RR.

28. See Jon J. Masters, "Limiting Director Liability Exposure in Strategic Matters," Appendix to Ronald E. Berenbeim, "The Corporate Board: A Growing Role in Strategic Assessment," The Conference Board, Report 1152-96-RR. Masters cites *Paramount Communications, Inc.* v. *Time Inc.,* 571 A.2d 1140, 1153-4 (Del. 1990).

29. *The Will to Act,* p. 13.

30. *The Cadbury Report,* pp. 41–42.

31. Toronto Stock Exchange Committee on Corporate Governance in Canada, "'Where Were the Directors?' Guidelines for Improved Corporate Governance in Canada," December 1994, p. 4. [Hereinafter cited as *The Toronto Stock Exchange Report.*]

32. *The Vienot Report,* p. 8.

33. California Public Employees' Retirement System, "CALPERS Announces Top Ten Worst Companies," News Release, February 6, 1996, p. 3.

34. Berenbeim, pp. 3–4.

35. *The Cadbury Report,* p. 41.

36. *The Cadbury Report,* p. 12.

37. *The Toronto Stock Exchange Report.*

38. See Bacon.

39. *The Cadbury Report,* p. 27.

40. *The Vienot Report,* p. 19.

41. Charkham, pp. 92–93.

42. *CEPS,* p. 44.

43. Breeden, p. 91.

44. *CEPS,* p. 42.

45. A number of financial reporting statements have been streamlined. For example, a "landmark step" allows foreign companies to submit, without supplement, modification, or reconciliations, a cash flow statement prepared in accordance with International Accounting Standard IAS No. 7. This is a step back from the SEC's previous hard stance, which required five-year reconciliation statements under Generally Accepted Accounting Principles (U.S. GAAP).

46. The SEC reduced the public float threshold from $300 million to $75 million and cut the required reporting history from 36 months to 12 months.

This should reduce both the paperwork required to be filed with the SEC and the time taken by the agency to review it.

47. Kevin D. Cramer and Catherine M. Stavrakis, "SEC Simplifies Foreign Companies' Access to U.S. Markets," *International Securities Regulation Report,* Buraff Publications, May 3, 1994, pp. 50–54.

48. Karmel, p. 153.

49. The Conference Board's 1993 survey found 76 percent of board chairmen are also the company chief executive, as was the case with the earlier 1972 Conference Board survey. See Bacon.

50. Korn/Ferry International, "22nd Annual Board of Directors Study," 1995, p. 20.

51. California Public Employees' Retirement System, p. 2.

52. *The Will to Act,* p. 13.

53. *GM Guidelines,* p. 2.

54. *The Cadbury Report,* p. 21.

55. *The Toronto Stock Exchange Report,* p. 5.

56. *The Vienot Report,* p. 9.

57. The Working Group on Corporate Governance, pp. 141–3.

58. Korn/Ferry, p. 5.

59. Ibid., p. 23.

60. See Ronald E. Berenbeim, "Corporate Boards: CEO Selection, Evaluation and Succession," The Conference Board, Report No. 1103-95-RR, 1995.

61. Bacon, p. 5.

62. *The Will to Act,* p. 13.

63. James E. Burton, Kayla J. Gillan, Sheryl K. Pressler, and Richard H. Koppes, California Public Employees' Retirement System, Memorandum to Members of the Investment Committee, Subject: Corporate Governance Program, August 14, 1995, Agenda Item 11, p. 11.49.

64. See Ronald E. Berenbeim, "Corporate Boards: Improving and Evaluating Performance," The Conference Board, Report No. 1081-94-RR, 1994.

65. *GM Guidelines,* p. 4.

66. *NACD CEO/Director Performance Report,* p.14.

67. Ibid., p. 15.

68. Brancato, pp. 177–182.

69. Lawrence Perlman,"Corporate Governance: A Postmodernist View," *ISSUE ALERT,* Institutional Shareholder Services, Inc., Novebmer 1995, X, No. 1, p. 3.

70. Ronald E. Berenbeim, "Company Relations with Institutional Investors," The Conference Board, Report No. 1070-94-RR, 1994, p. 25.

71. Korn/Ferry, p. 26.
72. Perlman, p. 14.

III

HOW COMPANIES CAN ATTRACT THE INVESTORS THEY WANT

CHAPTER

5

MARKETING YOUR STOCK TO YOUR INVESTORS

As long as corporate executives believe securities markets to be efficient—in the traditional sense that markets are thought to incorporate all available information and appropriately price stock—they will ignore an important new development, *shareholder marketing,* or *targeting* the most desirable shareholders to have in a corporation's ownership base. John Wilcox, Chairman of a Wall Street firm that helps companies realize their full market valuation, says:

> The efficient market hypothesis has long provided corporate managers with an easy excuse to ignore problems relating to investors and the securities markets. Managers were allowed to feel that they could focus solely on business strategy and the market would take care of itself and grant them a fair value. This is not the case. The markets are now driven by many non-fundamental strategies and other forms of tail-chasing that often do not reward companies with the price multiple they deserve. It is the responsibility of corporate managers and directors to fight for the highest appropriate multiple.[1]

While an individual corporation may have no control over the frightening gyrations of the stock market, Wilcox contends that companies can

177

improve how their own individual stock is viewed by the markets if they manage and take steps to improve their stock ownership base. This chapter investigates the evidence on this issue. It dissects the investing public in a number of ways to assist corporations in their efforts to market their stock to the *right kinds of investors*. Ideally, if this strategy is successful, it will reduce the amount of stock in the hands of the *wrong kinds of investors*. If management has a strong, credible business and strategic plan, evidence presented here shows it is possible to attract investors who will better match management's expectations for future growth and accord it a valuation more consistent with its plans to generate sustained shareholder wealth. This can mean higher price-to-earnings multiples, which will bolster the corporation's sustained support for its stock price valuation and, all others things equal, provide it with a lower cost of capital.

As the discussion on relationship investing in Chapter 1 pointed out, certain investors as opposed to traders have been changing their behavior, even with regard to a takeover bid (e.g., for Chrysler), which would formerly have generated a "herd effect" to tender stock and effect a change in corporate control. Rather than being intimidated by the vicissitudes of stock market forces, it is now up to the corporation to analyze and then attempt to alter its stock ownership base to target those investors likely to remain loyal through temporary blips in their earnings. This strategy is similar to one which has long been employed by marketing managers to sell new products to special groups of customers. Shareholders are, in an important but not often realized sense, simply another breed of the corporation's customers. This chapter shows corporations how they can decide which investors are right for them and how to attract them.

WHAT IS A DESIRABLE SHAREHOLDER BASE?

The financial press is replete with descriptions of various types of investors and their approaches to participating in stock markets. In Chapter 1, the general categories of institutional investors were described, including corporate and public pension funds, insurance companies, investment managers, and bank trusts. As noted earlier, a large portion of the equities under the control of each type of investor is, however, managed by another type of investor. Thus, money shifts from a pension fund to a money manager or a bank, which actually makes the investment decisions, although they may well be operating under the guidelines established by the prime fiduciary. Latest data (see Chapter 1) show that pension funds held a total of $4.4 trillion in 1994 assets, but they allocated $2.53 trillion (56.4 percent of all their assets) to other managers, including insurance companies ($811 billion), banks ($933 billion), and investment advisers ($787 billion). This means that pension funds managed only 42.6 percent of their own assets in 1994, down slightly from 44 percent in 1993.[2] Overall, pension funds "held" 47.4 percent of 1994 institutional investor assets, but actually "managed" only 20.2 percent of them. Therefore, any analysis of a corporation's shareholder ownership base should incorporate an understanding of the investment style and the buy-and-sell behavior undertaken by the "hands-on" managers, regardless of who the primary fiduciary institution is. This section first discusses current investment styles, then turns to a specific analysis of varying segments of the portfolios of the institutional managers who have this "hands-on" authority to buy and sell stock.

Investment Styles

Everyone has a theory about how to invest in the stock market. The most prominent and currently fashionable strategies are described below.[3] Some of the terminology used on Wall Street has been changed, however, from its common parlance to better fit the redefinitions along the spectrum of investors versus traders discussed in Chapter 1 of this book. Investing styles which can be used alone or in various combinations include:

- Passive investors who index their stock.
- Quantitative traders (not quantitative investors).
- Top-down investors.
- Bottom-up investors.
- Momentum traders (not momentum investors).
- Growth investors.
- Value investors.

Passive investors invest in a basket of stocks, although they may tailor their definition of this basket to focus on certain sectors (e.g., an index of technology stocks) or regions (e.g., an index of Asian stocks). Quantitative traders ("quants") look at market activity and things other than a company's in-depth fundamentals, although they may run screens of one kind or another which include elements of a company's fundamentals. They may also focus on trends in price performance and/or employ technical analysis and/or program trading to assist their analysis.

Top-down investors tend to react to general events in the economy as a whole, then decide what industries (and companies) will be in favor. Bottom-up investors will look for companies with particular fundamental characteristics, especially management characteristics. Growth investors usually follow a bottom up approach to uncovering growth opportunities.

Momentum traders focus primarily on trends in, or the *momentum* of, earnings estimates made by Wall Street analysts. For example, assume a stock price is going up based on a favorable consensus of analysts' earnings projections, then the company announces there has been a strike, which the company says will result in a drop in this quarter's earnings. Analysts will cut their earnings estimates, causing a rapid sell off which drags down the price. When the situation improves, these same momentum traders quickly move back into the stock, and the stock price rises. This can result in the "roller coaster" effect shown in Figure 5–1. In December 1992, company XYZ has only approximately 3 percent of its shareholder base held by momentum investors. This rises to 18 percent in the next six months as their buying pushes up the stock price. Around September 1993, the company reports weaker than expected earnings, causing expectations of a possible earnings decline (even if only a small amount or a few cents a share). The momentum traders dump their stock, and the percentage of momentum traders in the company's ownership base declines to 7 percent—resulting in a sharp price drop. Shortly thereafter, a positive announcement is made and momentum traders flood back into the company, raising their owner-ship share to 16 percent and pushing the stock price back up. But, according to Richard Wines, senior managing director of Georgeson, this influx of momentum traders is "dynamite in a company's shareholder base," just waiting to be "detonated" by the least disappointment in expected earnings. This produces a volatile situation for a company because momentum in the sense used in the markets cannot continue forever. This situation has a further potential negative fallout, as some criticize executives for "manag-ing" their earnings flows to avoid being subject to the price swings gener-ated by the momentum traders—a particular problem for engendering investor confidence in international companies whose accounting standards vary, as discussed in Chapter 4.

Momentum traders should, however, be distinguished from the ana-lysts upon whose recommendations they base their buy-and-sell activity. Making this distinction should clear up part of the confusion about short-termism in the markets discussed in Chapter 1. Many Wall Street analysts use fundamental techniques of in-depth analysis and frequently know

FIGURE 5-1

Momentum Traders and Share Price Changes

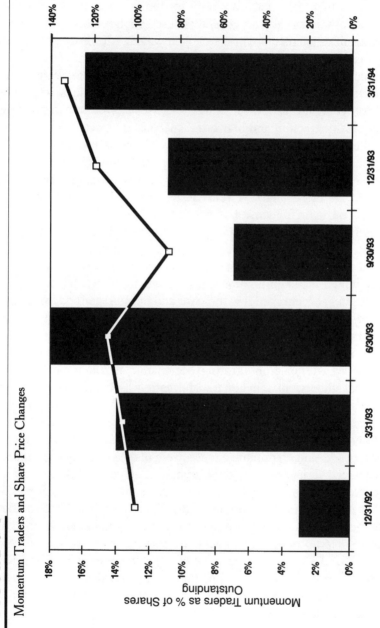

Source: Georgeson & Company Inc.

companies extremely well. They tend to make their earnings projections based on considerable, company-specific knowledge, and they may discount future trends and events they believe will have an impact on their estimates—which they make not only for the next quarter's results, but farther out into the future and, generally, based on the company's ability to generate a sustained increase in shareholder wealth. Momentum traders are acting, in essence, as derivatives of this fundamental analyst activity, since their rapid buy-and-sell strategy depends on uncovering variations in analysts' estimates and capturing swift movements in the markets, which they themselves generate in a self-fulfilling cycle. Most corporate executives fail to make this distinction and blame the analysts for stock price gyrations they, quite rightly, believe have no bearing on the company's fundamentals or its potential to generate future returns to shareholders.

This attitude does not properly reflect the fact that the role of Wall Street analysts has changed. Twenty years ago, the practice of analyzing companies on their fundamentals was a time-honored tradition and predominately favored as an investment strategy. The largest blocks of stock were placed by individuals in accounts with Wall Street investment firms or by "retail" individuals in brokerage accounts or mutual funds. Tax policies, which included high marginal income tax rates and low capital gains tax rates, encouraged low turnover and holding periods for stock of the tax-motivated "year and a day"—the length of holding which triggered the lower capital gains rate. Since the 1974 passage of ERISA, vast sums of institutional investor assets have come under management by pension funds who are exempt from taxation. Meanwhile, during the early 1970s, Wall Street underwent a major transformation as fixed brokerage fees, established for decades, were allowed to fluctuate. This ushered in a host of discount houses and resulted in consolidations on Wall Street which drastically reduced the number and influence of fundamental securities analysts. In addition, the simultaneous advent of the computer permitted an unprecedented variety of quantitative trading strategies. Institutions clearly now move stock prices and Wines estimates that the 100 largest are probably predominant in determining the valuation of the entire marketplace. These events have conspired to reduce the fundamental analysts' influence (in terms of actual number of trades if not necessarily in terms of knowledge of the companies they follow) and increase the market effects of participants such as momentum traders. Distinguishing between the relative contributions of these players in the markets is necessary to fully appreciate how important changes in ownership can be.

FIGURE 5–2

Percentage of Momentum Traders Within Each Type of Manager*

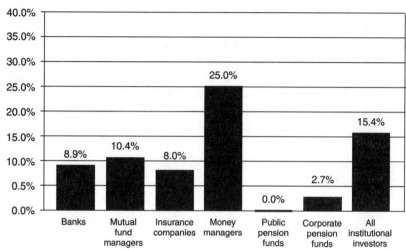

*Weighted by portfolio value.
Source: Georgeson & Company Inc.

As shown in Figure 5–2, momentum traders are more typical of some institutional money managers than others. Georgeson's analysis of the predominant portion of the U.S. universe of approximately 1,500 institutions shows that money managers use momentum trading to the greatest extent, with 25 percent of their trading activity devoted to momentum trading. In the mutual fund sector it is 10.4 percent, and for banks it is 8.9 percent. Corporate pension funds employ this strategy for only 2.7 percent of their trading, while public pension funds (which are largely indexed) practice no discernible momentum trading. Wines estimates that, weighted by portfolio value, approximately 15.4 percent of institutional trading activity is momentum trading. It is this special breed of trader—not the analyst or institutional investor community at large—that poses the greatest problem for the growth-oriented corporation.

A final distinction should be made on the subject of investment styles. To grow, a company obviously must balance its need to pay dividends and to plow back earnings into future growth prospects. While Warren Buffett's strategy (see Chapter 1) is focused entirely on growth, and Berkshire

Hathaway pays no dividends, this is a rare and somewhat purist approach. Generally, investors expect some combination of current payout and the potential for future shareholder returns (a combination of share price appreciation and dividend reinvestment). Growth investors tend to be content with companies who retain earnings to plow them back to generate future returns. Companies with a strategy to build sustained shareholder growth want to aggressively shift their shareholder base away from quantitative traders, program traders, top-down investors, momentum traders, and other "value" investors, and primarily towards "growth" investors (and to some extent, depending on the circumstances, bottom-up investors as well). Figure 5–3 is based on Georgeson's analysis of a number of major companies and shows that companies' stock prices frequently improve when the composition of their shareholder bases shifts from value to growth investors.

INSTITUTIONAL PORTFOLIO INVESTMENTS AND TURNOVER

Further information useful to corporations in their efforts to market their stock is obtained by analyzing the components of institutional investor portfolios, since a single institutional investor is likely to invest money in a number of different styles. Data on equity holdings by all investment entities which control over $100 million or more are contained in Form 13F, which must be filed with the U.S. Securities and Exchange Commission (SEC). These filings list the "ultimate managers" of equity managed by an investment manager or on behalf of another type of fiduciary, such as a pension fund. The Georgeson database of these filings reveals how the portfolios of each type of investment entity break down into specific investment components according to the strategies outlined in Box 5–1.

Table 5–1 details the equity allocation to various investment strategies for institutional investors who manage their own investments. It shows significant variation within the components of the total portfolios of the major categories of institutional investors. Data are based on the 13F filings described above, with supplementary surveys of other "poolings" of investments. As of September 30, 1995 detailed portfolio analysis is available for an estimated $3.2 trillion in equities, representing approximately 90 percent of total institutional investor equity holdings. Money managers have the largest share of equities under management, with $1.2 trillion or 39.5 percent of all equities (see Table 5–2). Banks manage the next largest quantity, $856 billion or 27.1 percent of the total. Mutual fund managers

FIGURE 5-3

Change in Shareholder Base from Value to Growth Investors

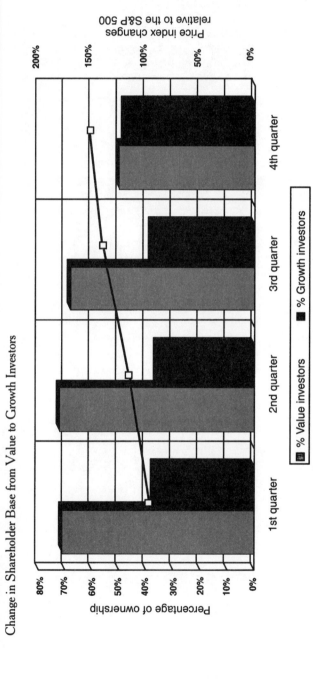

Source: Georgeson & Company Inc.

185

BOX 5–1

Institutional Investment Strategies

Aggressive Growth. Emphasis on projected three- to five-year earnings per share (EPS) growth potential, rather than historic or current EPS growth rates. Portfolios tend to have high tolerance for risk and be concentrated in biotech, technology, or emerging companies.

Growth. Somewhat more risk averse than aggressive growth. Prepared to accept lower growth potential. More emphasis on historical performance above market growth rates, including historic profitability measures, such as return on equity, and gross margins.

Growth at a reasonable price (GARP). Investment in stocks that offer above market sustainable growth at market or lower P/E multiples. Companies more likely to have healthy balance sheets, strong cash flows, strong franchises and to have demonstrated consistent growth in operating income.

Balanced. Investment style may include both top-down and bottom-up methods to uncover companies trading at below a fair market or appraised value. Portfolio elements may be combined to resemble a market portfolio.

Classic-value. Pursues the Graham-Dodd (authors of a classic textbook on the subject of security analysis) low relative price earnings ratio, price to book, or ratio of market value to appraised intrinsic value. Stocks generally trade at a substantial discount to market averages or multiples and are generally sold when they are no longer trading at an appropriate discount.

Value-income. Value-based, but emphasis on dividend payout capability and higher yields than the market. Yield hurdles generally imposed. Purchase of stocks with price earnings ratios less than the market but which offer higher-than-market yields.

Income. Primary focus on current dividend streams paid out. Concentrates on more mature companies with solid balance sheets and proven history of uninterrupted dividend payout. Strict yield hurdles.

Indexed. Invested in leading stock indexes, such as the Standard and Poor's 500.

Source: Georgeson & Company, Inc.

TABLE 5-1

Investment under Management by Institutions: Equity Allocation to Varying Investment Strategies During 1995

($ millions)

	Aggressive Growth	Growth	GARP	Balanced*	Classic Value	Value/ Income	Income	Indexed Only	Total
Corporate pensions	1,382	43,281	12,123	2,705	2,890	9,755	630	11,074	83,840
Public pension funds	neg.	16,174	1,009	31,652	27,669	1,392	neg.	156,489	234,385
Mutual fund managers	98,424	71,297	214,799	2,387	12,142	96,893	27,399	neg.	523,341
Money managers	144,120	323,003	216,677	58,345	220,607	232,022	39,302	12,336	1,246,412
Insurance companies	18,655	113,870	35,130	5,101	24,907	4,242	1,861	8,956	212,722
Banks	9,078	146,263	6,257	150,752	77,094	172,985	11,796	281,394	855,619
Total	271,659	713,888	485,995	250,942	365,309	517,289	80,988	470,249	3,156,319**

Notes:

Data calculated for year ended September 30, 1995.

All data weighted by value of portfolio devoted to each investment strategy.

* Balanced encompasses a variety of investment strategies and may include some indexed investments.

**Detailed portfolio analysis covers approximately 90% of total institutional investor holdings.

Source: *The Brancato Report on Institutional Investment*, 3, ed. 2 (May 1996). Calculated using the Georgeson & Company Inc. database.

TABLE 5-2

Investment Under Management by Institutions: Percentage of Equity Portfolio Allocated to Varying Investment Strategies During 1995

	Aggressive Growth	Growth	GARP	Balanced*	Classic Value	Value/ Income	Income	Indexed Only	Total
Corporate pensions	1.6%	51.6%	14.5%	3.2%	3.4%	11.6%	0.8%	13.2%	2.7%
Public pension funds	neg.	6.9	0.4	13.5	11.8	0.6	neg.	66.8	7.4
Mutual fund managers	18.8	13.6	41.0	0.5	2.3	18.5	5.2	neg.	16.6
Money managers	11.6	25.9	17.4	4.7	17.7	18.6	3.2	1.0	39.5
Insurance companies	8.8	53.5	16.5	2.4	11.7	2.0	0.9	4.2	6.7
Banks	1.1	17.1	0.7	17.6	9.0	20.2	1.4	32.9	27.1
Total	8.6%	22.6%	15.4%	8.0%	11.6%	16.4%	2.6%	14.9%	100.0%

Notes:

Data is calculated for year ended September 30, 1995.

* Balanced encompasses a variety of investment strategies including some indexed investments.

Source: *The Brancato Report on Institutional Investment*, 3, ed. 2 (May 1996). Calculated using the Georgeson & Company Inc. database.

control investments of $523 billion or 16.6 percent of the total. Insurance companies invest relatively little in equities compared to debt, but they tend to manage most of their own money—they accounted for only $213 billion or 6.7 percent of all equities. Public pension funds, with their large, internally managed indexed portfolios, managed $234 billion or 7.4 percent of the total. Finally, corporate pension funds, which tend to place investments with bank custodians or external managers, manage internally only $84 billion or 2.7 percent of total equities.

Of perhaps even more interest to the corporation's analysis of how to improve its shareholder ownership base is the diversification of portfolio investments among the strategies outlined in Box 5–1. Money managers concentrate their investments in growth (25.9 percent of their holdings are placed with this strategy in mind), followed by value/income (18.6 percent). They place 11.6 percent of their portfolios in aggressive growth investments (which are accompanied by the highest turnover of any of the strategies). Data in Table 5–3 show annual turnover at an extremely high 88 percent for the stocks in the aggressive growth part of the portfolios of money managers. Mutual fund managers turn over the percent of their portfolios devoted to aggressive growth stocks less than half that turnover amount—39 percent.

As would be expected, turnover of indexed money is the lowest—compared to an average turnover of 42.6 percent for all institutions managing their own money, average portfolio money devoted to indexation turned over only 11.4 percent. At this turnover rate, it would take nearly 10 years to trade the stocks in these indexed portfolios, compared to having nearly all the portfolio trading every year (an average turnover of 88 percent) for money manager investments categorized as aggressive growth.

Turnover, however, is not always detrimental because it provides market liquidity. But there appears to be an important relationship, which is not only intuitive but statistically demonstrable, between turnover and the movement of stock price relative to how the overall market moves. This relationship is referred to as a stock's beta (or its *market risk*). This is the difference between how the price of an individual stock behaves and how the market as a whole (measured by some general index such as the S&P 500) behaves. A stock with a beta of 1 would move exactly as the market moves (a proposition which passive indexers depend on). A stock with a beta over 1 is "riskier" in the sense that it fluctuates more than the overall market; conversely a stock with a beta under 1 is "less risky" in the sense that it fluctuates less than the overall market. Figures 5–4 and 5–5 show the

TABLE 5-3

Investment Under Management by Institutions: Turnover by Investment Strategy During 1995

	Aggressive Growth	Growth	GARP	Balanced*	Classic Value	Value/ Income	Income	Indexed Only	Total
Corporate pensions	N/A	13.7%	53.7%	48.0%	28.4%	25.9%	12.6%	17.3%	24.8%
Public pension funds	neg.	75.0	12.3	24.9	37.9	16.1	neg.	11.3	20.7
Mutual fund managers	39.0	62.1	42.5	25.2	69.3	27.3	43.7	neg.	42.3
Money managers	88.0	60.8	56.3	48.0	60.8	44.6	54.4	42.6	59.2
Insurance companies	54.4	44.1	44.1	52.7	58.5	44.3	35.9	34.9	46.4
Banks	19.9	37.4	38.1	35.3	31.5	28.8	37.8	9.1	25.3
Overall average	65.8%	50.9%	49.0%	37.4%	52.7%	35.6%	47.6%	11.4%	42.6%

Notes:

Data calculated for year ended September 30, 1995.   N/A = not available

All data weighted by value of portfolio devoted to each investment strategy.

* Balanced encompasses a variety of investment strategies and may include some indexed investments.

Source: *The Brancato Report on Institutional Investment*, 3, ed. 2 (May 1996). Calculated using the Georgeson & Company Inc. database.

F I G U R E 5–4

High-Turnover Institutions versus Beta

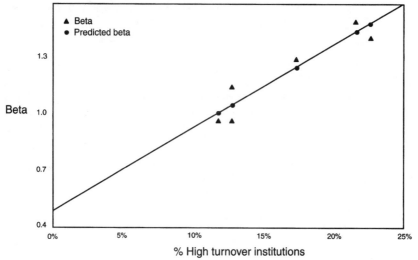

Source: Georgeson & Company Inc.

F I G U R E 5–5

Low-Turnover Institutions versus Beta

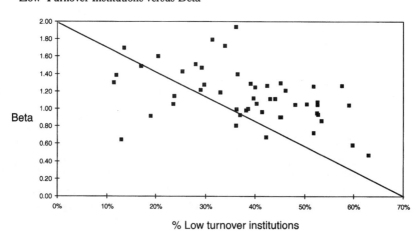

Source: Georgeson & Company Inc.

relationship between high- and low-turnover institutional ownership and beta for a Georgeson sample of companies in a single industry or peer group. There is a clear correlation between ownership by high-turnover institutions and higher betas as well as between ownership by low-turnover institutions and lower betas. Companies have come to live with near-term swings and fluctuations in their stock price, and, as discussed in Chapter 1, they say they do not significantly alter future plans because of these near-term swings—they "ride them out." However, it is clear that reducing the degree to which a stock price fluctuates provides the company with a more stable and predictable basis for planning its strategy and compensating its executives (to be discussed in Chapter 6). Clearly, minimizing price fluctuations is desirable for companies. This is why growth-oriented companies will want to move their shareholder ownership base to lower turnover, higher growth institutional investors.

HOW TO CHANGE A CORPORATION'S OWNERSHIP BASE

A company should take the following steps to improve its shareholder ownership base:

- Analyze the current shareholder profile to get as far as possible behind holders of record to determine who is making the ultimate investment decision.
- Investigate the shareholder base of the company's peer group, by type of investor and by region or other important factor.
- Target those shareholders a company believes will be most beneficial to it in terms of sharing its goals and expectations, e.g., a growing company that can attract more growth-oriented investment managers will almost certainly see its valuation increase.
- Formulate an effective strategic message to communicate to shareholders, which will convince them the company can achieve its growth objectives.
- Devise methods to contact and communicate with the desired shareholders in the same highly organized manner as a company might design and undertake a major marketing effort for a new product.
- Measure the success of the targeting effort by tracking those investors who have the "buying capacity" as against the current ownership base to determine how the base is changing.

- Track changes (hopefully increases) in stock price valuation, accompanied by higher price-to-earnings multiples, as desired investors with lower turnover and more stability replace traders.
- Track reductions in cost of capital as stock price stabilizes and, ideally, stock valuation increases.

The case of Digital Equipment illustrates positive and, according to Georgeson, typical results. In December 1994, the stock price was in the $35 per share range, and the company was in the process of what it hoped would be a turnaround. Its share ownership base was analyzed and found to have a high proportion of "quants" and other high-turnover owners. A detailed analysis was then conducted to come up with a list of owners who would have lower turnover characteristics and would be oriented to better match the company's fundamental strategic plans. These buyers were organized and rated (top 10, next 15, next 25) according to a range of factors, including their investment strategies, inclination to purchase Digital's stocks, fundamental and price-to-earnings profile, and so on—those institutions that could do the most for Digital in supporting sustained valuation and stability. The plan was to alter the company's ownership base by convincing the targeted institutions to do more buying than selling; similarly, the nontargeted institutions would ideally do more selling than buying.

The results of Digital's efforts during 1995 are shown in Figure 5–6. Overall, targeted institutions were buyers of 21 million shares, but sold only 7 million. By contrast, nontargeted institutions were buyers of only 3 million shares but sellers of approximately 7 million shares. Ownership composition was moving in the desired direction. In the process, total institutional ownership was also increasing; however, it was considered more important to have the right kind of institutions buying the stock than whether total institutional ownership increased.

The key measure of success of Digital's effort is shown in Figure 5–7, which tracks the strong upward movement in its stock price from the $30 to $35 range in the beginning of 1995 to the $60 to $65 range by the end of the year—an average gain of approximately 88 percent. This stock price gain must be seen primarily as the result of market response to improved conditions at the company, as well as expectations that these improvements would continue. Shareholder targeting can play an important role in helping to reinforce positive fundamentals to ensure not only fair valuation in the stock price but also reduced volatility. Subsequent movements in the price of the stock will also be determined by a combination of fundamentals and

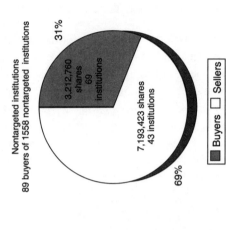
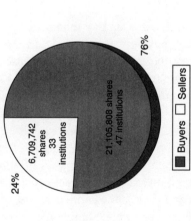

FIGURE 5-6

Digital Equipment—Institutional Targeting During 1995

Target Rank	# of Buyers	# of Sellers	Positions Unchanged
Top ten (1–10)	4	0	6
Next fifteen (11–25)	9	3	3
Next twenty five (26–50)	5	5	15
Next fifty (51–100)	13	10	27
Next one hundred (101–200)	16	15	69
Additional Targets (19)	5	4	10
Total	**47**	**33**	**120**

	Shares Bought	Shares Sold
Top ten (1–10)	1,821,371	0
Next fifteen (11–25)	7,224,298	(939,499)
Next twenty five (26–50)	1,039,902	(1,702,737)
Next fifty (51–100)	6,766,523	(941,533)
Next one hundred (101–200)	4,333,714	(3,125,973)
Additional Targets (19)	2,217,011	(5,609,394)
Total	**21,185,808**	**(6,709,742)**

Nontargeted institutions
89 buyers of 1558 nontargeted institutions

31%
3,212,760 shares 69 institutions
7,193,423 shares 43 institutions
69%

Buyers ☐ Sellers

Targeted institutions
47 buyers of 200 targeted institutions

76%
6,709,742 shares 33 institutions
21,105,808 shares 47 institutions
24%

Buyers ☐ Sellers

Source: Georgeson & Company Inc.

195

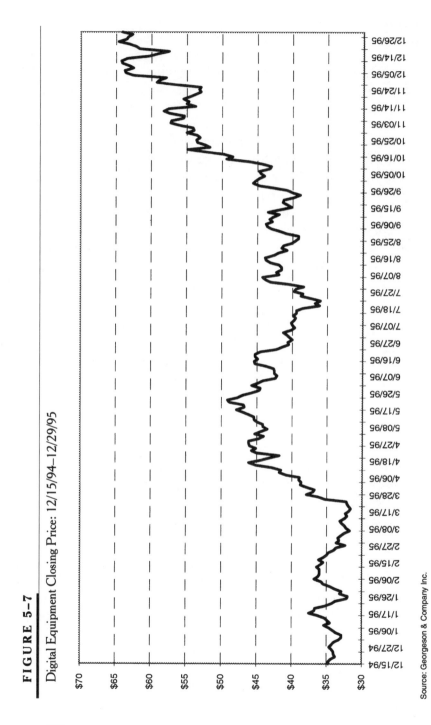

FIGURE 5-7

Digital Equipment Closing Price: 12/15/94–12/29/95

Source: Georgeson & Company Inc.

overall market conditions, although targeting can, here again, support a company's strategy to achieve full valuation. Moreover, according to Richard Wines of Georgeson: "the way these fundamental results and expectations get incorporated into market value is through the buy decisions of those institutions willing to pay appropriately for the story—the very institutions we attempted to identify in our targeting analysis."

Corporate CEOs and other senior executives tend to have strong personalities which allow them to take control of situations and move things forward. It is therefore especially frustrating for them to feel so little control over the movements of stock markets which place value for everything that they do in a single stock price statistic. While many executives say that they ignore short-term swings in their stock price, and certainly many do not base their future plans on such short-term swings, a stable and positive stock valuation can be of enormous benefit—and comfort—as company executives build value for the future.

ENDNOTES

1. John C. Wilcox, "What Types of Institutional Investors Would Your Company Like to Attract?," mimeographed notes from presentation at The Conference Board Seminars, *Access to U.S. Capital Markets: What Companies Should Know About U.S. Markets and Institutional Investors,* Melbourne and Sydney, June 15–16, 1995. p. 6.
2. *The Brancato Report on Institutional Investment,* 3, ed. 1, (January 1996), pp. 52-53.
3. Discussion of strategies is drawn from transcribed presentation by Richard A. Wines, "Valuation and Ownership," The Conference Board's Working Group on Key Measures of Corporate Performance, New York City, April 12, 1994.

6

ALIGNING THE INTERESTS OF INVESTORS AND CORPORATIONS

No issue promises more future unrest for the corporation—and its investors—than the widening gulf between executive and worker compensation. The outcry has mounted as proxy statements filed during the spring of 1996 revealed record levels of 1995 executive compensation paid while corporations continued massive layoffs and gave remaining workers meager increases. Although compensation policies might ordinarily be considered an internal corporate matter to be determined at the discretion of management, public pressure in the United States has been so great as to affect actions by both the SEC and the U.S. Congress. In 1992, the SEC began permitting shareholder proposals on executive compensation to be included in proxy statements, and landmark legislation was passed by Congress in 1993 adding Section 162(m) to the Internal Revenue Code, which limits the tax deductibility for executive compensation paid in excess of $1 million, unless shareholders approve and pay is tied to performance.[1] Additional legislative and shareholder proxy voting initiatives, proposed by public lawmakers as well as union-related pension funds, would tie the maximum amount of senior executive compensation to a multiple of wages paid to rank-and-file employees.

These proposals are clearly precipitated by a widening earnings gap. While CEO annual salary and bonuses climbed 10.4 percent in 1995, U.S. wages and benefits rose only 2.9 percent from 1994 to 1995, the smallest advance in 14 years. Meanwhile, the pay for white-collar workers grew only 4.2 percent, matching the smallest increase (which occurred in 1994) since 1977. In a study conducted by the consulting firm Pearl Meyer & Partners Inc. for *The Wall Street Journal,* CEOs in a sample of 30 major companies were found to have received 1995 pay which was 212 times the pay of the average American employee; this represents nearly a fivefold increase since 1965 when the multiple was 44.[2]

In May 1996, the White House called a summit of business leaders to focus on the "responsibilities" of businesses in society, with the disparity between worker and senior executive compensation high on its agenda. This issue is volatile, as Yale Professor Paul W. MacAvoy and noted attorney Ira M. Millstein observe:

> The issue of appropriate pay has the potential to be explosive politically for executives. In an election year, public outrage can translate into more government regulatory or tax policy when candidates for office tap into such a reaction. Prior to the 1992 election, then-candidate Bill Clinton criticized excessive salaries awarded to top executives, especially in light of the decline in the competitive position of U.S. industry in the global economy. . . . In this election cycle, compensation is again an issue as primary campaign rhetoric against layoffs jars against reports of huge pay packages to executives. To prevent another round of regulation, executives and board compensation committees should re-examine the compensation system from its basics to its embellishments, and come up with ways to set compensation packages that prevent excessive inexplicable awards.[3]

Moreover, the debate over compensation has also highlighted the potential conflict between two of the corporation's stakeholders—its investors and its employees. Corporations have simultaneously initiated massive layoffs and paid relatively low salaries to their remaining workers, while they have earned record profits. From 1990 to 1995, corporate profits rose 75 percent from $176 billion to $308 billion, while worker layoffs increased 39 percent (from 316,047 workers laid off in 1990 to 439,882 workers laid off in 1995), and blue-collar worker pay increased only 16 percent, from an average of $22,976 in 1990 to $26,652 in 1995.[4]

Although it is not widely publicized (or the media choose to ignore it), there has been a major shift, especially within the United States, away from paying large sums for top executive fixed base salary (and for directors' retainers and pensions) towards variable pay tied to performance. Paying executives more for performance, even when that pay includes large grants of stock options, has tended to satisfy investors as long as it is accompanied by stock price increases. MacAvoy and Millstein make this point by citing a 1995 study conducted by Russell Reynolds Associates and the Wirthlin Group in which 97 percent of investment institutions and fund managers surveyed favored linking CEO compensation with perform- ance, where performance primarily means higher stock price.[5] Although total CEO compensation (annual salary, bonus, and stock options) rose 92 percent, from an average $1.95 million in 1990 to $3.75 million in 1995, profits rose 75 percent and stock prices are at their all-time high. For example, in 1995, Coco-Cola paid its CEO Roberto Goizueta only 7 percent more in base compensation, but the board gave him a million-share stock option grant (worth approximately $25.6 million in May 1996), while stock price soared 44.2 percent. With returns in this range, few sharehold- ers have complained. As long as profits and stock prices are climbing and options are issued in a reasonable way and not repriced[6] after the fact, executives appear to be earning their pay and satisfying their shareholders.

Viewed from the worker perspective, on the other hand, profits and stock prices may be little more than abstract concepts (unless, of course, workers own stock in the company). Even if workers own stock, the growing disparity between executive and worker pay, with or without stock, can foster low employee morale to the detriment of the growth of the corporation. The chief means of reconciling this brewing conflict is for the corporation to fully implement a strategic performance measurement sys- tem to measure its key drivers of success and replace its current compensa- tion system with one which is tied not to stock price alone but to strategic measures of corporate success as well. Furthermore, compensation systems tied to strategic measures of success must be implemented throughout the entire company, not merely for the top executives and directors. This should help to align the interests of all the company's employees—executives, directors, and white- and blue-collar workers—with investors who are interested in sustained growth which produces a stream of favorable share- holder returns. Finally, true alignment of interests through strategic meas- ures of success will go far to answer the question: which stakeholders should the company consider most important? A proper strategy to achieve strate- gic success will automatically incorporate and balance the interests of all the other major stakeholders—customers, employees, the community—while satisfying shareholders by providing them with sustained returns on their investments.

This chapter discusses disclosure requirements for executive compensation in the United States, the United Kingdom, and Canada—the primary countries which accept the premise that compensation should be disclosed to the public; emerging and contrasting trends in top executive compensation in these three countries; the debate over paying stock as part of executive and directors' compensation; and the development and use of both financial and nonfinancial strategic measures of success to design corporate compensation packages and to align the interests of the company's investors with those of its employees and other critical stakeholders.

COMPENSATION DISCLOSURE IN THE UNITED STATES, THE UNITED KINGDOM, AND CANADA

The U.S. system of compensation disclosure for CEOs and senior executives has set the pace for Canada and, to a certain extent, the United Kingdom. Pressures militating against high CEO pay have been especially acute in the United Kingdom, as formerly state-owned companies have privatized and executive pay packages have come under scrutiny in new, publicly held companies. On the Continent, however, there is little movement to require U.S.-style, extensive compensation disclosure. Indeed, some companies so carefully guard their top executive compensation data that one prominent banking official in France indicated that compensation was masked behind secret codes even within the bank itself. This is not to say that the media in France and other countries on the Continent have not made projections—and accusations—but executives and regulators have thus far resisted all efforts directed towards making compensation data public.

In the United States, however, during the early 1990s, the Securities and Exchange Commission undertook a major review of its shareholder voting and proxy regulations, which also included a review of executive compensation disclosure regulations. At the same time, there was a public uproar in Congress over the issue of excessive executive compensation, fueled by the perception that executives were being paid unfairly high amounts, as the country lost its competitive edge in the world, struggled during a recession, company profits fell, and unemployment escalated. Numerous pieces of legislation to limit executive compensation were introduced in the Congress, and one significant bill passed which limits the deductibility of executive compensation in excess of one million dollars, unless shareholders approve the compensation and it can be shown to be linked to corporate performance. In contrast with the Congressional approach of limiting compensation unless certain actions are taken, the SEC has consistently taken the position that *disclosure* rather than *regulation* to impose dollar compensation limits is desirable. The SEC's position is based on the belief that the disciplinary effect of the markets, aided by full and fair disclosure mandated by SEC rules, should ultimately operate to curb any perceived abuses in the area of executive pay.

In February 1992, the SEC began to reinforce shareholder monitoring of executive compensation by changing its interpretation of the "ordinary business" exclusion of Rule 14a-8(c)(7) to permit shareholders to express their views on executive and director compensation through the vehicle of shareholder proposals carried in registrant proxy statements. Then, on October 15, 1992 the SEC adopted new executive compensation disclosure requirements for proxy statements and other reports filed by domestic reporting companies. The regulations require the following be included in the registrant company's proxy statement:

1. A summary table containing detailed information on the total compensation for the last three years for the CEO and each the four other most highly paid executives.

2. A performance graph comparing the companies' five-year cumulative total shareholder returns with those of other companies in a peer group and/or compared to the Standard and Poor's 500 average or other broad equity market index.

3. A compensation committee report describing the factors affecting the committee's decisions regarding CEO and other executive compensation and discussing the relationship between such compensation and the company's performance in the past fiscal year.

4. Option/stock appreciation rights tables disclosing various information regarding stock options and stock appreciation rights (SARs), including potential appreciation rates and unrealized gains on outstanding options.

5. Expanded disclosure for incentive stock option repricings, potential lack of independence of compensation committee members, and details of new compensation plans subject to shareholder approval.

The SEC's rigorous new executive compensation disclosure standards were partially the result of mounting shareholder demands for concise yet understandable information on precisely how and how much senior managers and directors of public companies are paid. Even more importantly, the new standards compel board compensation committees to explain the extent to which executive pay awards are linked to corporate performance. Armed with this information, shareholders have penalized directors for abusive compensation practices at the corporate ballot box. In sum, strong shareholder demand for quantified, individualized compensation data— typically expressed in the form of inquiries as to how executive and/or director compensation leads to improved corporate performance—have forced companies to furnish far more disclosure during recent years than had ever been the case.

Canada acted quickly and closely followed the SEC's 1992 initiatives. In October 1993, the Ontario Securities Commission (OSC) introduced U.S.-style disclosure requirements for executive compensation in information circulars and annual filings. The requirements mandate the disclosure of executive compensation components in summary tables and the statement of factors and criteria used to set compensation levels. Most provincial jurisdictions have either adopted or acknowledged compliance with the new Ontario rules pertaining to the disclosure of executive compensation.[7]

In the United Kingdom, a follow-up report to *The Cadbury Report* dealt with executive compensation, which had become a prominent issue there as well. In July 1995, the U.K. Greenbury Study Group (headed by Sir Richard Greenbury, Chairman of Marks and Spencer) published its "Code of Best Practice" on the determination and disclosure of the pay and other issues relating to the board of directors[8] of publicly traded companies in the U.K. These recommendations were then adopted as a listing requirement by the London Stock Exchange on board pay and remuneration practices.[9] Companies whose years end on and after December 31, 1995 are required to disclose full details of all elements in the remuneration package of each director (both executive and nonexecutive) in their annual reports. (See Box 6–1 for the major provisions of the Greenbury Report.) As in the United States, remuneration committees must disclose factors and criteria used to determine remuneration packages. Table 6–1 provides a comparison between the prominent disclosure requirements and forms of compensation in the United States, the United Kingdom, and Canada.

Since the issuance of the Greenbury report, there have been two significant pronouncements by U.K. institutional investors. In July 1995,

TABLE 6-1

Summary of Top Executive Compensation Practices in the United States, the United Kingdom, and Canada

	Executive Compensation Disclosure Requirements	CEO Annual Cash Compensation by Industry Sector	Annual Incentive Plans	Long-Term Incentive Plans	Perquisites and Personal Benefits	Employment/Service Contracts
United States	October 1992, U.S. SEC introduced new rules on disclosure of executive compensation.	U.S. CEO base salary, annual bonus, and total cash highest in all industries except insurance and commercial banking.	1. Prevalence over 90 percent. 2. Awards paid in cash and/or stock. 3. Directly tied to both financial and non-financial performance measures.	1. Stock options. 2. Restricted stock. 3. Long-term performance unit/share plans.	1. Cars/car allowances. 2. Financial planning.	SEC requires disclosure of terms and conditions of employment/ services contracts with a named executive.
United Kingdom	July 1995, Greenbury Study Group published its "Code of Best Practice" on disclosure of board of directors' pay. October 1995, The London Stock Exchange amended *Listing Rules* with the "Code."	U.K. CEO base salary highest in nonfinancial services. U.K. CEO annual bonus and total cash highest in nonfinancial services.	1. Prevalence of 83 percent. 2. Awards paid normally cash and rarely in stock. 3. Financial performance measures increasingly augmented with nonfinancial measures.	1. Stock options. 2. Cash based: — stock appreciation rights. — long-term cash bonus plans. 3. Stock plans linked to annual bonus and/or future company performance.	1. Cars/car allowances. 2. Private health insurance.	The London Stock Exchange requires employment/services contracts of executive directors to be available for inspection.
Canada	October 1993, Ontario Securities Commission (OSC) introduced U.S.-style disclosure requirements for executive compensation.	Canadian CEO annual cash compensation ranked second behind the United States in most industry sectors.	1. Average prevalence of 90 percent. 2. Awards paid in cash and/or stock. 3. Both financial and nonfinancial measures used to set annual incentives.	1. Stock options. 2. Long-term unit/share plans. 3. Restricted stock.	1. Cars/car allowances. 2. Financial planning. 3. Club memberships. 4. Supplemental retirement plans (SERPS).	OSC requires disclosure of terms and conditions of employment/services contracts with a named executive.

Source: Marc-Andreas Klein, "Top Executive Compensation: A Comparison Between U.S., U.K. and Canada," The Conference Board, Report No. 1155-96-RR, p. 8.

203

BOX 6–1

The Greenbury Study Group

Set up by the Confederation of British Insurers in January 1995, the Greenbury Study Group was chaired by Sir Richard Greenbury, Chairman of Marks and Spencer. The group's mandate was to examine the structure within which executive compensation for publicly traded companies is determined and disclosed and codify a set of recommendations that would consolidate and improve on the many extant sets of guidelines. The group included nominees from the Institute of Directors, the Association of British Insurers, the National Association of Pension Funds, and the London Stock Exchange.

The Study Group published its report in July 1995. The report includes a Code of Best Practice, which is divided into four sections:

Section A   Composition and role of the remuneration committee
Section B   Disclosure and approval provisions for the remuneration committee's report to shareholders
Section C   Remuneration policy and the interaction of the elements of remuneration
Section D   Service contracts and compensation payments

In summary, the guidelines discuss the following requirements for a company's annual report:

- Explanation of company policy on executive remuneration, including the various components of remuneration; measures used to gauge performance and chosen performance criteria; pension provisions; contracts of service; compensation commitments in the event of early termination; and peer groups used for determining pay.

- Disclosing all the elements of the remuneration of named directors (including directors based wholly or mainly overseas).

- Divulging payments and benefits not previously disclosed, e.g., unfunded pension promises.

- A statement on the degree of compliance with the Greenbury Code.

(continued)

Greenbury—Concluded

THE LONDON STOCK EXCHANGE *LISTING RULES*

In its October 1995 Amendment No. 6 to the *Listing Rules,* the London Stock Exchange adopted large parts of the Greenbury Study Group's recommendations. It should be noted that the latter are not part of (and so do not carry the same weight as) the Listing Rules, but are annexed to them. For companies listed on the London Stock Exchange, a report from the remuneration committee will be required in annual reports for companies with fiscal years ending on or after 31 December 1995. In practice, this means that the first reports which have been prepared to meet the new requirements are unlikely to appear before April 1996. This does not mean, however, that current reports are failing to meet some or all of the requirements of the Greenbury Code.

DIFFERENCES BETWEEN THE LISTING RULES AND GREENBURY

There are three main areas that are either treated differently or await clarification:

- *Disclosure of pension.* The method to be used in disclosing the cost of directors' pensions benefits is still under review, with a consultation exercise by the Institute of Actuaries and the Faculty of Actuaries in progress during early 1996.

- *Approval of long-term incentive (LTI) arrangements by shareholders.* This Greenbury requirement was omitted from the Listing Rules, except as a recommendation in the Best Practice Provisions. The issue is still under review.

- *Disclosure of amounts earned under long-term incentive plans.* Greenbury calls for actual and potential payments to be shown in a table, in common with share option details. This is not required by the Stock Exchange, but a listing rule deals with the disclosure of LTI proceeds in the remuneration committee's report.

Source: Marc-Andreas Klein, "Top Executive Compensation: A Comparison Between U.S., U.K. and Canada," The Conference Board, Report No. 1155-96-RR, pp. 17–18.

in a letter clarifying its attitude towards the acceptability of companies' new incentive arrangements, PDFM (a major pension fund management company) formulated a set of basic principles which it recommends be built into any remuneration scheme to ensure that the community of interest between a company and its shareholders is reinforced. These include visibility of pay and the use of shares rather than cash, after a minimum performance period of three years, as the method of reward in incentive schemes. Then, in January 1996, Standard Life, a major U.K. institutional investor, sent a letter to the FT-SE 100 companies which sets out guidelines for combining the chairman and chief executive roles; the use of nonexecutive directors on boards and committees; remuneration disclosure; performance conditions in share options and other long-term plans; and directors' service contracts.

TRENDS IN EXECUTIVE COMPENSATION

Total compensation packages are typically designed to attract exceptionally qualified executives, retain them, motivate them in the short and long term, provide recognition, and provide security. According to the National Association of Corporate Directors' Blue Ribbon Commission Report on Executive Compensation, total compensation for an executive can be defined as the sum of annualized pretax base salary, annual bonus, estimated grant value of medium- or long-term incentive compensation, and the value of qualified and supplemental benefits, including deferred compensation and perquisites.[10]

A typical senior U.S. executive today might receive some or all of the following (see Box 6–2 for an explanation of key terms):

- Base salary.
- Annual bonus or short-term incentive.
- Medium- or long-term incentives that may include:
  - stock options
  - stock appreciation rights (SARs)
  - restricted stock
  - phantom stock
  - performance units paid in the form of stock or cash.
- Tax-qualified or broad-based benefit plans that may include:
  - pension plans
  - medical and dental plans
  - savings plans

BOX 6–2

Elements in Typical U.S. Executive Pay Plans

1. **Base salary** reflects the impact of experience and sustained performance. Salary is usually set on the basis of "market rate" (what similar companies pay for similar jobs).

2. **Annual bonus** rewards achievement of an annual target. Most typically a percent of profits goes into a pool, which is allocated to the participants, usually on the basis of each one's contribution to annual profitability as measured by growth in earnings per share or rate of return on equity.

3. **Long-term incentives** are designed to reward future performance for periods greater than one year. They are subdivided into the following:

   a. **Performance unit or share plans**: awards of cash or stock related to financial measures, most often cumulative increases in earnings per share over a three- to five-year period.

   b. **Stock options:** nontransferable rights to purchase shares of employer stock at a fixed price over a stated period (usually 10 years). Increases in share price over time increase the potential value of stock or the actual value of stock acquired and held. Incentive stock options (ISOs) meet Internal Revenue Code requirements. SARs are stock appreciation rights that give a recipient, in lieu of exercising one stock option in whole or in part, the right to receive an amount in cash or stock equal to appreciation in the stock price since the date of the grant.

   c. **Restricted stock:** grants of shares of stock or stock equivalents restricted from sale or transfer for a period of continued employment (anywhere from 3 to 10 years).

   d. **Phantom stock:** analogous to company stock most often used by private companies or divisions of public corporations. Conceptually similar to an SAR.

Source: The Conference Board

- life insurance plans
- disability plans.

■ Supplemental benefit plans that may include:
  - deferred compensation plans
  - supplemental executive retirement plans (SERPs)
  - excess retirement plans
  - supplemental medical and disability plans
  - supplemental life insurance plans.

■ Perquisites that may include:
  - club memberships
  - financial planning or counseling
  - use of company automobiles and company planes
  - airline club memberships
  - chauffeurs.

According to the William M. Mercer, Inc. annual executive pay survey conducted for *The Wall Street Journal*,[11] chief executive officer salaries and annual bonuses in a sample of 350 of the largest U.S. corporations grew to a median $1.43 million in 1995, up 10.4 percent from $1.29 million in 1994. This was the second fastest growth rate since 1988 and only slightly lower than the 11.4 percent growth from 1993 to 1994, although considerably higher than the 8.1 percent increase registered during the period 1992 to 1993. Data for total compensation (including base salary, annual bonus, gains from the exercise of stock options, long-term incentive payouts, and the value of restricted stock at the time of grant) show CEO compensation increasing 14.3 percent to $1,992,490, the highest figure since 1989, when *The Wall Street Journal's* annual survey began. Table 6–2 shows CEO compensation for the five highest paid CEOs in each of seven major industry groupings in the Mercer-*Wall Street Journal* survey.

A comparison between the pay of U.S., U.K., and Canadian CEOs and other senior executives in 1994 was undertaken by Marc-Andreas Klein at The Conference Board, in collaboration with Monks Partnership Limited of the United Kingdom. The study provides comparative analyses of disclosure requirements, executive compensation data, and annual and long-term compensation standards and practices of the largest publicly traded companies in the United States, the United Kingdom, and Canada. The sample consists of 1,660 companies segmented into 10 industry categories.

Klein finds that, when company size is equalized among the three countries, total current compensation (salary plus bonus) tends to be highest among U.S. companies. Table 6–3 provides an overview of annual com-

TABLE 6-2

CEO Compensation in 1995: Five Highest Paid CEOs as Measured by Total Direct Compensation in Selected Industry Sectors

Company	Executive	1995 Salary ($000)	1995 Bonus ($000)	1995 Salary + Bonus ($000)	Percent Change from 1994	Long-Term Compensation— Option Grants ($000)	Long-Term Compensation— Other ($000)	Total Direct Compensation ($000)	Present Value of Option Grants ($000)
Basic Materials									
Alcoa	Paul H. O'Neill	750.0	1,250.0	2,000.0	37.9	8,603.1	0.0	10,603.1	10,581.8
Hercules	Thomas L. Gossage	837.5	1,020.0	1,857.5	23.6	0.0	5,351.6	7,209.1	3,891.6
Cyprus Amax Minerals	Milton H. Ward	620.0	1,700.0	2,320.0	N/A	0.0	1,522.5	3,842.5	N/A
Hanna (M.A.)	Martin D. Walker	640.0	540.0	1,180.0	4.2	1,866.1	337.5	3,383.6	661.9
Phelps Dodge	Douglas C. Yearley	640.0	642.9	1,282.9	14.5	2,070.3	0.0	3,353.2	3,042.5
Energy									
Enron	Kenneth L. Lay	990.0	1,440.0[4,6]	2,430.0[4,6]	N/A[3]	4,936.6	421.9	7,788.5[4,6]	1,722.7[6]
Exxon	Lee R. Raymond	1,400.0	1,000.0	2,400.0	29.7	2,994.1	1,573.0	6,967.1	3,009.2
Occidential	Ray R. Irani	1,900.0	872.0	2,772.0	0.0	0.0	2,459.4	5,231.4[7]	1,188.0
Chevron	Kenneth T. Derr	1,000.0	721.0	1,721.0	1.2	0.0	1,958.5	3,679.5	1,137.5
Texaco	Alfred C. DeCrane, Jr.	977.5	862.81	1,840.3	20.9	976.4	777.5	3,594.2	2,721.0[1]
Industrial									
AlliedSignal	Lawrence A. Bossidy	2,000.0	2,350.0	4,350.0	20.0	4,055.6	0.0	8,405.6	N/A
Engelhard	Orin R. Smith	735.0	925.0	1,660.0	24.8	5,966.8	412.3	8,039.1	4,586.3
Burlington Northern	Robert D. Krebs[5]	525.0	530.3	1,055.3	N/A[3]	6,021.3	641.6	7,718.1	2,533.6[1]
Armstrong	George A. Lorch	587.9	929.4	1,516.9	31.9	33.6	3,909.8	5,460.4	5,335.8
R.R. Donnelley	John R. Walter	900.0	555.0	1,455.0	12.4	365.9	3,142.7	4,963.6	3,874.5[2]
Cyclical									
Goodyear	Stanley C. Gault	1,020.0	1,155.0	2,175.0	0.8	12,005.0	1,348.1	16,518.1	2,271.4
Walt Disney	Michael D. Eisner	750.0	14,021.2	14,771.2	38.6	0.0	0.0	14,771.2	N/A
ITT	Rand V. Araskog	2,000.0	2,330.8	4,330.8	7.5	0.0	5,343.8	9,674.6	6,749.0[2]
Kodak	George M.C. Fisher	2,000.0	2,282.5	4,282.5	12.2	0.0	5,010.1	9,292.6[8]	923.9
Harcourt General	Robert J. Tarr, Jr.	1,500.0	1,125.0	2,625.0	7.1	5,291.1	0.0	7,916.1	N/A

(Continued)

N/A = not available.

TABLE 6–2 Concluded

Company	Executive	1995 Salary ($000)	1995 Bonus ($000)	1995 Salary + Bonus ($000)	Percent Change from 1994	Long-Term Compensation— Option Grants ($000)	Long-Term Compensation— Other ($000)	Total Direct Compensation on ($000)	Present Value of Option Grants ($000)
Noncyclical									
Colgate-Palmolive	Reuben Mark	984.7	1,000.0	1,984.7	-15.9	11,567.3	1,516.1	15,068.1	1,566.9[1]
Coca-Cola Co.	Roberto C. Goizueta	1,680.0	3,200.0	4,880.0	11.6	6,565.6	1,463.6	12,909.2	21,241.7
PepsiCo	D. Wayne Calloway	925.0	2,425.0	3,350.0	13.8	7,966.2	0.0	11,316.2	94.7
Schering-Plough	Robert P. Luciano	1,140.7	1,227.5	2,368.2	4.1	3,283.0	3,125.0	8,776.2	1,025.2
IBP	Robert L. Peterson	1,000.0	5,278.3	6,278.3	28.8	0.0	0.0	6,278.3	849.6
Technology									
General Electric	John F. Welch, Jr.	2,000.0	3,250.0	5,250.0	20.7	5,315.6	11,425.0	21,990.6	5,590.4
Compaq Computer	Eckhard Pfeiffer	1,125.0	2,500.0[9]	3,625.0	2.1	12,492.9	0.0	16,117.9	9,873.1
IBM	Louis V. Gerstner Jr.	2,000.0	2,775.0	4,775.0	3.8	132.9	8,319.0	13,226.9	3,354.9
Motorola	Gary L. Tooker	990.0	1,030.0	2,020.0	2.0	7,046.4	1,800.0	10,866.4	2,417.6
Texas Instruments	Jerry R. Junkins	792.1	1,750.0	2,542.1	31.9	7,713.5	0.0	10,255.6	2,478.2[2]
Financial									
Morgan Stanley	Richard B. Fisher	477.3[4]	4,187.0[4]	4,664.3[4]	N/A[3]	5,178.4	2,072.3[4]	11,915.1[4]	N/A
BankAmerica	Richard M. Rosenberg	841.7	3,700.0	4,541.7	44.6	0.0	7,312.5	11,854.2	1,757.8
American Int'l	Maurice R. Greenberg	1,000.0	3,150.0	4,150.0	10.7	6,833.7	0.0	10,983.7	2,004.6
Group									
Charles Schwab	Charles R. Schwab	800.0	8,606.2	9,406.2	187.4	0.0	0.0	9,406.2	7,194.8
Bear Stearns	James E. Cayne	200.0	7,500.9	7,700.9	N/A[3]	912.6	0.0	8,613.5[10]	N/A

1. A portion of 1995 grants were reload options. 2. A portion of 1995 grants were performance options. 3. Percent change not meaningful. 4. Data not valid for comparison (e.g., partial-year data). 5. New CEO for 1995. 6. A portion of bonus was replaced with stock options. 7. Does not include tax reimbursement in excess of $400,000. 8. Does not include $1,982,891 of principal and interest forgiven on two loans. 9. Does not include $1,250 deferred unfunded bonus. 10. Does not include $1,303,122 preferential earnings pursuant to Capital Accumulation Plan. N/A = not available.

Source: William M. Mercer, Inc., "The Boss's Pay: Executive Pay Survey," *The Wall Street Journal*, April 11, 1996, pp. R15–17.

TABLE 6-3

Median Annual Cash Compensation: Companies of $4.6 billion in Annual Sales in the United States, the United Kingdom, and Canada

CEO Compensation

	1992		1993				1994			
	Median Base Salary ($000)	Median Total Cash Compensation[1] ($000)	Median Base Salary ($000)	Percent Change of Medians 1992–1993	Median Total Cash Compensation ($000)	Percent Change of Medians 1992–1993	Median Base Salary ($000)	Percent Change of Medians 1993–1994	Median Total Cash Compensation ($000)	Percent Change of Medians 1993–1994
United States	675	1,156	750	11	1,323	14	796	6	1,483	12
United Kingdom	405	470	425	5	525	12	435	2	550	5
Canada	559	802	662	4	908	13	638	3	1,034	14

1. Total Cash Compensation is the sum of base salary and annual bonus.

Compensation of the Four Highest Paid Executives (excluding the CEO)

	1992		1993				1994			
	Median Base Salary ($000)	Median Total Cash Compensation[1] ($000)	Median Base Salary ($000)	Percent Change of Medians 1992–1993	Median Total Cash Compensation ($000)	Percent Change of Medians 1992–1993	Median Base Salary ($000)	Percent Change of Medians 1993–1994	Median Total Cash Compensation ($000)	Percent Change of Medians 1993–1994
United States	296	428	312	5	498	16	330	6	530	6
United Kingdom	235	270	250	6	300	11	260	4	310	3
Canada	249	326	299	20	390	20	302	1	471	21

1. Total Cash Compensation is the sum of base salary and annual bonus.

Source: Marc-Andreas Klein, "Top Executive Compensation: A Comparison Between U.S., U.K. and Canada," The Conference Board, Report No.1155-96-RR, pp. 11–12.

pensation for the CEO and the four highest paid executives in companies with average annual sales of approximately U.S. $4.6 billion from 1992 to 1994. The findings indicate that, during the three-year period, 1992 to 1994:

- CEO base salary and total cash (base salary plus annual bonus) were highest among U.S. companies, followed by Canada and U.K.
- U.S. CEO base salary and total annual cash exhibited highest growth from 1992 to 1994, followed by Canada and the U.K.
- Canadian four highest paid executives' base salary and total annual cash showed the strongest increase from 1992 to 1994, followed by the United States and the United Kingdom.

The Conference Board's study attributes most of the variation in compensation between the United States, the United Kingdom, and Canada to the impact of the annual bonus. Annual bonus plans are almost universal among publicly traded companies in all three countries, although they are utilized much more in the United States than in the others. In an attempt to link executive compensation to company performance, annual incentive plans are increasingly tied to both financial and nonfinancial measures.

- Annual executive compensation in U.S. corporations typically consists of salary (fixed annual pay) and bonus (variable annual pay). Popular types of plans are profit-sharing and threshold plans. Annual bonuses are directly tied to financial performance measures, such as earnings per share and return on equity, and increasingly to nonfinancial measures, such as quality or customer satisfaction. Bonuses are usually paid in cash and/or stock. Over 90 percent of all publicly traded companies have an annual bonus plan in place for their top executives.
- In U.K.-based companies, annual compensation typically also consists of salary (fixed annual pay) and bonus (variable annual pay). The Greenbury Group's *Code of Best Practice* recommends that the level of annual bonus be tied to company performance. Remuneration committees set annual incentive pay based on both financial and nonfinancial performance measures. Approximately 83 percent of publicly listed companies in the United Kingdom have annual bonus plans in place for their board of directors (e.g., senior executives).
- Within Canadian companies, annual executive compensation plans also consist of salary and bonus. Popular types of annual

bonus are profit-sharing and performance target plans. The Ontario Securities Commission also requires that executive compensation committees disclose the factors and criteria used to set executive compensation. Canadian companies increasingly use both financial and nonfinancial measures to set annual variable compensation. An average of 90 percent of Canadian publicly traded companies have annual incentive plans in place. Bonuses are either awarded in cash and/or stock.[12]

As Table 6–4 shows, the U.S. bonus is significantly higher, as a percentage of base salary, than in the other two countries. That is, in the mix of fixed pay (salary) versus pay-at-risk (bonus), there is more emphasis on pay-at-risk in the United States. As a result, the relatively good corporate performance in 1994 is reflected in the bonuses paid for that year's performance. Since in the United Kingdom and Canada there is more emphasis on the fixed, or salaried, component of pay, the impact of company performance on total compensation is not as visible. Table 6–4 shows the percentage of CEO annual bonus as a percentage of base salary for a range of industry groupings in the United States, the United Kingdom, and Canada. In every case, the percent of bonus is higher in the United States and in some cases, significantly higher. For example, in the manufacturing sector, when ad-

TABLE 6-4

Median CEO Annual Bonus as a Percentage of Base Salary: Comparison of Companies of $4.6 Billion in Annual Sales in the United States, the United Kingdom, and Canada in 1994

	U.S.	U.K.	Canada
Manufacturing	79	24	61
Food, Tobacco, and Kindred Products	81	29	*
Chemicals, Petroleum, & Pharmaceuticals	81	14	61
Machinery, Primary & Fabricated Metals	72	25	61
Nonfinancial Services	60	34	43
Media & Leisure	73	32	*
Trade (Retail and Wholesale)	51	35	24
Utilities	36	21	*

*Insufficient Data.

Source: Marc-Andreas Klein, "Top Executive Compensation: A Comparison Between U.S., U.K. and Canada," The Conference Board, Report No. 1155-96-RR, p. 21.

justed for the same size ($4.6 billion) company, CEOs in the United States received an annual 1994 bonus which equaled 79 percent of their base salary; in the United Kingdom CEOs received an annual bonus of only 24 percent of their base salary; in Canada—following closest behind the United States—CEOs received an annual bonus which was 61 percent of their base salary.

Comparisons between smaller companies with median annual revenues of $500 million in the United States, the United Kingdom, Germany, France, and Italy show similar trends (see Table 6–5). The United States is highest in overall total compensation, but has the lowest base salary as a percent of total pay and the highest bonus as a percent of total pay.

COMPENSATION TO BE PAID IN STOCK?

Sarah Teslik, Executive Director of The Council of Institutional Investors, wrote a Council newsletter article entitled "Let Them Eat Stock," in which she argues that companies should align the interests of their shareholders with those of their executives and directors. There are two principal methods suggested by a broad consensus of shareholders and other participants in the corporate governance process, such as the National Association of Corporate Directors (NACD). These methods are (1) paying executives and directors more in stock and less in cash and (2) requiring them to own stock in multiples of their compensation or retainer fees (for directors this is frequently couched in terms that directors should own stock worth five times their basic retainer). Tying stock to compensation has become a kind of "mantra" in the United States, although it is not so widely favored in the United Kingdom. According to the 1995 *Report of the NACD Blue Ribbon Commission on Director Compensation: Purposes, Principles and Best Practices:*

- The level of directors' pay has increased dramatically over the past decade.
- There has been a corresponding increase in activity and professionalism of boards.
- Contributing to this rise are new forms of director pay: stock, stock options, and benefits.
- Stock and stock options tie the interests of directors to those of shareholders.
- Benefits serve no such purpose.

TABLE 6-5

Average Compensation of Chief Executives at Companies With Median Annual Revenues of $500 Million: Comparative Compensation Data in the United States, the United Kingdom, Germany, France, and Italy

	Base Salary	% of Total Pay	Annual Bonus	% of Total Pay	Employee Benefits	% of Total Pay	Long-Term Incentives	% of Total Pay	Perquisites	% of Total Pay	Total Compensation
United States	$438,000	40.4%	$227,000	20.9%	$106,000	9.8%	$288,000	26.5%	$26,000	2.4%	$1,085,000
Britain	315,000	57.1	63,000	11.4	75,600	13.7	63,000	11.4	35,000	6.3	551,600
Germany	290,000	54.0	96,000	17.9	67,000	12.5	46,000	8.6	38,000	7.1	537,000
France	265,960	54.8	49,532	10.2	71,890	14.8	53,660	11.1	43,962	9.1	485,004
Italy	241,000	75.8	60,000	18.9	7,000	2.2	0	0	10,000	3.1	318,000

Note: Employee benefits include retirement and health benefits; French benefits figure also includes mandatory employer contributions to social security. Long-term incentives include share options and stock plans. Perquisites include noncash compensation, such as company car, chauffeur, etc. Study is based on national companies and excludes operating units of multinational companies. All figures are based on current currency conversions. Percentages for each country may not total 100 percent due to rounding.

Source: Hewitt Associates Data as cited in Tara Parker-Pope, "So Far Away," *The Wall Street Journal*, April 11, 1996, p. R12.

BOX 6-3

NACD's Blue Ribbon Commission on Directors' Compensation: Six Recommended "Best" Practices

1. Establish a procedure to determine the compensation program in an objective way.

2. Set a stock ownership target for each director and a time for the target to be met.

3. Define the desirable total value of all forms of director compensation.

4. Pay directors solely in the form of equity and dismantle existing benefit programs.

5. Adopt a policy not to hire a director/director's firm for services to the corporation.

6. Disclose fully in the proxy statement the value of all elements of compensation.

Professor Robert Stobaugh of the Harvard Business School (a chairman of the NACD Blue Ribbon Commission on Directors' Compensation) is also a director of Ashland Oil Company and has long advocated compensation in stock and ownership of stock in multiples of pay. Others in the corporate sector concur. For example, in its 1995 proxy statement, the Campbell Soup Company "subscribes to sharply increasing the at-risk portion of director compensation," and the "core concept . . . that directors should walk in the shoes of the Shareowners." Campbell Soup requires that directors own at least 3,000 shares within three years of election (with an approximate value as of January 1, 1996 of $180,000) and that annual board retainers be paid 100 percent in stock.[13]

The NACD and shareholder groups want to see more stock in the typical package for executives and directors. (See Box 6–3.) Phantom stock, representing half the retainer and fees and paid in actual shares after retirement, is one way. Existing deferred compensation plans, allowing directors the option of deferring some or all of current payment until retirement and taking it in stock value, is another. One difficulty is actually placing a current price on the future cash payout of existing retirement plans and converting those to a comparable stock value.

Until 1995, it was widely regarded by managements and consultants that pensions should be a part of the compensation package because they allowed boards to remain competitive in their recruitment of appropriately talented and committed members. Most institutional investors, like CalPERS, agree that directors should be fairly compensated for their work; the debate centers on how to structure that compensation. Tom Flanagan of the Investors' Rights Association of America (IRAA) believes that "if directors need retirement money, it should come from the success of the stock in the market."[14]

Directors' pensions became a particular focus of institutional investor attack during the proxy seasons of 1995 and 1996, especially from union-related pension funds angry over the disparity in pay between rank-and-file workers and executives and directors. By February 1996, the Investor Responsibility Research Center (IRRC) had reported that limits on pensions for nonemployee directors were the second most popular issue, with 45 resolutions filed during the first two months of the 1996 proxy season, 2 omitted and 8 withdrawn. The Conference Board reports this growing interest in directors' retirement benefits:

> Other shareholder groups have directly opposed pensions, including the Investors' Rights Association of America (IRAA, newest of the shareholder activist groups), and labor unions, including the International Union of Operating Engineers, the Teamsters, and Communication Workers of America. The unions have made elimination of outside director pensions a leading issue among resolutions proposed at shareholder meetings in 1995 and will keep it a leading issue in the 1996 proxy season. IRAA alone submitted 24 proposals to eliminate pensions for directors in 1995. In 1996, they expect to submit twice as many proposals and it is expected that the number dealing with pensions will continue to escalate. . . .
>
> IRAA has been the most outspoken advocate of revisions in directors' compensation and has paid particular attention to retirement plans in this year's and last year's proxy season. Labor unions have also turned their attention to "pensions" paid to outside directors. Bill Patterson, director of corporate affairs for the Teamsters and co-chair of the Council of Institutional Investors, says in regard to a resolution presented to Philip Morris shareholders to end pensions: "Giving a director a pension [that becomes effective after five years' service] sends the wrong signal that, if you don't rock the boat for five years, you will get a pension." Among those making proposals to restrict

or do away with directors' retirement plans are the Teamsters, the International Union of Operating Engineers, the United Brotherhood of Carpenters & Joiners, the International Brotherhood of Electrical Workers, and Communication Workers of America.[15]

A number of companies have responded to this pressure by altering their approaches to paying directors retirement benefits, with some shifting from cash to stock. The American Society of Corporate Secretaries carried out a survey among its members in January 1996: In response, 51 companies reported having terminated, replaced, or amended (restricted) retirement plans for outside directors (880 said no, they have not terminated, replaced, or amended such a plan).[16] Of those responding, 298 report having a director pension plan and 634 say they do not have a plan. The Society also asked respondents: "If amended or replaced, by what means?" In response:

- 17 companies indicated they are freezing the plan.
- 11 have closed the plan to new participants.
- 9 reported a buyout, making annual stock grants in the future.
- 7 reported a buyout, converting vested benefits to stock.

The directors' pension benefit issue has become extremely volatile and serves as a warning that union-related pension funds will not only join, but in many cases surpass, the public employee activist funds in pressuring to reform company compensation packages.

Arguments to Limit or Restructure Stock-Related Compensation

Pressure to align compensation with stock comes not only from the institutional investor activists, but also from some directors' groups as well as certain corporations. Yet others in the corporate sector have argued either to limit the practice or remove it altogether. Hoffer Kaback, president of the New York investment firm Gloucester Capital Corp., serves as a director of two New York Stock Exchange–listed companies and one NASDAQ company. Kaback disagrees with the NACD's report advocating broader use of paying in stock and requiring ownership of multiples of stock as means to link the interests of shareholders with executives and directors. He argues that these practices involve: "(a) practical complexities, (b) leaps of illogic, (c) unmanageable and distasteful results, (d) a misguided tying of director compensation to market performance of the company's stock, and (e) perverse results detrimental to good corporate governance."[17] Kaback argues that paying executives (or most commonly directors) purely in stock produces taxable income without cash (although the use of various forms of either restricted or unrestricted and phantom stock may mitigate the negative tax effects). But Kaback argues that it is wrong to place a director into a negative cash flow of any amount as a direct consequence of board service, since, irrespective of their net worths, directors may sometimes be illiquid. He also argues a broader issue—that owning stock may give rise to serious conflicts of interest: "For many corporations, the board consists in substantial part of independent directors who bring to the boardroom their business judgment and outside perspective but otherwise have little or no direct connection to the business. Some believe that that is its own virtue."[18] He also challenges the wisdom of linking the performance of the executive with the performance of the company's stock.

> Significant is the misguided apparent assumption that price appreciation of the corporation's stock measures the contribution of the company's board, and price depreciation means the board is deficient. This assumed causal linkage may be present in some situations, but, as a general rule, it does not apply.
>
> Can price appreciation/depreciation occur irrespective of the quality of the board's performance? Clearly the answer is yes. If a bear market emerges and takes the company's stock price with it, then, in that case, a director who had performed admirably for several years would, in a Stock Comp/Stock Own [paying in stock and requiring ownership of multiples of stock] environment, see the dollar value of this compensation for past good service substantially cut. Moreover, if paying directors a fixed number of shares were the mechanism used for a particular company's version of Stock Comp, then the director's present compensation would also be reduced by a bear market. Similarly, a bull market can cause substantial price appreciation of a company's stock (thereby enriching a Stock Comp/Stock Own board) even though that board's collective IQ does not exceed that of a vegetable patch.[19]

MacAvoy and Millstein also take note of this flaw: "in an extended bull market, executives may gain a benefit for which they cannot and should not take credit."[20] They recommend modifying the approach to granting stock options to executives and directors by linking the value of the grant to the company's performance rather than the stock market's performance. Their approach would factor out the effect of variations in stock market prices by indexing options to changes in the overall market. Under such a plan, executives would garner achievement rewards based on changes in their company's share price only if they exceeded changes in a market or industry stock price index. For example, awards would be made to executives only if, at the end of the year, stock price exceeded the beginning year price plus the change in the Dow Jones Industrial average (or some other, more specific industry-related index).

> Thus, if from 1996 to 1997 the DJIA rises by 10%, each percentage point over 10% a particular company's stock price rises could represent a point in which the option is "in the money," or a point for which the option which may be exercised at a profit above the previous year's price. . . .
>
> If the company stock price and the DJIA index both go down, the system could be the same: if the company stock price declines less than the index, then there are gains in the executive's options. If market prices go down $10, while this company's stock goes down $9, then the adjusted price against the base increases by $1 times the number of options. With a million options, the executive receives one million dollars more in his compensation package—a justifiable return for increasing the company's stock price against the market.[21]

These types of indexed systems, it is argued, set up more meaningful incentive plans because executives are rewarded only for outperforming the market. This is very much along the lines of the current thinking in the United Kingdom. As Klein from The Conference Board observes, the recommendations and "Code of Best Practice" of the Greenbury Group stress that the level of annual bonuses should be tied to company performance judged against a financial measure such as profit, cash flow, or earnings per share, and augmented with nonfinancial performance measures such as customer satisfaction and quality. When determining total cash compensation for directors (e.g., executives) in the United Kingdom, it is common practice first to establish an appropriate market-related base salary. Target values for annual incentives are then set accordingly, to bring total compensation to the desired level—but only for outstanding performance.

Like the U.S. and Canadian practices, U.K.-based companies have an annual bonus plan for most of their senior executives. Eligibility for annual bonus plans varies by industry sector. The food, drink, and tobacco industry in the United Kingdom demonstrates the highest prevalence, with 94.7 percent. The lowest incidence is in the building and construction industry, with 70.7 percent.

In the United Kingdom, one of three practices is generally used as a basis for determining the potential value of the bonus award:

1. The target or standard bonus for acceptable results.
2. The upper limit on annual bonus as a percentage of salary.
3. The actual bonus received during the last year.

The most common target bonus at the executive level in a parent or subsidiary company in the United Kingdom is 20 percent of salary. A minority of companies set higher target bonuses for the chief executive or managing director level than for other members of the same board. In many plans, the upper limit is twice the target. For example, if the target is 20 percent of base salary, the upper limit will be 40 percent of salary. For executives and other directors (e.g., executives) of companies with annual sales higher than £500 million, the majority of executives receive between 30 and 60 percent of base salary. In smaller companies, the bonus plan might not have a formal upper limit. In these cases, if a link to company performance exists, the bonus might simply be a percentage of all profits or all profits above a threshold—a practice that is also common among both U.S. and Canadian companies.

The increasing trend towards pay for performance in the United Kingdom requires companies, and specifically remuneration committees, to identify appropriate performance measures used to set executive variable compensation. The list of preferred performance measures used by corporations with annual sales greater than £500 million shows that earnings per share is the most popular measure used to evaluate chief executives (52 percent) followed by group profit (42 percent). In addition, 32 percent of chief executives in the United Kingdom are evaluated according to so-called "job-related measures." These measures generally take one of two main forms:

- Financial performance measures, which relate to the role of the individual (e.g., turnover for the sales director or production costs for the manufacturing director).
- Quantitative or other qualitative measures, which relate to specific key tasks for the year (e.g., opening up a new territory, launching a new product, or introducing an appraisal system).

Thus, nonfinancial measures are receiving increased attention in U.K. companies, particularly in view of the new disclosure requirements set forth in the Greenbury report.

Institutional Investor Concerns

Jon Lukomnik, Deputy Comptroller for Pensions, New York City Comptroller's Office, sees no one governance issue as more directly representing a transfer of wealth from shareholders to management than executive compensation. According to Lukomnik, focusing on the compensation issue is also an easy way to understand whether the board of directors is putting the shareholders' interests first and to ask the fundamental question, are corporate directors executing their proper authority? And while executive compensation is currently the focus of most of the contention, directors' own compensation is increasingly of shareholder concern as well.

Many large institutional investors candidly state they are not in a position to analyze the nuances of individual company pay packages. Kurt N. Schacht, general counsel of the State of Wisconsin Investment Board, says that institutional investors are focused on four key compensation issues:

1. The extent to which management has a significant stock ownership stake in the company.

2. The fairness of issuing stock options and other grants to executives.

3. Designing pay-for-performance packages that provide a meaningful correlation between corporate results and compensation.

4. The role of the compensation committee and its proper determination and processes.[22]

In support of these principles, the State of Wisconsin Investment Board has actively opposed compensation packages which result in what it considers to be unfair dilution, and it has been especially adamant about opposing repricing stock options which enable executives to take advantage of stock options even if the company's stock has fallen to lower prices than when the options were originally offered. Richard M. Schlefer, assistant vice president of the College Retirement Equities Fund, agrees that evaluating executive compensation is generally so complex that the investor can only recommend the following general policies, standards, and processes for setting executive compensation:

- Compensation should include salary and performance components.

- Salary should have a defined relationship to salaries in industry peer groups.

- Total compensation should be adequate to attract, motivate, and retain quality talent.

- Performance measures should relate to key characteristics accepted within the particular industry to measure success.
- Performance should be measured over time periods adequate to assess and link actual performance with responsibilities.
- Compensation should be determined by the compensation committee of a board and care should be taken to avoid interlocking compensation committee memberships with other boards.
- Stock options and restricted stock awards should be integrated with other elements of compensation to formulate a competitive package.
- The board should set forth annually in the proxy statement the criteria used to evaluate performance of the chief executive officer and other senior management. TIAA-CREF supports the spirit of the SEC rules on enhanced executive compensation disclosure and compensation committee reports to shareholders.
- TIAA-CREF opposes any ban on "golden parachute" severance agreements. We abstain on resolutions calling for prior shareholder ratification of golden parachute severance agreements, but TIAA-CREF supports resolutions that call for shareholder approval of golden parachutes that exceed Internal Revenue Service guidelines.
- Stock option, stock purchase, stock appreciation rights, savings, pensions, bonus, and management incentive award proposals are scrutinized closely by TIAA-CREF. Consideration should be given to the need of the company to attract, motivate, and reward people. This must be balanced against the concerns of shareholders. TIAA-CREF had developed guidelines for voting proxies on these issues.

Notwithstanding these general principles, TIAA-CREF notes that certain types of executive compensation practices raise warnings or "red flags" to institutional investors. While Schlefer notes considerable difficulty in obtaining valid company-specific data, a company's *policies,* which now must be disclosed in its proxy statement, can raise "red flags," which call for further research. Red flags may be a sign of procedural faults in the development of a compensation plan or may reveal a history of abusive practices. TIAA-CREF will also vote against a plan that does not raise a red flag if the company's current practice or history of awards causes serious concerns about the way the plan would be administered. For example, a red flag would be raised if the total potential dilution from existing and proposed compensation plans exceeds 15 percent over the duration of the plan or 1.5 percent per year. TIAA-CREF may permit an exception to this policy in the case of plans proposed by companies in high-technology industries, which routinely pay executives more in stock and for which coverage extends through at least middle management levels. Also, TIAA-CREF says it may increase the threshold of dilution to 20 percent for firms whose market equity capitalization is under $100 million. TIAA-CREF, like the State of Wisconsin Investment Board and other U.S. institutional investors, is similarly interested in opposing abusive compensation practices which dilute shareholder value and reward executives even if stock price has not appreciated (such as proposals to reprice stock options).

While some institutions see paying in stock as an incentive that links the interests of shareholder to those of management and directors, others have objected to payments in stock directly or indirectly via options as "too much of a good thing," potentially diluting the value of outstanding stock currently held by these institutions. In a study done by Pearl Meyer & Partners Inc. and cited in *The Wall Street Journal's* annual compensation review, approximately 7 percent of the stock in the United States' 200 largest publicly traded industrial and service companies was allocated to equity compensation plans as a percentage of shares outstanding in 1989; by 1995, the amount had risen to 10 to 11 percent.[23] Companies with extremely high amounts of stock allocated to equity compensation plans (as a percentage of shares outstanding) include Merrill Lynch & Co. (41.1 percent), Morgan Stanley Group Inc. (39.6 percent), J.P. Morgan & Co. (30.3 percent), Time Warner Inc. (22.8 percent), and AlliedSignal Inc. (22.7 percent).

Typically, a company receives shareholder approval to issue new stock at a later date for an option plan; however, many shareholder activists have opposed such issuance on the grounds of excessive dilution. The State of Wisconsin Investment Board (SWIB) opposed stock awards at the Chicago-based Information Resources Inc., which added 500,000 shares to one of its three stock option plans, after repricing at deep discounts some options the previous year to account for a drop in the stock market's price. The dilutive effect was estimated at 50 percent. Reportedly, at a February 20, 1996 meeting with SWIB, the company agreed not to reprice options, except "under extraordinary circumstances."[24] Other companies reportedly feeling pressure to scale back options include Cirrus Logic Inc., Cigna Corp, J.P. Morgan & Co., Kmart, General Motors, Columbia Gas System Inc., and Mobil Corp.—and the trend is increasing.

> According to the IRRC [Investor Responsibility Research Center], shareholders were nearly five times more likely to oppose a new stock-option plan in 1995 than they were in 1988. Though not a single new stock plan proposed by a major U.S. company failed in 1995, the IRRC says shareholders opposed new plans about 17% of the time and opposed adding shares to existing plans about 22% of the time. (The center defines opposition as votes against a plan, as well as abstentions.) Moreover, 14% of new plans [in 1995] received less than 70% of shareholder support, compared with 7.4% of new plans in 1994.[25]

The tension is clearly rising between paying in stock as a means to link shareholder interests with those of executives and directors and diluting the total shares outstanding. Even if significant dilution is not an immediate threat, the issue is rapidly coming to the forefront of the governance debate. The solution is to combine (or replace entirely if companies so choose) stock-based incentive plans with plans that link compensation to the corporation's strategic financial and nonfinancial drivers of success.

LINKING PAY TO PERFORMANCE

For some years, companies, especially in the United States, have been experimenting with ways to pay their executives based on innovative measures of corporate performance other than stock price and cumulative shareholder returns. For top executives, there was an extra incentive to develop performance-based pay packages following enactment in 1993 by the U.S. Congress (and signing by the President) of the Omnibus Budget Reconciliation Act of 1993, which added Section 162(m) to the Internal Revenue Code. As mentioned earlier in this chapter, this provision denies a publicly held company a deduction for compensation paid to certain top executives to the extent that the compensation exceeds $1 million per executive in a taxable year. The compensation applies to most forms of compensation, including cash, stock, and stock options. The Internal Revenue Service issued proposed regulations on December 15, 1993 to provide guidance on some of the broader issues raised by Section 162(m). In order to qualify for the exclusion for performance-based compensation, compensation must satisfy the following requirements: (1) it is payable solely on account of the attainment of one or more performance goals; (2) the performance goals are established by a compensation committee consisting of at least two directors, all of whom must be "outside" directors; (3) the material terms of the compensation and performance goals are disclosed to and approved by the corporation's shareholders in a separate vote before the compensation is paid; and (4) the compensation is paid after the compensation committee certifies that the goals have been achieved.

In a study entitled *Top Executive Pay for Performance*,[26] Marc-Andreas Klein of The Conference Board analyzed *Fortune's* largest 100 companies from 1991 through 1994 to determine the extent to which top executive compensation is related to corporate performance in addition to stock price performance. Klein found:

- The proportion of top executive pay is increasingly variable rather than fixed.
- Both financial and nonfinancial indicators are used to set compensation.
- CEO base salary and annual bonus are tied to improvements in pretax profit margins and return on equity.
- Long-term CEO compensation correlates strongly with total cumulative shareholder returns.

The analysis also compares key elements of median annual and long-term compensation to changes in median total cumulative shareholder returns, median pretax profit margins, and median return on equity. To examine the relationship between compensation and company performance, a review of trends is supplemented by a correlation analysis. All elements of profitability and compensation increased from 1991 through 1993, and the study finds:

- Total cumulative shareholder returns grew 11.6 percent from 1991 to 1992 and 17.3 percent from 1992 to 1993.
- CEO median base salary also grew, although at a lesser rate—10.8 percent from 1991 to 1992 and 4.6 percent from 1992 to 1993.
- Annual bonuses grew faster than median total cumulative shareholder returns from 1991 to 1992 (33.1 percent) but slower from 1992 to 1993 (15.9 percent).
- Like that for CEOs, median compensation for the four highest paid executives compared to median total cumulative shareholder returns rose.

- Median CEO restricted stock in dollar value grew somewhat faster than median shareholder returns from 1991 to 1992 and significantly faster from 1992 to 1993.
- Median pretax profit margins improved slightly during the period, as did median return on equity.

Correlation analysis supports the conclusion that companies link compensation to certain indicators of performance Most notably, the shorter-term elements of annual and bonus are linked to operational changes as reflected by changes in pretax profit margins, whereas the long-term elements of compensation appear to be linked to longer-term indicators such as cumulative shareholder returns. For example:

- CEO annual base salary and annual bonus showed a particularly strong correlation with pretax profit margins and return on equity, although a relatively low correlation existed with total cumulative shareholder returns.
- All long-term CEO compensation components, such as restricted stock, stock options, and long-term incentive plan payouts, were found to be highly correlated with total cumulative shareholder returns, although no significant correlation was found with pretax profit margin or return on equity.
- Base salaries allocated to the four highest paid executives are also strongly correlated to total cumulative shareholder returns.
- Annual bonus, however, demonstrates only a relatively modest correlation with cumulative shareholder returns.
- Restricted stock and stock options/SARs granted the four top executives, as with CEO grants, also showed a strong correlation with total cumulative shareholder returns.

The *Fortune* 100 companies were also found to use both financial and nonfinancial performance measures to set top executive compensation. Data were obtained by examining proxies that require companies to state in their compensation committee report criteria for making compensation decisions for top executive officers. As shown in Table 6–6, of the 100 sample companies, 37 percent used return on equity as a component in their calculations of the annual compensation. Net income was the next most frequently used factor (32 percent of the companies), followed by earnings per share (29 percent), stock price appreciation (27 percent), and pretax profit (23 percent). Stock price appreciation was by far the most often cited

TABLE 6-6

Summary of Financial Performance Measures Used to Determine Compensation of Top Executives in Fortune 100 Companies: 1993

Performance Measures[1]	Annual Compensation (% of Companies)	Long-Term Compensation (% of Companies)
Pretax Profit	23%	16%
Operating Profit	16	7
Net Income	32	15
Economic Value Added[2]	1	0
Earnings Per Share	29	26
Return on Equity	37	32
Return on Assets	19	14
Return on Capital Employed	6	5
Revenue	20	12
Working Capital	5	5
Cash Flow	12	9
Inventory	2	3
Receivables	1	0
Price Competition	0	3
Cost Reduction	13	3
Stock Price Appreciation	27	52

1. Companies may use more than one to set compensation.

2. The total cost of the company's or business unit's capital. Variable pay is based on year-to-year improvements.

Source: Marc-Andreas Klein, "Top Executive Pay for Performance," The Conference Board, Report No. 1113-95-RR, 1995, p. 15.

measure to set long-term variable compensation (52 percent of the companies), followed by return on equity (32 percent), and earnings per share (26 percent). The findings indicated that operating measures such as annual net income were given much greater emphasis in setting annual compensation (32 percent of companies) than in establishing long-term compensation (15 percent). Companies typically used more than one measure to determine both annual and long-term compensation.

Another step in the analysis determined how the median weights associated with the various financial performance measures were used to determine long-term variable compensation. Where companies used stock price appreciation as one of the measures to set long-term compensation and provided weighted data, they based 58 percent of this compensation on stock price appreciation results. Other financial performance measures ranged from a 33 percent weight given to pretax profit to 50 percent for net income, earnings per share, return on equity, and cash flow.

While these financial data are illuminating, the striking thing about the report was the extent to which companies reported using nonfinancial measures as a basis for establishing a portion of top executive compensation (see Table 6–7). Companies typically used more than one nonfinancial measure to determine compensation. However, in contrast to financial performance measures, the same types of nonfinancial criteria were most often used to set both annual and long-term variable compensation. The compensation committee reports in the companies' proxy statements indicated that 50 percent of the 100 sample companies explicitly stated that their top executives were evaluated on the basis of overall corporate performance. Forty-nine percent of the sample companies also evaluated their executives on an individual and business-unit level. "Stakeholder interests" and "organization and business development" were the next most cited factors, with 27 percent of the companies using these measures to help set annual variable compensation. Twenty-two percent also used these measures to determine long-term variable compensation. "Stakeholder interests" were defined by companies to encompass such issues as public affairs, civic involvement, and environmental concerns. "Organization and business development" issues ranged from restructuring to team management. Quality and customer satisfaction were also frequently used in computing annual variable compensation (25 percent and 24 percent, respectively). Both categories were used (quality by 12 percent of companies and customer satisfaction by 10 percent) to set long-term variable compensation.

Calculations were then made of the median weights associated with the various nonfinancial performance measures used to determine annual variable compensation. For example, to establish annual variable compensation, companies providing weights showed that they based 70 percent of this compensation on corporate performance. Other nonfinancial performance measures included using both customer satisfaction and quality at 20 percent each as the basis for determining compensation.

Designing a compensation system tied to both stock and strategic measures of success, as well as implementing this system throughout the entire company—for directors, executives, and employees—can help all parties interested in the sustained well-being of the company focus on its

TABLE 6-7

Summary of Nonfinancial Performance Measures Used to Determine Top
Executive Compensation in Fortune 100 Companies: 1993

Performance Measures	Annual Compensation (% of Companies)	Long-Term Compensation (% of Companies)
Customer satisfaction	24%	10%
Quality	25	12
Market share	10	8
New product development	12	9
Ethics	5	4
Workplace issues[1]	10	10
Stakeholder interests[2]	27	22
Organization and business development[3]	27	22
Individual and business unit performance	49	45
Corporate performance	50	46

1. Work force diversity, people development, high-performance workplace.

2. Public affairs, civic involvement, environmental issues.

3. Divestiture, restructuring, rational of capital expenditure, business planning process, team management (management strategies).

Source: Marc-Andreas Klein, *Top Executive Pay for Performance,* The Conference Board, Report No. 1113-95-RR, 1995, p. 16.

key drivers of success. This should also align the interests of the company's managers, directors, and employees with those of its investors—as opposed to its traders—who also have an interest in seeing the company achieve sustained growth.

STRATEGIC PERFORMANCE MEASURES: CREATING AND COMMUNICATING FIRM VALUE

Earlier sections of this book have demonstrated that all investors do not have the same investment style and trading behavior. Thus, strategic performance measurement information will probably not be used directly by most "quants" or traders, although it will eventually make its way into their quarterly earnings screens. Performance measures, however, can make a considerable difference to investors interested in sustained shareholder value. The questions are: how does one find those investors, and what does one communicate to them?

As described in Chapters 1 and 5, this is not as easy as it sounds, since a large portion of the equities under the control of each type of investor are managed by another type of investor. Thus, money shifts from a pension fund to a money manager or a bank, which actually makes the investment decisions. Data show that for institutions with the "hands on" management authority over equities as of September 30, 1995, money managers controlled 39.5 percent of equity management, banks 27.1 percent, mutual fund managers 16.6 percent, public pension funds 7.4 percent, insurance companies 6.7 percent, and corporate pension funds 2.7 percent. Moreover, turnover patterns vary considerably among institutions, as money managers have the highest average overall turnover of 59.2 percent (the portfolio turned over each year) and public pension funds, with their high proportion of indexed equities, have the lowest turnover at 20.7 percent (mutual fund managers have an average 42.3 percent turnover, banks 25.3 percent turnover, and corporate pension funds 24.8 percent turnover). Finally, turnover varies within the portfolios of each type of institution. For example, "aggressive growth" stocks in the portfolios of money managers turn over an average of 88 percent, whereas "income" stocks in their portfolios turn over only 54 percent and "value/income" stocks turn over only 45 percent. The "classic value" stocks in the portfolios of corporate pension funds turn over only 28.4 percent, while the indexed portion of the portfolios of public pension funds turn over only 11 percent.[27]

While an individual corporation may have no control over the seemingly meaningless gyrations of the stock market, companies can improve how their own individual stock is viewed by the markets if they analyze who holds their stock and then take steps to improve their stock ownership base. Some investors do rate companies on their intangibles and are prepared to stick with a company if they believe it will generate sustained shareholder value (Chrysler's fending off its recent bid from Tracinda is a good example). Clearly, and as the data in this book show, institutions do not all behave in the same manner. The key is to replace high-turnover shareholders and other momentum traders with investors interested in the corporation's ability to generate sustained shareholder value.

If successful, *the shareholder marketing and targeting approach* described in this book can accord a company a valuation more consistent with its plans to focus on the intangible drivers of success in order to create sustained investor wealth. This can mean higher price-to-earnings multiples, which will bolster support for the company's sustained stock price valuation and, all others things equal, provide it with a lower cost of capital.

All the Conference Board case study companies described in Chapter 2 originally developed their strategic performance measures in response to internal needs, not as a result of pressures to make this information available either to analysts or institutional investors. Indeed, as discussed earlier, there are serious problems in disclosing measures that are largely internal, not standardized among companies or industries, and subject to internal process changes as strategic options change and corporate focus shifts. Even so, some companies are searching for ways to disclose their strategic measures, especially in light of mounting pressure from certain large institutional investors, such as the California Public Employees' Retirement System (CalPERS), to meet with managements and boards of directors to discuss strategic issues.

Measures companies consider worthwhile and sufficiently objective to develop and possibly disclose were suggested (see Chapter 2) by Price Waterhouse's Change Management Team:

- Average time to market for new products.
- Design for manufacturability (a series of factors that indicate how easy it is to make the new product).
- New product sales dollars as a percentage of total sales dollars.
- Number of engineering changes after production release.
- Number of part numbers (and percentage of parts standardized among products).
- Concept-to-customer time milestones met.
- R&D investment as a percentage of sales.
- Planned and actual return on new product investment.
- Target product cost achievement.[28]

At the Bank of Montreal, Executive Vice President and Chief Financial Officer Robert Wells believes that "it is imperative to find the drivers that are critical to the success of your business, and to structure your performance measurement around these few items. We also believe that part of the success you gain from focusing on Performance Measurement comes from communicating these measures publicly to all stakeholders."[29] The Annual Report for the Bank of Montreal spells out a number of strategic goals, measurements, and accomplishments.

In by far the most comprehensive disclosure of intangibles, Skandia has created an entire supplement to its annual report entitled *Intellectual Capital: Value Creating Processes.* A "Skandia Navigator" leads the reader through the strategic processes the company considers most important for its future renewal and development. A Navigator section appears for each major business segment, providing a short series of numbers and ratios which quantifies the year-to-year change in such intellectual capital assets as:

- Satisfied customer index.
- Customer loyalty (measured in years).
- Empowerment indexes for each business area.
- Number of strategic alliances.
- Repeat ratio for reinsurance business.
- Quality index.
- Information technology (IT) expense/administrative expense (an increase in this ratio is desirable to the extent it reflects additional resources devoted to IT).
- Changes in the company's IT literacy.
- Service awards by a prominent industry organization.
- Processing time for new contracts.

Skandia measures some of these items internally, while others are measured for the company through an annual survey. For example, the empowerment index is from a recurring Swedish Institute of Public Opinion Research (SIFO) survey and was created to measure employee motivation, support in the organization, sensitivity to quality demands, matching of responsibility and authority, and competence. The scale is from 0 to 1,000. (For example, in the 1995 supplement to its annual report, Skandia reports that the empowerment index for its Vesta Commercial Divisions rose from 681 in 1994 to 702 in 1995.)

Efforts to develop new performance measurements appear to be farther along outside the United States, primarily because shareholder litigation is less common and companies feel more confident disclosing "soft" and "forward-looking" information. That situation could change in the United States following the passage of the Private Securities Litigation Reform Act of 1995. Title I provides a safe harbor (companies cannot be sued) for certain statements companies choose to disclose, raises pleading standards for fraud actions (making it harder to bring a suit), and limits attorneys' fees in class actions (where a single shareholder brings an action on behalf of a class or group of shareholders). It is possible that the quality and quantity of information companies make available to the public will increase as a result of this legislation, although changes have been minimal during the 1996 proxy season and will probably remain so until the first test litigation is resolved.

Even prior to enactment of this law, some U.S. companies had voluntarily begun to increase disclosure of forward-looking information and intangibles, with Whirlpool a major example. Such disclosure, however, is still relatively rare in the United States. At an April 1996 Securities and Exchange symposium entitled "Financial Accounting and Reporting of Intangible Assets," most commentators agreed that nonfinancial performance measurement information would best be disclosed in supplements to the financials rather than attempting to standardize and audit measures sufficiently to include them in the 10K annual reports or other required filings. These measures could be "auditable" in the sense that industrywide generally accepted accounting principles could be applied to them, as they are to the corporation's vast and complex financial statements. The accounting profession has begun to discuss this issue with several committees formed by various industry groups, including the Association for Investment Management and Research (AIMR), the Financial Accounting Standards Board (FASB), and a committee of the major accounting professional association, the AICPA's Special Committee on Financial Reporting. Development of voluntary, self-regulated standards for the use of nonfinancial measures would give companies and investors added confidence that these measures could not be manipulated.

Expanded use of key strategic drivers of success to better manage businesses and set compensation could not only better link the interests of investors with corporations, it could reduce the tension that arises as managers and directors attempt to reconcile conflicts in deciding to whom the corporation owes its allegiance: the shareholders or its other constituents such as customers, employees, and the community. Fashioning true strategic drivers of success incorporates the best balance of the interests of all these stakeholders, removing the tension between satisfying one group at the expense of another.

Corporations must develop and utilize strategic measures of performance to run their businesses as well as to compensate their employees and directors. And investors must pay attention to these measures of performance if they want to behave like owners interested in the sustained economic value of the firm. These joint actions by corporations and investors are the key to the genuine creation of corporate value.

ENDNOTES

1. In 1993, the United States Congress passed and the President signed the Omnibus Budget Reconciliation Act of 1993, adding Section 162(m) to the Internal Revenue Code. This provision denies a publicly held company a deduction for compensation paid to certain top executives to the extent that the compensation exceeds $1 million per executive in a taxable year. The compensation applies to most forms of compensation, including cash, stock, and stock options. The IRS issued proposed regulations on December 15, 1993, to provide guidance on some of the broader issues raised by Section 162(m).

2. Joann S. Lublin, "The Great Divide," *The Wall Street Journal*, April 11, 1996, p. R1.

3. Paul W. MacAvoy and Ira M. Millstein, "Linking Executive Compensation to Company, Not Stock Market, Performance," Special Report on Executive Compensation, National Association of Corporate Directors, April 11, 1996, pp. 1–2.

4. John A. Byrne, "How High Can CEO Pay Go?," Business Week, April 22, 1996, pp. 100–101.

5. MacAvoy and Millstein, p. 2.

6. Many institutions have opposed the repricing of stock options (to lower the price at which the option becomes exercisable) as removing the incentive normally associated with the granting of stock options.

7. For a more complete discussion of Canadian and U.K. disclosure developments see Marc-Andreas Klein, "Top Executive Compensation: A Comparison Between U.S., U.K., and Canada," The Conference Board, Report No. 1155-96-99.

8. The term *board of directors* in the United Kingdom refers to its executive management team and not to a U.S.- or Canadian-style board of directors comprised of outside directors.

9. Klein, pp. 17–18.

10. Guidelines for Corporate Directors: Report of the NACD Blue Ribbon Commission on Executive Compensation: Guidelines for Corporate Directors, National Association of Corporate Directors, Washington, DC, 1993, p.7.

11. William M. Mercer, Inc., "The Boss's Pay: Executive Pay Survey," *The Wall Street Journal*, April 11, 1996, pp. R15–17.

12. Klein, pp. 9–12.

13. Hoffer Kaback, "The Case for Cash for Directors," *Directors and Boards*, Winter 1996, p. 16.

14. Thomas E. Flanagan, "Directors' Pensions—One Shareholder's View," *Directorship: Significant Issues Facing Directors: 1996* (Greenwich, CT: Directorship, Inc., and the Institute for Research on Boards of Directors), pp. 8–5.

15. Kay Worrell, Carolyn Brancato, and Charles Peck, "Directors' Retirement Benefits," The Conference Board, white paper, April 1996, p. 8.

16. Communications between Kay Worrell of The Conference Board and Blanca Rossbach from The American Society of Corporate Secretaries, New York, as cited in Worrell, Brancato, and Peck, p. 8.

17. Kaback, p. 15.

18. Ibid., p. 18.

19. Ibid.

20. MacAvoy and Millstein, p. 3.

21. Ibid.

22. Kurt N. Schacht, General Counsel, State of Wisconsin Investment Board. Comments before the Investor Responsibility Research Center's 1994 Forum for Shareholders and Corporations: Voting on Executive Pay, New York City, October 13, 1994.

23. Sarah Bowen, "ENOUGH!: Shareholders Like the Idea of Using Stock as a Pay Incentive. But Now, Some Say, It Has Gone Too Far." *The Wall Street Journal*, April 11, 1996, p. R6.

24. Ibid., p. R6.

25. Ibid.

26. See Marc-Andreas Klein, "Top Executive Pay for Performance," The Conference Board, Report No. 1113-95-RR.

27. See *The Brancato Report on Institutional Investment*, 3, ed. 2 (May 1996); calculations based on the Georgeson & Company, Inc. database.

28. The Price Waterhouse Change Integration Team, *The Paradox Principles: How High-Performance Companies Manage Chaos, Complexity, and Contradiction to Achieve Superior Results* (Burr Ridge, IL: Irwin Professional Publishing, 1996), p. 250.

29. Letter from R.B. Wells, executive vice president and chief financial officer, Bank of Montreal, to the author, dated December 20, 1995.

INDEX